Complete French Grammar

PRACTICE
MAKES
PERFECT

Complete French Grammar

Annie Heminway

McGraw Hill

New York Chicago San Francisco Lisbon London Madrid Mexico City
Milan New Delhi San Juan Seoul Singapore Sydney Toronto

ISBN 978-0-07-148284-4
MHID   0-07-148284-9

e-ISBN 978-0-07-159435-6
e-MHID   0-07-159435-3

Library of Congress Control Number 2006931668

Interior design by Village Typographers, Inc.

McGraw-Hill books are available at special quantity discounts to use as premiums and sales promotions or for use in corporate training programs. To contact a representative, please e-mail us at bulksales@mcgraw-hill.com.

This book is printed on acid-free paper.

Contents

Introduction

Practice Makes Perfect: Complete French Grammar is designed as a review and study tool for the advanced beginner and intermediate student of French. The grammar explanations given in each unit include comparisons that provide ample practice of the material along with appropriate, useful vocabulary. Instructions for each exercise are given in French, enabling the student to anticipate the task that follows while, at the same time, practicing vocabulary in context. The variety of exercises makes them suitable for a range of different learning styles; open-ended exercises are included to encourage creative answers and to increase confidence in using French for normal everyday communication.

Each unit can be studied independently to suit individual needs in a specific area. For the student seeking additional practice at the high school or college level, these units, taken individually or as a whole, provide an opportunity to learn and review French grammar using contemporary language and examples.

New vocabulary is incorporated within the exercises or is highlighted in boxes. The glossaries include words appropriate to this level and make it easy to quickly review or learn new vocabulary. Finally, the verb charts serve as a quick grammar reference.

Learning another language requires dedication, time, and ultimately, frequent practice. By using what the students already know, by making connections with their first language, and by building on that base, the foundation for their future learning is strengthened. By including a number of cognates of English words in the vocabulary, both advanced beginners and intermediate students are given numerous opportunities to reinforce what they already know as they continue to advance their knowledge of French.

**PRACTICE
MAKES
PERFECT**

Complete French Grammar

The present tense of regular -er verbs

·1·

Before studying the present tense in French, you need to be familiar with the grammatical terms in chapters presenting verbs. To conjugate a verb in the present tense, you'll need to find the *root* (or *stem*) of a verb to which you'll add the *ending* corresponding to the desired *tense*. The root of the verb is found in its *infinitive* form. In English, the infinitive is preceded by the preposition *to: to say, to wear.* Infinitives in French are not preceded by an equivalent of the preposition *to.* They are identified according to groups by their endings: **-er, -ir, -re, -oir.**

Regular -er verbs in the present

Let's start with the infinitives of verbs of the first group, ending in **-er**, such as **regarder** (*to look at*) and **chanter** (*to sing*). Most verbs that end in **-er** in the infinitive follow the same conjugation. The pattern is easy. You remove the **-er** ending of the verb to get the root: **parler** (*to speak*) → **parl-**. Then, you add the endings corresponding to the subject pronoun.

The endings for the **-er** regular verbs are: **-e, -es, -e, -ons, -ez, -ent.** The **-e, -es,** and **-ent** endings of the verbs are all silent. The final **-s** of **nous, vous, ils, elles** links with verbs beginning with a vowel sound, making a **z** sound. This is called a **liaison**.

Let's conjugate the verb **parler** (*to speak*). Note that, as in English, conjugated forms are preceded by a *subject pronoun:*

je parl**e**	*I speak*	nous parl**ons**	*we speak*
tu parl**es**	*you speak*	vous parl**ez**	*you speak*
il parl**e**	*he speaks*	ils parl**ent**	*they (m., m./f.) speak*
elle parl**e**	*she speaks*	elles parl**ent**	*they (f.) speak*
on parl**e**	*one/they/we speak*		

Here are some questions using **parler**:

Parlez-vous italien?	*Do you speak Italian?*
Combien de langues **parles-tu?**	*How many languages do you speak?*

Chanter (*to sing*) follows the same pattern:

je chant**e**	*I sing*	nous chant**ons**	*we sing*
tu chant**es**	*you sing*	vous chant**ez**	*you sing*
il chant**e**	*he sings*	ils chant**ent**	*they (m., m./f.) sing*
elle chant**e**	*she sings*	elles chant**ent**	*they (f.) sing*
on chant**e**	*one/they/we sing*		

To recapitulate, here are the subject pronouns with their English equivalents:

je	*I*
tu	*you* (singular familiar)
il	*he, it* (masculine)
elle	*she, it* (feminine)
on	*one, we, they*
nous	*we*
vous	*you* (singular formal and all plurals)
ils	*they* (masculine or mixed masculine and feminine)
elles	*they* (feminine)

There are two ways of saying *you* in French. Use **tu** to talk to friends, family members, children, and animals. Use **vous** when you are addressing a stranger, someone you don't know well, or to maintain a certain degree of distance or respect.

The pronoun **on** takes on different meanings. It may mean *one, we,* or *they* depending on how it is used. See the examples below.

Ici, **on parle** japonais.	*Japanese is spoken here.*
On ne devrait pas se comporter ainsi.	*One should not behave this way.*
On va au cinéma ce soir? (*familiar*)	*Shall we go to the movies tonight?*
En Espagne, **on mange** des tapas.	*In Spain, they eat tapas.*
On est tous d'accord. (*familiar*)	*We all agree.*

Here are some common regular **-er** verbs:

accepter	*to accept*
aimer	*to like, to love*
annuler	*to cancel*
apporter	*to bring*
attraper	*to catch*
augmenter	*to increase*
bavarder	*to chat*
casser	*to break*
chercher	*to look for*
commander	*to order*
couper	*to cut*
danser	*to dance*
déjeuner	*to have lunch*
demander	*to ask*
dessiner	*to draw*
donner	*to give*
emprunter	*to borrow*
enlever	*to remove*
étudier	*to study*
exprimer	*to express*
gagner	*to win, to earn*
garder	*to keep*
habiter	*to live*
laver	*to wash*
manger	*to eat*
mériter	*to deserve*
oublier	*to forget*
porter	*to carry*
prêter	*to lend*

refuser	*to refuse*
regarder	*to watch*
saluer	*to greet*
sauter	*to jump*
tomber	*to fall*
travailler	*to work*
visiter	*to visit (a place)*

EXERCICE
1·1

Mettre les verbes entre parenthèses au présent.

1. Lucie ___travaille___ (travailler) à Lyon.

2. Mon frère et moi, nous ___acceptons___ (accepter) votre invitation.

3. M. et Mme Benoît ___cherchent___ (chercher) un appartement.

4. Tu ___apporte___ (apporter) toujours des fleurs.

5. Vous ___bavardez___ (bavarder) sur la terrasse.

6. Je ___commande___ (commander) une soupe de légumes.

7. Ils ___habitent___ (habiter) en Normandie.

8. Elle ___déjeune___ (déjeuner) avec sa belle-sœur.

9. Vous ___dessinez___ (dessiner) très bien.

10. Nous ___visitons___ (visiter) le château de Fontainebleau.

EXERCICE
1·2

Traduire en français.

1. We refuse the invitation.
   ___Nous réfusons l'invitation___

2. She cancels the trip.
   ___elle annule l'excursoin___

3. He speaks French.
   ___Il parle francai___

4. You bring some flowers. (*formal*)
   ___Vous apportez les fleurs.___

5. I cut the bread.
   ___Je coupe le pain___

6. They are having lunch with Julie.

Ils déjeunent avec Julie

7. He borrows ten euros.

Il emprunte dix euros

8. I order a dessert.

Je commande un dessert

9. You study Russian. (*informal*)

Vous etudez russe

10. They are looking for a good restaurant.

Ils cherchent un bon restaurant

VOCABULAIRE

à midi	*at noon*	**le samedi,**	*on Saturdays, on*
à minuit	*at midnight*	**le dimanche**	*Sundays*
aujourd'hui	*today*	**cette semaine**	*this week*
demain	*tomorrow*	**le mois prochain**	*next month*
hier	*yesterday*	**le mois dernier**	*last month*
après-demain	*the day after tomorrow*	**à la fin du mois**	*at the end of the*
avant-hier	*the day before yesterday*		*month*
le matin	*in the morning*	**au début de l'année**	*at the beginning of*
l'après-midi	*in the afternoon*		*the year*
le soir	*in the evening*	**de temps en temps**	*from time to time*
toujours	*always*	**parfois**	*sometimes*
souvent	*often*		

-er verbs with spelling and stem changes

Some -**er** verbs, otherwise regular, show spelling or stem changes in the present tense, largely to maintain pronunciation. These can be learned according to their groups.

Verbs ending in -cer

Some spelling changes occur with some -**er** regular verbs. With verbs ending in -**cer**, such as **prononcer** (*to pronounce*) the -**c**- becomes -**ç**- before the letter **o**. The cedilla (**ç**) under the **c** is needed to keep the soft pronunciation of the **c** in the infinitive form.

je prononce	*I pronounce*	nous prononçons	*we pronounce*
tu prononces	*you pronounce*	vous prononcez	*you pronounce*
il/elle prononce	*he/she pronounces*	ils/elles prononcent	*they pronounce*

Here are a few examples of other -**cer** verbs:

nous annonçons	*we announce*
nous avançons	*we move forward*

nous balançons	we swing
nous commençons	we start
nous défonçons	we smash in
nous déplaçons	we move
nous devançons	we get ahead of
nous effaçons	we erase
nous épiçons	we spice
nous façonnons	we craft, we manufacture
nous finançons	we finance
nous grimaçons	we make faces
nous influençons	we influence
nous laçons	we lace up, we tie
nous menaçons	we threaten
nous perçons	we pierce
nous plaçons	we place
nous ponçons	we sand
nous remplaçons	we replace
nous renonçons	we give up

EXERCICE 1·3

Mettre au présent les verbes entre parenthèses.

1. Nous _commençons_ (commencer) à huit heures le matin.

2. Vous _avancez_ (avancer) rapidement.

3. Je _déplace_ (déplacer) les meubles du salon.

4. Nous _devançons_ (devancer) nos concurrents. (rivals)

5. Nous _annonçons_ (annoncer) une augmentation de salaire au début de l'année.

6. Tu _effaces_ (effacer) le tableau.

7. Nous _remplaçons_ (remplacer) toute l'équipe.

8. Ils _exercent_ (exercer) une grande influence.

9. Nous _finançons_ (financer) ce projet.

10. Elle _menace_ (menacer) de partir.

Verbs ending in -ger

With verbs ending in **-ger**, such as **voyager** (*to travel*), the **-g-** becomes **-ge-** before the letter **o**.

je voyage	*I travel*	nous voyageons	*we travel*
tu voyages	*you travel*	vous voyagez	*you travel*
il/elle voyage	*he/she travels*	ils/elles voyagent	*they travel*

Here are other common **-ger** verbs:

nous bougeons	*we move*
nous changeons	*we change*

nous corrigeons	*we correct*
nous dégageons	*we release, we free*
nous déménageons	*we move (house)*
nous encourageons	*we encourage*
nous exigeons	*we demand*
nous hébergeons	*we host*
nous mangeons	*we eat*
nous mélangeons	*we mix*
nous nageons	*we swim*
nous négligeons	*we neglect*
nous partageons	*we share*
nous plongeons	*we dive*
nous protégeons	*we protect*
nous rangeons	*we put away*
nous vengeons	*we avenge*

EXERCICE
1·4

Mettre au présent les verbes entre parenthèses.

1. Vous _melangez_ (mélanger) les ingrédients.

2. Je _range_ (ranger) mes affaires.

3. Nous _exigeons_ (exiger) votre présence à la réunion.

4. Ils _demenagant_ (déménager) demain.

5. Elle _héberge_ (héberger) ses amis.

6. Vous _corrigez_ (corriger) les exercices.

7. Nous _mangeons_ (manger) sur la terrasse à midi.

8. Tu _nage_ (nager) dans la piscine.

9. Nous _encourageons_ (encourager) ces jeunes talents.

10. Souvent, il _change_ (changer) d'avis.

Verbs ending in -e + consonant + -er

With some verbs composed of **-e** + consonant + **-er**, such as **acheter** (*to buy*), some accent changes occur. An **accent grave** is added in all but the first- and the second-person plural.

j'achète	*I buy*	nous achetons	*we buy*
tu achètes	*you buy*	vous achetez	*you buy*
il/elle achète	*he/she buys*	ils/elles achètent	*they buy*

Here are a few other verbs following the same pattern:

achever	j'achève	*I complete*
emmener	j'emmène	*I take along, I escort*
enlever	j'enlève	*I remove*
lever	je lève	*I raise*

mener	je mène	I lead
peser	je pèse	I weigh
semer	je sème	I sow

With some verbs composed of **-é** + consonant + **-er**, such as **répéter** (*to repeat*), changes may also occur. The **é aigu** changes to an **è grave** in all but the first- and second-person plural.

je répète	I repeat	nous répétons	*we repeat*
tu répètes	*you repeat*	vous répétez	*you repeat*
il/elle répète	*he/she repeats*	ils/elles répètent	*they repeat*

Here are a few other verbs following the same pattern:

céder	je cède	I yield
célébrer	je célèbre	I celebrate
considérer	je considère	I consider
déléguer	je délègue	I delegate
espérer	j'espère	I hope
exagérer	j'exagère	I exaggerate
gérer	je gère	I manage
lécher	je lèche	I lick
posséder	je possède	I own
préférer	je préfère	I prefer
révéler	je révèle	I reveal

Verbs ending in -e + l + -er

Some verbs composed of **-e + l + -er**, such as **épeler** (*to spell*), sometimes take two **l**s in all but the first- and second-person plural.

j'épelle	I spell	nous épelons	*we spell*
tu épelles	*you spell*	vous épelez	*you spell*
il/elle épelle	*he/she spells*	ils/elles épellent	*they spell*

Here are a few other verbs following the same pattern:

appeler	j'appelle	I call
ensorceler	j'ensorcelle	I bewitch
étinceler	j'étincelle	I sparkle, I glitter
ficeler	je ficelle	I tie
niveler	je nivelle	I level
rappeler	je rappelle	I remind, I call back
renouveler	je renouvelle	I renew

EXERCICE

1·5

Mettre au présent les verbes entre parenthèses.

1. Il _renouvelle_ (renouveler) son passeport.

2. J'_emmène_ (emmener) ma nièce à l'opéra.

3. Vous _achetez_ (acheter) un kilo de haricots.

4. Le sorcier _ensorcelle_ (ensorceler) le public.

5. Elle _____espère_____ (espérer) aller à Paris en mai.

6. Vous _____exagérez_____ (exagérer).

7. Elle _____s'appelle_____ (s'appeler) Juliette.

8. Ces diamants _____étincellent_____ (étinceler) de mille feux.

9. Il _____répète_____ (répéter) mille fois la même chose.

10. Nous _____célébrons_____ (célébrer) son anniversaire.

EXERCICE
1·6

Mettre au présent les verbes entre parenthèses.

1. Aujourd'hui, il _____achète_____ (acheter) du poisson au marché.

2. Ils _____travaillent_____ (travailler) le samedi.

3. Vous _____empruntez_____ (emprunter) de l'argent à la banque.

4. Tu _____aime_____ (aimer) voyager en bateau.

5. Nous _____renonceons,_____ (renoncer) à notre projet.

6. Je _____habite_____ (habiter) au dixième étage.

7. L'après-midi, elle _____préfère_____ (préférer) aller dans le parc.

8. Comment _____s'appelle_____ (s'appeler) sa sœur?

9. De temps en temps, nous _____bavardons_____ (bavarder) pendant la pause-café.

10. Il vous _____rappelle_____ (rappeler) avant midi.

EXERCICE
1·7

Faire correspondre les deux colonnes.

_1._	1. Il épelle (spell)	a.	dans l'Atlantique
_e_	2. Je regarde	b.	à midi et demi
___	3. Nous habitons	c.	la comédienne malade
_a._	4. Tu aimes nager	d.	Amélie
_b_	5. Ils déjeunent toujours	e.	la télévision
_d._	6. Vous chantez	f.	son voyage au Japon
_c_	7. Elle remplace	g.	à la fin du mois

substitute

_____d._ 8. Je m'appelle   h. au troisième étage

_____f._ 9. Elle annule   i. le mot

_____h_10. Nous déménageons   j. une belle chanson

When is the present tense used in French?

The present indicative is used in a number of ways:

◆ To make a general statement and to describe ongoing actions in the present. It can be translated in three different ways.

Valérie **parle** à son ami Ludovic.	Valérie is talking (talks, does talk) to her friend Ludovic.
Il **regarde** les étoiles dans le ciel.	He is looking (looks, does look) at the stars in the sky.

◆ To express a close future

Il **part** demain soir.	He'll leave tomorrow night.
On **parle** de cela en fin de semaine.	We'll discuss this at the end of the week.

◆ To express a habitual action

Tous les jours, le soleil **se lève**.	The sun rises every day.
D'habitude, j'**achète** la viande dans cette boucherie.	Usually I buy meat in this butcher shop.

◆ To describe a past action closely connected to the present

Claude **revient** d'Asie et c'**est** la pagaille au bureau!	Claude just returned from Asia and chaos started in the office!
À peine rentrés et les problèmes **commencent** déjà.	They have just come back and the problems have already started.

◆ To express a historical fact

Flaubert **publie** Madame Bovary et c'**est** le scandale!	Flaubert published Madame Bovary and the scandal broke out!
Le président **arrive** en Chine et c'**est** la débâcle!	The president arrived in China and it was a complete disaster!

◆ To describe past events more dramatically

La reine **avance** vers le trône.	The queen moved toward the throne.
Et son pire ennemi **entre** dans la salle.	And his worst enemy walked into the room.

◆ To express an action in the process, **être en train de** + the infinitive form of the verb is used.

Un instant, s'il vous plaît, je **suis en train de parler** à Rémi.	One moment, please, I am talking to Rémi.
Qu'est-ce que tu **es en train de faire**?	What are you doing?

*Reformuler les phrases en utilisant **être en train de** + infinitif.*

1. Nous chantons une chanson.

   Nous sommes en train de chanter une chanson

2. Elle dessine un mouton. (draw)

   elle est en train de dessine un mouton

3. Je travaille dans la cuisine.

   Je suis en train de travailler dans la cuisine

4. Tu effaces le tableau.

   Tu es en train d'efface le tableau.

5. Vous étudiez l'histoire européenne.

   Vous êtes en train d'etudie l'histoire européenne

6. Nous bavardons dans le jardin.

   Nous sommes en train de bavarder dans le jardin.

7. Il corrige les copies.

   Il est en train de corriger les copies

8. Tu laves la chemise.

   Tu es en train de laver la chemise,

9. Je range mes affaires.

   Je suis en train de range mes affaires

10. Elle mange une omelette aux champignons.

    Elle est en train de mange une omelette aux champignons

One more use of the present tense: depuis

The present tense is used to express an action that began in the past and continues in the present. Note that in English, the past tense is used. There are different ways to formulate the questions, using either **depuis**, **il y a... que**, **cela (ça) fait... que**.

Let's start with **depuis**. To ask a question about the duration of an action, use **depuis quand** (*since when*) or **depuis combien de temps** (*how long*).

Depuis combien de temps habites-tu à Nice?	*How long have you been living in Nice?*
—J'habite à Nice **depuis trois ans**.	*—I have been living in Nice for three years.*

Depuis quand travaillez-vous chez L'Oréal?	*How long have you been working at L'Oréal?*
—Je travaille chez L'Oréal **depuis trois mois.**	*—I have been working at L'Oréal for three months.*
Il y a combien de temps que vous connaissez M. Blier?	*How long have you known Mr. Blier?*
—**Il y a quelques années que** je connais M. Blier.	*—I have known Mr. Blier for a few years.*
Ça fait combien de temps que vous avez ce dictionnaire?	*How long have you had this dictionary?*
—**Ça fait cinq ans que** j'ai ce dictionnaire.	*—I have had this dictionary for five years.*

EXERCICE 1·9

Répondre aux questions en utilisant le présent et **depuis.**

1. Depuis combien de temps chante-t-elle dans cette chorale? (trois ans)

   Elle chante dans cette chorale depuis trois ans.

2. Depuis combien de temps partages-tu cet appartement? (six mois)

   Je partage cet appartement depuis six mois

3. Depuis combien de temps nage-t-il dans cette piscine? (un mois)

   Il nage dans cette piscine depuis un mois

4. Depuis quand habitez-vous à Montpellier? (2004)

   J'habite à Montpellier depuis 2004

5. Depuis combien de temps possède-t-il cette propriété? (dix ans)

   Il possède cette propriété depuis dix ans.

6. Depuis combien de temps regardez-vous cette émission? (des années)

   Il y a quelques années que je regarde cette émission

7. Depuis quand travaille-t-il dans cette entreprise? (2002)

   Je travaille dans cette entreprise depuis 2002

8. Depuis combien de temps portez-vous des lunettes? (dix ans)

   Je porte des lunettes depuis dix ans.

9. Depuis quand est-il président? (2005)

   Il est président depuis 2015

10. Depuis combien de temps ce magasin est-il fermé? (deux mois)

    Ça fait deux mois que ce magasin est fermé

*Traduire les phrases suivantes en utilisant **vous** et l'inversion si nécessaire.*

1. I study French.

   J'étud la francai

2. I spell my name.

   J'épelle mon nom,

3. They are moving tomorrow.

   Ils demenagen' demai

4. She likes to travel by boat.

   Elle aim voyage e bateau

5. How long have you been studying French?

   Depuis combu de tens elude tu la francai

6. You repeat the sentence. (*informal*)

   Tu répe't la phrase.

7. We are financing the project.

   Nous francai le projet

8. She cancels the meeting.

   Elle annule la reunion

9. How long have you been living in this house?

   Depuis cabu de l'temp habler vas dans cette mais?

10. I weigh the vegetables.

    Je pès les légumes.

The present tense of -ir and -re verbs

-ir verbs in the present

We studied the **-er** verbs in the first chapter. Now, let's explore the **-ir** and **-re** verbs. The **-ir** verbs follow two different conjugation patterns.

Type 1 verbs drop the **-ir** of the infinitive, add an **-iss-** to the plural form, and then insert the appropriate ending.

choisir to choose			
je chois**is**	*I choose*	nous chois**issons**	*we choose*
tu chois**is**	*you choose*	vous chois**issez**	*you choose*
il/elle chois**it**	*he/she chooses*	ils/elles chois**issent**	*they choose*

Many other verbs follow the same conjugation.

accomplir	*to accomplish*	**nous accomplissons**	*we accomplish*
adoucir	*to soften,*	**nous adoucissons**	*we soften,*
	to mellow		*we mellow*
agrandir	*to enlarge*	**nous agrandissons**	*we enlarge*
applaudir	*to applaud*	**nous applaudissons**	*we applaud*
bâtir	*to build*	**nous bâtissons**	*we build*
bénir	*to bless*	**nous bénissons**	*we bless*
éclaircir	*to lighten, to clear*	**nous éclaircissons**	*we lighten, we clear*
s'épanouir	*to bloom,*	**nous nous**	*we bloom,*
	to blossom	**épanouissons**	*we blossom*
s'évanouir	*to faint*	**nous nous**	*we faint*
		évanouissons	
finir	*to finish*	**nous finissons**	*we finish*
grandir	*to grow up*	**nous grandissons**	*we grow up*
grossir	*to put on weight*	**nous grossissons**	*we put on weight*
investir	*to invest*	**nous investissons**	*we invest*
maigrir	*to lose weight*	**nous maigrissons**	*we lose weight*
mincir	*to slim down*	**nous mincissons**	*we slim down*
obéir	*to obey*	**nous obéissons**	*we obey*
pâlir	*to turn pale*	**nous pâlissons**	*we turn pale*
rafraîchir	*to refresh*	**nous rafraîchissons**	*we refresh*
ralentir	*to slow down*	**nous ralentissons**	*we slow down*
réfléchir	*to think, to reflect*	**nous réfléchissons**	*we think, we reflect*
remplir	*to fill*	**nous remplissons**	*we fill*
réussir	*to succeed*	**nous réussissons**	*we succeed*
rougir	*to blush*	**nous rougissons**	*we blush*
saisir	*to seize*	**nous saisissons**	*we seize*
vieillir	*to grow old*	**nous vieillissons**	*we grow old*

Type 2 **-ir** verbs drop the **-ir** of the infinitive, then add the appropriate ending, *without* the **-iss-** in the **nous** and **vous** forms. These groups of **-ir** verbs can be termed irregular. Let's look at the examples below:

sortir *to go out*

je **sors**	*I go out*	nous **sortons**	*we go out*
tu **sors**	*you go out*	vous **sortez**	*you go out*
il/elle **sort**	*he/she goes out*	ils/elles **sortent**	*they go out*

Study the first-person conjugations of the following **-ir** verbs.

bouillir	*to boil*	**je bous**	*I boil*	**nous bouillons**	*we boil*
courir	*to run*	**je cours**	*I run*	**nous courons**	*we run*
couvrir	*to cover*	**je couvre**	*I cover*	**nous couvrons**	*we cover*
cueillir	*to pick*	**je cueille**	*I pick*	**nous cueillons**	*we pick*
dormir	*to sleep*	**je dors**	*I sleep*	**nous dormons**	*we sleep*
fuir	*to flee*	**je fuis**	*I flee*	**nous fuyons**	*we flee*
mentir	*to lie*	**je mens**	*I lie*	**nous mentons**	*we lie*
mourir	*to die*	**je meurs**	*I die*	**nous mourons**	*we die*
obtenir	*to get*	**j'obtiens**	*I get*	**nous obtenons**	*we get*
offrir	*to offer*	**j'offre**	*I offer*	**nous offrons**	*we offer*
ouvrir	*to open*	**j'ouvre**	*I open*	**nous ouvrons**	*we open*
partir	*to leave*	**je pars**	*I leave*	**nous partons**	*we leave*
sentir	*to feel,*	**je sens**	*I feel, I smell*	**nous sentons**	*we feel,*
	to smell				*we smell*
servir	*to serve*	**je sers**	*I serve*	**nous servons**	*we serve*
souffrir	*to suffer*	**je souffre**	*I suffer*	**nous souffrons**	*we suffer*

EXERCICE
2·1

Mettre les verbes entre parenthèses au présent.

1. Nous (cueillir) _cueillons_ des fleurs dans le jardin.

2. Ils (finir) _finissent_ à dix-huit heures.

3. Je (remplir) _remplis_ les verres des invités.

4. Nous (investir) _Investissons_ dans l'immobilier. *j'investis*

5. Ils (mentir) _mentent_ à la police.

6. Tu (ouvrir) _ouvres_ les fenêtres du salon.

7. Vous (réfléchir) _réfléchissez_ à leur proposition.

8. Je (sentir) _sens_ les bonnes odeurs de la cuisine.

9. Ils (offrir) _offrent_ toujours les mêmes fleurs.

10. Il (mourir) _meurt_ de faim.

Faire correspondre les deux colonnes.

__h.__ 1. Il agrandit

__j.__ 2. Le public applaudit

__a__ 3. Nous choisissons

__e__ 4. La voiture ralentit

__i__ 5. Je vous offre

__b__ 6. Tu ouvres

__d__ 7. Ils dorment bien

__f__ 8. Il bout (boil)

__g__ 9. Vous réussissez

__c__ 10. Je cours

a. un bon vin

b. la porte

c. très vite

d. la nuit

e. en voyant le gendarme

f. d'impatience

g. à l'examen

h. la photo

i. des chocolats pour votre anniversaire

j. l'artiste

*Traduire les phrases suivantes en utilisant **vous** si nécessaire.*

1. We are leaving at ten. nous partons a dix heures

2. She opens the door. elle ouvre la porte

3. You pick some flowers in Florence's garden. vous cueillez des fleurs dans le jardin de Florence

4. The car is slowing down. la voiture ralentit

5. We are going out tonight. Nous sortons ce soir

6. She seizes the opportunity. Elle saisit l'occasion

7. She blushes easily. Elle rougit facilement

8. They run fast. Ils courent vite

9. She solves the mystery.

Elle résout la mystère

10. They sleep in Sonia's bedroom.

Ils dorment dans la chambre de Sonia

VOCABULAIRE

Quelle langue parlez-vous?

l'allemand (*m.*)	*German*	l'italien (*m.*)	*Italian*
l'anglais (*m.*)	*English*	le japonais	*Japanese*
l'arabe (*m.*)	*Arabic*	le polonais	*Polish*
le chinois	*Chinese*	le portugais	*Portuguese*
le créole	*Creole*	le russe	*Russian*
l'espagnol (*m.*)	*Spanish*	le swahili	*Swahili*
le français	*French*	le wolof	*Wolof*
l'hindi (*m.*)	*Hindi*		

-re verbs in the present

For regular -**re** verbs, remove the -**re** ending and follow the pattern below.

vendre to sell

je vend**s**	*I sell*	nous vend**ons**	*we sell*
tu vend**s**	*you sell*	vous vend**ez**	*you sell*
il/elle vend	*he/she sells*	ils/elles vend**ent**	*they sell*

Here are other verbs that are conjugated in the same way:

attendre	*to wait*	**j'attends**	*I wait*
défendre	*to defend, to forbid*	**je défends**	*I defend, I forbid*
descendre	*to go down*	**je descends**	*I go down*
détendre	*to release, to relax*	**je détends**	*I release, I relax*
entendre	*to hear*	**j'entends**	*I hear*
étendre	*to spread out, to extend*	**j'étends**	*I spread out, I extend*
mordre	*to bite*	**je mords**	*I bite*
perdre	*to lose*	**je perds**	*I lose*
prétendre	*to claim*	**je prétends**	*I claim*
rendre	*to give back, to return*	**je rends**	*I give back, I return*
répandre	*to spread, to spill*	**je répands**	*I spread, I spill*
répondre	*to answer*	**je réponds**	*I answer*
tendre	*to stretch, to hold out*	**je tends**	*I stretch, I hold out*
tordre	*to twist*	**je tords**	*I twist*

Mettre au présent les verbes entre parenthèses.

1. Nous (répondre) __répondons__ aux questions du professeur de français.
2. La presse anglaise (répandre) __répand__ une rumeur inquiétante.
3. Vous (rendre) __rendez__ les livres à la bibliothèque.
4. Ils (vendre) __vendent__ des fruits et légumes au marché.
5. Je (descendre) __descends__ l'escalier à toute vitesse.
6. Tu (attendre) __tu attends__ l'autobus depuis dix minutes.
7. Il me (tendre) __tend__ la main pour me dire bonjour.
8. Elle (perdre) __perd__ toujours ses clés.
9. Il (prétendre) __il prétend__ être le plus intelligent.
10. Ils (étendre) __étendent__ leur action à d'autres domaines.

Faire correspondre les deux colonnes.

__h__ 1. Le chat mord   a. le train

__e__ 2. Je perds toujours   b. toutes sortes de marchandises

__g__ 3. Elle prétend   c. au questionnaire

__i__ 4. Nous entendons   d. leurs activités à l'étranger

__a__ 5. Tu attends   e. mon parapluie

__c__ 6. Je réponds   f. l'atmosphère

__b__ 7. Ce magasin vend   g. être très riche

__j__ 8. L'étudiant rend   h. la souris

__d__ 9. Ils désirent étendre   i. du bruit dans la rue

__f__ 10. Son humour détend un peu j. trois livres à la bibliothèque

Irregular -re verbs

Some fairly common **-re** verbs are irregular. Let's look at **prendre** (*to take*):

je **prends**	*I take*	nous **prenons**	*we take*
tu **prends**	*you take*	vous **prenez**	*you take*
il/elle **prend**	*he/she takes*	ils/elles **prennent**	*they take*

And its variations:

apprendre	*to learn*	**j'apprends**	*I learn*
comprendre	*to understand*	**je comprends**	*I understand*
entreprendre	*to undertake*	**j'entreprends**	*I undertake*
surprendre	*to surprise, to discover*	**je surprends**	*I surprise, I discover*

EXERCICE 2·6

Mettre au présent les verbes entre parenthèses.

1. Nous (prendre) _prenons_ le petit déjeuner à huit heures.

2. Il (entreprendre) _entreprend_ toujours des choses dangereuses.

3. Je (apprendre) _j'apprends_ l'allemand.

4. Vous (comprendre) _comprenez_ son hésitation.

5. Ils (apprendre) _apprendent_ à conduire.

6. Il (surprendre) _surprend_ le secret.

7. Vous (prendre) _prenez_ de longues vacances.

8. Nous (comprendre) _comprenons_ le chinois.

9. Tu (prendre) _prenas_ une autre direction.

10. Elle (comprendre) _comprend_ tout.

EXERCICE 2·7

*Traduire les phrases suivantes en utilisant **vous** si nécessaire.*

1. He is learning Chinese.

   il apprend le Chinois

2. She takes the subway every day.

   elle prend le métro tous les jours

3. He often loses his keys.

   il perd souvent ses clefs

4. I can hear Pierre on the street.

   j'entends Pierre dans la rue

5. He claims to be the king's brother.

   il prétend être le frère du roi

6. You answer quickly.

   Vous répondez rapidement

7. She sells flowers.

   elle vend des fleurs

8. We go down the Champs-Élysées.

   Nous descendons le CE

9. I am going down.

   je descends

10. We are waiting for an answer.

    nous attendons une réponse

The interrogative form

In French there are three ways of asking questions. You can do an inversion of the subject and the verb, use the **est-ce que** form, or simply use the affirmative form with an upward intonation. Let's start with the inversion:

Comprenez-vous la question?	*Do you understand the question?*
Parlez-vous espagnol?	*Do you speak Spanish?*

If the third-person singular of a verb ends with a vowel, a **-t-** is inserted to facilitate the pronunciation.

Parle-t-elle russe?	*Does she speak Russian?*
Voyage-t-il souvent en Europe?	*Does he often travel to Europe?*

A more colloquial way of asking a question is to use the **est-ce que** form in front of the *subject + verb*.

Est-ce que vous habitez à New York?	*Do you live in New York?*
Est-ce que tu sors ce soir?	*Are you going out tonight?*

Est-ce que becomes **est-ce qu'** before a vowel.

Est-ce que vous courez dans le parc?	*Do you run in the park?*
Est-ce qu'ils vendent des timbres?	*Do they sell stamps?*

A third way of asking a question, colloquially, is keeping the order *subject + verb* and speaking with an upward intonation.

Tu finis à cinq heures?	*You're finishing at five o'clock?*
Vous investissez en Asie?	*You're investing in Asia?*

Mettre les phrases suivantes à la forme interrogative en utilisant l'inversion.

1. Ils remplissent les formulaires.

   remplissent-ils les formulaires

2. Il réfléchit au problème.

   réfléchit-il au problème

3. Vous aimez aller au théâtre.

   aimez-vous aller au théâtre

4. Elle préfère voyager en Italie.

   préfère-t-elle voyager en Italie

5. Tu écoutes le discours du président.

   écoutes-tu le discours du président

6. Ils influencent le public.

   influencent-ils le public

7. Elle annule son voyage au Brésil.

   annule-t-elle son voyage au Brésil

8. Tu travailles le jeudi.

   travailles-tu le jeudi

9. Vous apportez un nouveau livre.

   apportez-vous un nouveau livre

10. Elle agrandit les photos.

    agrandit-elle les photos

*Mettre les phrases suivantes à la forme interrogative en utilisant la forme **est-ce que**.*

1. Ils parlent de la nouvelle transaction.

   est-ce qu'

2. Elle apprend le portugais.

   est-ce qu'

3. Vous commandez une bouteille de vin blanc.

est-ce que vous commandez une bouteille de vin blanc

4. Tu demandes une augmentation de salaire.

est-ce que tu demandes une augmentation de salaire

5. Ils financent un grand projet.

est-ce qu'ils financent un grand projet

6. Vous choisissez une autre direction.

est-ce que vous choisissez une autre direction

7. Ils finissent tard.

est-ce qu'ils finissent tard

8. Il prétend être pauvre.

est-ce qu'il prétend être pauvre

9. Ils défendent cette théorie.

est-ce qu'ils défendent cette théorie

10. Vous descendez par l'escalier.

est-ce que vous descendez par l'escalier

The negative form

To make a sentence negative, you simply place **ne... pas** around the verb.

Elle **travaille** le lundi.	*She works on Mondays.*
Elle **ne travaille pas** le lundi.	*She does not work on Mondays.*
Il **répond** à la lettre.	*He answers the letter.*
Il **ne répond pas** à la lettre.	*He does not answer the letter.*

If the **ne** precedes a verb starting with a vowel or a mute **h**, **ne** becomes **n'**.

J'**habite** à Strasbourg.	*I live in Strasbourg.*
Je **n'habite pas** à Strasbourg.	*I do not live in Strasbourg.*
Elle **aime** les marguerites.	*She likes daisies.*
Elle **n'aime pas** les marguerites.	*She does not like daisies.*

Aside from **ne... pas**, there are other negations, constructed in the same way.

Il **n'attend personne**.	*He is not waiting for anybody.*
Tu **ne** voyages **jamais** en hiver.	*You never travel during the winter.*
Il **n'a plus de** patience.	*He has no patience left.*
Elle **ne** répond **rien**.	*She does not answer anything.* (She answers nothing.)
Ce **n'est guère** raisonnable.	*It's hardly reasonable.*

Mettre les phrases suivantes à la forme négative.

1. Il encourage ses employés.

   Il n'encourage pas ses employés

2. Ils visitent le musée.

   Ils ne visitent pas le musée

3. Tu gagnes à la loterie.

   Tu ne gagnes pas à la loterie

4. Elle enlève son chapeau.

   Elle n'enlève pas son chapeau

5. Vous exprimez vos opinions.

   Vous n'exprimez pas vos opinions

6. Tu pèses les fruits.

   Tu ne pèses pas les fruits

7. Il danse la valse.

   Il ne danse pas la valse

8. Vous corrigez les copies des étudiants.

   Vous ne corrigez pas les copies des étudiants

9. Nous étudions l'arabe.

   Nous n'étudions pas l'arabe

   (lose weight)

10. Il maigrit en vacances.

    Il ne maigrit pas en vacances

The negation ni... ni...

The negation **ni... ni...** precedes each noun that it negates. In addition, the negative particle **ne** (**n'**) comes directly before the verb. When the definite article **le, la, l', les** is used before the noun, the definite article remains when the verb is negative.

Il aime **le** café et **le** chocolat.	*He likes coffee and chocolate.*
Il **n'**aime **ni le** café **ni le** chocolat.	*He likes neither coffee nor chocolate.*
Elle aime **le** bleu et **le** jaune.	*She likes blue and yellow.*
Elle **n'**aime **ni le** bleu **ni le** jaune.	*She likes neither blue nor yellow.*

When the indefinite or partitive article is used before the noun in the affirmative sentence, the article disappears when the verb is made negative.

Elle commande **de l'**eau et **du** vin.	*She orders water and wine.*
Elle **ne** commande **ni** eau **ni** vin.	*She orders neither water nor wine.*
Il vend **des** oranges et **des** mangues.	*He sells oranges and mangoes.*
Il **ne** vend **ni** oranges **ni** mangues.	*He sells neither oranges nor mangoes.*

EXERCICE

2·11

*Traduire les phrases suivantes en utilisant **vous** et l'inversion si nécessaire.*

1. I am learning Japanese.

   J'apprends le Japonais

2. He does not speak Italian.

   Il ne parle pas l'Italien

3. She eats neither meat nor cheese.

   elle ne mange ni viande ni fromage

4. They never listen to anybody.

   Ils n'écoutent jamais personne

5. You work late.

   Vous travaillez tard

6. They like neither tea nor coffee.

   Ils n'aiment ni le thé ni le café

7. Do you understand the question?

   comprenez-vous la question?

8. We pick flowers in the garden.

   Nous cueillons des fleurs dans le jardin

9. He never takes off his hat.

   il n'enlève jamais son chapeau

10. She never lies.

    elle ne ment jamais

·3· To be and to have

The verb **être** (to be)

The verbs **être** (*to be*) and **avoir** (*to have*) are essential verbs you need to memorize. They are both irregular. Let's start with **être**:

je **suis**	*I am*	nous **sommes**	*we are*
tu **es**	*you are* (familiar)	vous **êtes**	*you are*
il/elle **est**	*he/she is*	ils/elles **sont**	*they are*

Note that the -**s** of **vous** is pronounced as a **z** when followed by the vowel **ê**- in **êtes**.

Elle **est** américaine.	*She is American.*
Vous **êtes** brésilien?	*Are you Brazilian?*

VOCABULAIRE

agréable	*pleasant*	heureux,	*happy, content,*
amusant(e)	*funny*	heureuse	*glad*
beau, bel, belle	*beautiful*	jeune	*young*
bon, bonne	*good*	libre	*free*
charmant(e)	*charming*	nouveau, nouvel,	*new*
cher, chère	*expensive*	nouvelle	
créatif, créative	*creative*	petit(e)	*small*
efficace	*efficient*	sec, sèche	*dry*
frais, fraîche	*fresh, cool*	sympathique	*nice, friendly*
gentil(le)	*kind, nice*	vieux, vieil, vieille	*old*
grand(e)	*tall*		

EXERCICE
3·1

Mettre au présent les verbes entre parenthèses.

1. Le château (être) _____est_____ vieux.

2. Nous (être) _____sommes_____ libres demain soir.

3. Les produits (être) _____sont_____ beaucoup trop chers.

4. Tu (être) _____es_____ plus jeune que lui?

5. Elles (être) _____*sont*_____ vraiment charmantes.

6. Vous (être) _____*êtes*_____ occupé cet après-midi?

7. Ce (être) _____*C'est*_____ un nouveau livre.

8. Leurs méthodes (ne pas être) _____*ne sont pas*_____ très efficaces.

9. Est-ce qu'il (être) _____*est*_____ aussi amusant que son frère?

10. Je (être) _____*suis*_____ un peu en retard.

EXERCICE

3·2

Répondre aux questions à la forme affirmative.

1. Est-ce qu'ils sont en retard?

   Oui, ils sont en retard.

2. Le climat est sec?

   Oui, le climat est sec.

3. Êtes-vous libre ce soir?

   Je suis libre ce soir.

4. Est-il heureux?

   Il est heureux.

5. Est-ce qu'elle est sympathique?

   Oui, elle est sympathique.

6. Ce restaurant français est cher?

   Oui, ce restaurant est cher.

7. Êtes-vous fatigué?

   Oui, je suis fatigué.

8. Est-ce que nous sommes à la bonne adresse?

   Oui, nous sommes à la bonne adresse.

9. Ce film est amusant?

   Oui, ce film est amusant.

10. Le musée est ouvert?

    Oui, le musée est ouvert.

The verb avoir (to have)

The verb **avoir** (*to have*) also has an irregular conjugation.

j'**ai**	*I have*		nous **avons**	*we have*
tu **as**	*you have*		vous **avez**	*you have*
il/elle **a**	*he/she has*		ils/elles **ont**	*they have*

Note that the **-s** of **nous**, **vous**, **ils**, **elles** is pronounced **z** when followed by a vowel.

Il**s ont** une belle maison.	*They have a beautiful house.*
Vou**s avez** un instant?	*Do you have a moment?*

Note that **un**, **une**, and **des** change to **de** or **d'** when the verb is in the negative form.

Tu as **des** amis à Paris?	*Do you have friends in Paris?*
Non, je **n'**ai **pas d'**amis à Paris.	*No, I do not have friends in Paris.*
Il a **des** enfants?	*Does he have (any) children?*
Non, il **n'**a **pas d'**enfants.	*No, he does not have (any) children.*

The verb **avoir** is used in many common idiomatic expressions. Here are a few examples:

j'ai de la chance	*I am lucky*
j'ai besoin de…	*I need …*
j'ai chaud	*I am hot, warm*
j'ai envie de…	*I feel like …*
j'ai faim	*I am hungry*
j'ai froid	*I am cold*
j'ai honte	*I am ashamed*
j'ai l'air de…	*I seem, I look …*
j'ai mal	*I have a pain, it hurts*
j'ai peur	*I am afraid*
j'ai (trente-cinq) ans	*I am (thirty-five) years old*
j'ai raison	*I am right*
j'ai soif	*I am thirsty*
j'ai tort	*I am wrong*

When referring to the state of one's body, French uses **avoir mal à** (*having an ache or pain*).

J'ai **mal à la tête**.	*I have a headache.*
Il a **mal au bras**.	*His arm hurts.*

When **avoir mal à** is followed by a verb, it means *to have trouble doing something.*

Nous **avons du mal à accepter** sa décision.	*We have trouble accepting his decision.*
Elle **a du mal à monter** l'escalier.	*She has trouble climbing the stairs.*

EXERCICE
3·3

Mettre au présent les verbes entre parenthèses.

1. Nous (avoir) _avons_ quelques minutes.

2. Tu (ne pas avoir) _n'as pas_ assez d'arguments.

3. Je (avoir) _j'ai_ une grande estime pour lui.

4. Vous (avoir) _avez_ des amis à Londres?

5. Elle (avoir) _____ a _____ beaucoup de chance dans les affaires.

6. Ils (avoir) _____ ont _____ une réunion à quinze heures.

7. Tu (avoir) _____ as _____ une maison à la campagne?

8. Nous (ne pas avoir) _____ n'avons pas _____ besoin de son aide.

9. Vous (ne pas avoir) _____ n'avez pas _____ toujours raison.

10. Je (avoir) _____ j'ai _____ froid.

Faire correspondre les deux colonnes.

_g_	1. J'ai faim, alors	a. au casino
_j_	2. Il a peur	b. à la tête
_a_	3. Ils ont de la chance	c. fatigué
_i_	4. L'étudiant de français a besoin	d. il ouvre la fenêtre
_b_	5. Tu as mal	e. de longues vacances
_h_	6. Il a tort, alors	f. elle boit un verre d'eau
_c_	7. Vous avez l'air	g. je mange quelque chose
_e_	8. Ils ont très envie (feel like)	h. il présente ses excuses
_d_	9. Il a chaud, alors	i. d'un nouveau dictionnaire
_f_	10. Elle a soif, alors	j. des fantômes

*Traduire les phrases suivantes en utilisant **vous** et l'inversion si nécessaire.*

1. I am tired.

_____ Je suis fatigué _____

2. He is very hungry.

_____ Il a faim _____

3. They are always right.

_____ Ils ont toujours rais— _____

4. Are they French?

_____ Sont-ils français _____

5. Are you afraid of his reaction?

Avez-vous peur de sa réaction, (f.).

6. He is ashamed.

il a honte (ashamed)

7. They have a dog.

Ils ont un chien.

8. She has a new hat.

elle a un nouveau chapeau

9. It's very expensive.

C'est très cher

10. Close the window. We are cold.

Fermez la fenêtre. Nous avons froid.

The -oir verbs

The **-oir** verbs do not all follow the same conjugation pattern. We'll start with the very useful verb **savoir** (*to know*). **Savoir** means *to know a fact, to know how to do something* from memory or study.

je **sais**	*I know*	nous **savons**	*we know*
tu **sais**	*you know*	vous **savez**	*you know*
il/elle **sait**	*he/she knows*	ils/elles **savent**	*they know*

Elle **sait jouer** du piano.	*She can play the piano.*
Il **sait** ce poème par cœur.	*He knows this poem by heart.*
Ils **savent gérer** leurs affaires.	*They know how to manage their business.*

Note that **savoir** is sometimes translated by *can*. Before a dependent clause or before an infinitive, only **savoir** can be used.

Je ne sais pas **où il est**.	*I don't know where he is.*
Il sait **qu'elle est occupée**.	*He knows she is busy.*

EXERCICE 3·6

Mettre au présent les verbes entre parenthèses.

1. Est-ce que vous (savoir) __savez__ jouer au poker?

2. Je (savoir) __sais__ que Laurent est un bon musicien.

3. Elle (ne pas savoir) __ne sait pas__ s'il travaille lundi.

4. Nous (savoir) __savons__ utiliser cet ordinateur.

5. Tu (savoir) _____sais_____ parler espagnol?

6. Est-ce que tu (savoir) _____sais_____ parler anglais?

7. Il (ne pas savoir) _____ne sait pas_____ faire la cuisine.

8. (Savoir) _____savez_____ -vous quand ils partent?

9. Tu (savoir) _____sais_____ si ce restaurant est cher?

10. Vous (savoir) _____savez_____ où se trouve la Bastille?

Connaître

When learning the verb **savoir**, you also need to become acquainted with the verb **connaître**, in order to understand when to use one or the other. **Connaître** means *to know, to be acquainted with, to be familiar with*. In a figurative way, it means *to enjoy, to experience*. It is always followed by a direct object; it is never followed by a dependent clause.

je **connais**	*I know*	nous **connaissons**	*we know*
tu **connais**	*you know*	vous **connaissez**	*you know*
il/elle **connaît**	*he/she knows*	ils/elles **connaissent**	*they know*

Elle **connaît** bien Paris.	*She knows Paris well.*
Connaissez-vous les Tavernier?	*Do you know the Taverniers?*
Son nouveau roman **connaît** un grand succès.	*His new novel is enjoying great success.*

EXERCICE
3·7

Conjuguer le verbe **connaître** *au présent.*

1. Ils _____connaît_____ bien la Normandie.

2. Nous _____connaissons_____ Julien depuis trois ans.

3. Ce nouveau club _____connaît_____ un grand succès.

4. Je _____connais_____ ce fait.

5. Cet artisan _____connaît_____ son métier.

6. Vous _____connaissez_____ cette chanson?

7. Est-ce que vous _____connaissez_____ un bon restaurant italien?

8. Je _____connais_____ Paris comme ma poche.

9. Il _____connaît_____ cette méthode à la perfection.

10. _____Connaissez_____ -vous l'œuvre de Victor Hugo?

Connaître ou *savoir?*

1. Est-ce que tu _____ sais _____ pourquoi il est absent?

2. Elle _____ sait _____ cette chanson par cœur.

3. Tu _____ sais _____ jouer au base-ball?

4. Nous _____ connaissons _____ la fille de José.

5. Je ne _____ sait _____ pas à quelle heure ouvre la banque.

6. Ils _____ connaissent _____ un bon dentiste.

7. Ce nouveau produit _____ connaît _____ un grand succès sur le marché.

8. Vous _____ connaissez _____ Bertrand?

9. Il _____ sait _____ qu'il n'est pas qualifié pour ce travail.

10. Nous ne _____ connaissa _____ pas ce quartier.

The verbs pouvoir and vouloir

Pouvoir (*can, may*) expresses ability and capability.

je **peux**	*I can*	nous **pouvons**	*we can*
tu **peux**	*you can*	vous **pouvez**	*you can*
il/elle **peut**	*he/she can*	ils/elles **peuvent**	*they can*

Elle ne **peut** pas **venir** aujourd'hui.	*She cannot come today.*
Est-ce que tu **peux** lui **téléphoner**?	*Can you call him?*
Je **peux** vous **donner** des renseignements?	*May I give you some information?*

When asking permission with inversion in formal style, the first-person singular of **pouvoir** takes a different form.

Puis-je vous aider?	*May I help you?*
Puis-je vous donner un conseil?	*May I give you a piece of advice?*

Another formal way of asking questions is to use the conditional form of **pouvoir**. We'll cover this in more depth in Chapter 12.

Pourriez-vous **résoudre** ce problème?	*Could you solve this problem?*
Pourriez-vous **annuler** notre vol?	*Could you cancel our flight?*

The verb **vouloir** (*to want*) is used to express wishes and desires. It is also used for a polite request in the conditional form.

je **veux**	*I want*	nous **voulons**	*we want*
tu **veux**	*you want*	vous **voulez**	*you want*
il/elle **veut**	*he/she wants*	ils/elles **veulent**	*they want*

Elle **veut** une augmentation.	*She wants a raise.*
Nous **voulons** une table près de la cheminée.	*We want a table by the fireplace.*
Je **voudrais** vous **parler**.	*I would like to speak with you.*

Mettre au présent les verbes entre parenthèses.

1. Nous (vouloir) _voulons_ une chambre qui donne sur le jardin.

2. Je (ne pas pouvoir) _ne peux pas_ assister à la réunion à quinze heures.

3. Je (vouloir) _veux_ vous parler avant jeudi.

4. Nous (pouvoir) _pouvons_ envoyer les documents par la poste.

5. Tu (vouloir) _veux_ venir ce soir?

6. Est-ce que vous (pouvoir) _pouvez_ écrire une lettre de recommandation?

7. Elle (pouvoir) _peut_ remplir ce formulaire.

8. Ils (vouloir) _veulent_ partir avant midi.

9. Vous (vouloir) _voulez_ prendre un verre?

10. Est-ce qu'ils (pouvoir) _peuvent_ arriver un peu plus tôt?

A number of other verbs ending in **-oir** are irregular. Let's look at a few examples in their first-person singular and plural forms:

apercevoir to see, to perceive			
j'aperçois	*I see, I perceive*	**nous apercevons**	*we see, we perceive*
décevoir to disappoint			
je déçois	*I disappoint*	**nous décevons**	*we disappoint*
devoir must, to have to			
je dois	*I must, I have to*	**nous devons**	*we must, we have to*
émouvoir to move, to stir			
j'émeus	*I move, I stir*	**nous émouvons**	*we move, we stir*
prévoir to foresee, to predict			
je prévois	*I foresee*	**nous prévoyons**	*we foresee*
promouvoir to promote			
je promeus	*I promote*	**nous promouvons**	*we promote*
recevoir to receive			
je reçois	*I receive*	**nous recevons**	*we receive*
valoir to be worth			
cela vaut	*it is worth*	**nous valons**	*we are worth*
voir to see			
je vois	*I see*	**nous voyons**	*we see*

Falloir and **pleuvoir** are used only in the third-person singular.

falloir	*to be necessary*	**il faut**	*it is necessary*
pleuvoir	*to rain*	**il pleut**	*it is raining*

EXERCICE
3·10

Mettre au présent les verbes entre parenthèses.

1. Je (apercevoir) _j'aperçois_ un château en haut de la colline.

2. Il (prévoir) _prévoit_ un avenir meilleur.

3. Il (pleuvoir) _pleut_ toujours dans cette région.

4. Nous (voir) _voyons_ une amélioration.

5. Tu (décevoir) _déçois_ ton professeur.

6. Cette organisation (promouvoir) _promouvoit_ la recherche scientifique.

7. Cela (valoir) _valut_ très cher.

8. Il (falloir) _faut_ apprendre les conjugaisons.

9. Cet écrivain (émouvoir) _émoutit_ le public.

10. Vous (recevoir) _recevez_ nos félicitations.

EXERCICE
3·11

*Mettre au présent les verbes entre parenthèses en utilisant **tu** et la forme **est-ce que** si nécessaire.*

1. Can you swim?
   Est-ce que tu sais nager

2. Can he cook?
   Est-ce qu'elle sait faire la cuisine

3. I don't know where he is.
   Je ne sais pas où il est

4. Can she fill out this form?
   Est-ce qu'elle peut remplir ce formulaire

5. She knows Caroline.
   Elle connaît Caroline

6. Do you know this French song by heart?
   française
   Est-ce que vous save cette chanson par cœur

7. It is raining in France.

Il pleut en France

8. You must arrive at noon.

Tu dois arriver à midi

9. He foresees a great improvement.

Il prévoit une grande amélioration

10. I see the castle.

Je peux voir le château

 **·4·**

More irregular verbs

The verb **aller** (*to go*)

Wherever you want to go, you'll need the verb **aller** (*to go*). It is an **-er** irregular verb, also used in many idiomatic expressions.

je **vais**	*I go*	nous **allons**	*we go*
tu **vas**	*you go*	vous **allez**	*you go*
il/elle **va**	*he/she goes*	ils/elles **vont**	*they go*

Ils **vont** à Paris à la fin du mois.	*They are going to Paris at the end of the month.*
Elle ne **va** pas à l'école demain.	*She is not going to school tomorrow.*

Use the preposition **à** (*to, at, in*) to say where you are going. Watch out for the contraction: **à** + **le** = **au** and **à** + **les** = **aux**.

Je vais **au** théâtre ce soir.	*I am going to the theater tonight.*
Elle va souvent **à l'**opéra.	*She often goes to the opera.*
Léa va **à la** bibliothèque.	*Léa is going to the library.*
Chloé veut aller **aux** États-Unis.	*Chloé wants to go to the United States.*

Aller is used in many common expressions.

Ça **va**?	*How are you? How are things going?*
Comment **allez**-vous?	*How are you?*
Ce tailleur vous **va** bien.	*This suit looks good on you.*
Comment **va** la famille?	*How is the family?*

VOCABULAIRE

lundi	*Monday*	**juin**	*June*
mardi	*Tuesday*	**juillet**	*July*
mercredi	*Wednesday*	**août**	*August*
jeudi	*Thursday*	**septembre**	*September*
vendredi	*Friday*	**octobre**	*October*
samedi	*Saturday*	**novembre**	*November*
dimanche	*Sunday*	**décembre**	*December*
janvier	*January*	**le printemps**	*spring*
février	*February*	**l'été** (*m.*)	*summer*
mars	*March*	**l'automne** (*m.*)	*fall*
avril	*April*	**l'hiver** (*m.*)	*winter*
mai	*May*		

The immediate future tense

Aller is also used to form the immediate future. So, to talk about what you are *going to do*, use **aller** in the present indicative followed immediately by a verb in the infinitive.

Je **vais acheter** une voiture en mai.	*I am going to buy a car in May.*
Nous **allons faire** un voyage en avril.	*We are going to go on a trip in April.*
Elle **va apprendre** le chinois.	*She is going to learn Chinese.*
Ils **vont** bientôt **déménager**.	*They're going to move soon.*

This construction can replace the present in colloquial speech.

Vous **déjeunez** avec nous?	*Are you having lunch with us?*
Vous **allez déjeuner** avec nous?	*Are you going to have lunch with us?*
Est-ce que tu acceptes leur offre?	*Are you accepting their offer?*
Est-ce que tu **vas accepter** leur offre?	*Are you going to accept their offer?*

And in everyday conversation, the immediate future is often used as a substitute for the future tense (*le futur simple*).

Vous **partirez** la semaine prochaine?	*You'll leave next week?*
Vous **allez partir** la semaine prochaine?	*You're going to leave next week?*
Vous **prendrez** des vacances?	*Will you take any vacation?*
Vous **allez prendre** des vacances?	*Are you going to take any vacation?*

EXERCICE 4·1

Mettre au présent les verbes entre parenthèses.

1. Nous (aller) __allons__ à la plage cet après-midi.

2. Ils (aller) __vont__ à Tahiti en décembre.

3. Je (aller) __vais__ chez le dentiste demain matin.

4. Le lundi, il (aller) __va__ à son cours d'anglais.

5. Vous (aller) __allez__ en vacances à la fin de la semaine.

6. Ça (aller) __va__ ?

7. Elle (aller) __va__ à la banque cet après-midi.

8. Je (aller) __vais__ en Afrique avec mes amis.

9. Il (aller) __va__ au match de base-ball ce soir.

10. Comment (aller) __allez__ -vous?

Mettre les phrases suivantes au futur immédiat.

1. Nous achetons une nouvelle machine à laver.

   Nous allons acheter une nouvelle machine à laver.

2. Il prend des vacances cet automne.

   Il va prendre des vacances cet automne.

3. Vous investissez au Japon.

   Vous allez investir au Japon.

4. Elle a vingt ans.

   Elle a avoir vingt ans.

5. Cette agence promeut cette marchandise.

   Cette agence va promouvoir cette marchandise.

6. Il est président.

   Il va être président.

7. Nous choisissons un cadeau.

   Nous allons choisir un cadeau.

8. Tu dînes au restaurant.

   Tu vas dîner au restaurant.

9. Ils déménagent en janvier.

   Ils vont déménager en janvier.

10. Elle travaille au centre-ville.

    Elle va travailler au centre-ville.

The verb **venir** (*to come*)

The verb **venir** (*to come*) and its derivatives, **devenir** (*to become*), **prévenir** (*to warn, to inform*), **survenir** (*to occur*), are all commonly used verbs. First, let's look at the conjugation:

je **viens**	*I come*	nous **venons**	*we come*
tu **viens**	*you come*	vous **venez**	*you come*
il/elle **vient**	*he/she comes*	ils/elles **viennent**	*they come*

Vous **venez** à huit heures ce soir?   *Are you coming at eight this evening?*
D'où **viennent**-ils?   *Where are they coming from?*
N'oubliez pas de nous **prévenir**.   *Don't forget to inform us.*

The immediate past

The verb **venir** (*to come*) in the present tense + **de**, combined with a verb in the infinitive, expresses an action that has just taken place. Although the construction **venir de** is in the present tense in French, it conveys an idea in the past in English.

Il **vient de partir**.	*He just left.*
Elle **vient de vendre** sa voiture.	*She just sold her car.*

EXERCICE
4·3

Mettre au présent les verbes entre parenthèses.

1. Il (venir) _vient_ d'Espagne.

2. Est-ce qu'elles (venir) _viennent_ ce midi?

3. Tu (venir) _viens_ avec nous?

4. Elle (venir) _vient_ du Canada.

5. Vous (revenir) _revenez_ des Maldives?

6. Elle nous (prévenir) _prévient_ [Inform] toujours à la dernière minute.

7. Nous (venir) _venons_ tous ce soir.

8. Il (devenir) _devient_ [become] fou avec tout ce travail.

9. Vous (revenir) _revenez_ cet après-midi?

10. Je (venir) _viens_ de la contacter.

EXERCICE
4·4

Mettre les phrases suivantes au passé immédiat.

1. Je téléphone à Bernard.   *he has just telephoned Bernard*
   Je viens de téléphoner à Bernard.

2. Il annule son vol.
   Il vient d'annuler son vol (flight)

3. Elle remplace tous ses meubles.
   elle vient de remplacer tous les meubles

4. La police révèle le secret.
   La police vient de révéler le secret

5. Vous commencez à travailler.
   Vous venez de commencer à travailler

6. Elle manque le train.

elle vient de manquer le train

7. Tu as trente ans. _avoir_

tu viens d'a trente ans

8. Il achève ses études.

il vient d'achève ses études

9. Nous parlons à la directrice.

Nous venons de parler à la directrice

10. Ils voient un bon film.

Ils viennent de voyer un bon film

EXERCICE
4·5

*Traduire les phrases suivantes en utilisant **tu** et l'inversion si nécessaire.*

1. Are you going to the movies on Sunday?

Vas-tu au cinéma au dimanche?

2. They are going to move soon.

Dé... qu'il... Ils vont bientôt déménager

3. How are you doing?

Comment va-tu ?

4. They are going to invest in Portugal.

Ils vont investir au Portugal

5. She's just started a new job.

elle vient de commencer un nouvel travail.

6. This hat looks good on you.

Cet chapeau te va bien à toi

7. They just canceled my flight.

Ils viennent d'annuler mon vol

8. He goes to the library on Saturdays.

il va à la bibliothèque le Samedi

9. She just called François.

elle vient d'appeler François

10. She is going to finish the book this afternoon.

elle vient de fini ce livre cet après-midi

Tenir

Another verb conjugated like **venir** is **tenir** (*to hold*):

here
tenir compte de
take into account
trans, trans   well well

je **tiens**	*I hold*	nous **tenons**	*we hold*
tu **tiens**	*you hold*	vous **tenez**	*you hold*
il/elle **tient**	*he/she holds*	ils/elles **tiennent**	*they hold*

Il **tient** ses gants à la main.   *He holds his gloves in his hand.*
Tiens la porte!   *Hold the door!*

Tenir has several different meanings.   *keep/s run (busmas) fit*

Le directeur ne **tient** jamais ses   *The manager never keeps his promises.*
    promesses.
Il **tient** son fils par la main.   *He is holding his son's hand.*
La caféine la **tient** éveillée.   *Caffeine keeps her awake.*
Ils **tiennent** un restaurant à Nice.   *They run a restaurant in Nice.*
Toutes ces affaires ne vont pas **tenir**   *All these things won't fit in your suitcase.*
    dans ta valise.
Ils **tiennent le rythme**.   *They are keeping up the pace.*
Elle **tient compte de** vos commentaires.   *She takes your comments into account.*
Tiens, tiens, c'est étrange...   *Well, well, this is strange . . .*
Tiens, prends ces trois livres.   *Here, take these three books.*

When used with the preposition **à** or **de**, **tenir** takes on another meaning.

Elle **tient à** ses bijoux.   *She is attached to her jewels.*   *attached to – à*
Ils **tiennent à** leurs habitudes.   *They are attached to their habits.*
Marc **tient à** vous voir.   *Marc insists on seeing you.*   *insists – à*
De qui **tient**-elle?   *Whom does she take after?*
Elle **tient de** sa mère.   *She takes after her mother.*   *takes after – de*

EXERCICE
4·6

Faire correspondre les deux colonnes.

  c   1. Il tient à sa voiture.   a. Il ressemble à sa parente.

  d   2. Il ne tient compte de rien.   b. Il veut discuter avec toi.

  e   3. Il ne tient pas ses promesses.   c. Il est attaché à cette chose.

  a   4. Il tient de sa sœur.   d. Il ignore tout.

  b   5. Il tient à te parler.   e. Il ne respecte pas ses engagements.

The verb faire (to do, to make)

Another verb you'll come across all the time is **faire** (*to do, to make*). Let's look at its conjugation:

je **fais**	*I do*	nous **faisons**	*we do*
tu **fais**	*you do*	vous **faites**	*you do*
il/elle **fait**	*he/she does*	ils/elles **font**	*they do*

Qu'est-ce que vous **faites** ce soir?	*What are you doing tonight?*
Nous **faisons** un gâteau.	*We're making a cake.*
Il ne sait pas quoi **faire**.	*He does not know what to do.*

Faire is also used in expressions relating to chores, activities, sports, etc.

Elle **fait les courses** ici.	*She shops here.*
Tu ne **fais** jamais **la cuisine**?	*You never cook?*
Il **fait le ménage** le samedi.	*He does the housecleaning on Saturdays.*
Viens **faire une promenade**!	*Come take a walk!*
L'enfant **fait la vaisselle**.	*The child is doing the dishes.*
Je ne veux pas **faire la queue**.	*I don't want to stand in line.*
Ça **fait combien**?	*How much does it cost?*
Tu **fais du vélo**?	*Do you ride a bike?*
Vous **faites du sport**?	*Do you play sports?*

Faire is used, with the impersonal third-person singular **il**, in most expressions relating to the weather.

Quel temps fait-il?	*What's the weather like?*
Il fait beau.	*It is nice.*
Il fait froid.	*It is cold.*
Il fait frais.	*It is cool.*
Il fait doux.	*It is mild.*
Il fait chaud.	*It is hot.*

A few verbs relating to the weather are used in the impersonal **il** form, without **faire**.

Il pleut.	*It is raining.*
Il neige.	*It is snowing.*
Il grêle.	*It is hailing.*
Il bruine.	*It is drizzling.*

EXERCICE
4·7

Mettre au présent les verbes entre parenthèses.

1. Qui (faire) _fait_ quoi dans cette entreprise?

2. Ils (faire) _font_ un grand voyage chaque année.

3. Tu (faire) _fais_ la cuisine?

4. Quel temps (faire) _fait_ -il à Rome aujourd'hui?

5. Nous (faire) _faisons_ une promenade dans les jardins du Luxembourg.

6. Elle (faire) _fait_ le marché le samedi matin.

7. On (faire) ___fait___ la queue depuis une demi-heure!

8. Ils (faire) ___font___ la sieste de trois à cinq heures.

9. Vous (faire) ___faites___ de l'exercice pour rester en forme?

10. Il (faire) ___fait___ des grimaces devant le miroir.

The causative form

The causative form is, in most cases, used to express the idea of *having something done by someone* or of *causing something to happen*. It is formed with the verb **faire** followed by an infinitive.

Elle **écrit** la lettre elle-même.	*She writes the letter herself.*
Elle **fait écrire** la lettre par sa secrétaire.	*She has the letter written by her secretary.*
Ils **envoient** le document.	*They send the document.*
Ils **font envoyer** le document.	*They have the document sent.*
Elle **fait** la robe.	*She is making the dress.*
Elle **fait faire** la robe.	*She is having the dress made.*

Mettre les phrases suivantes à la forme causative.

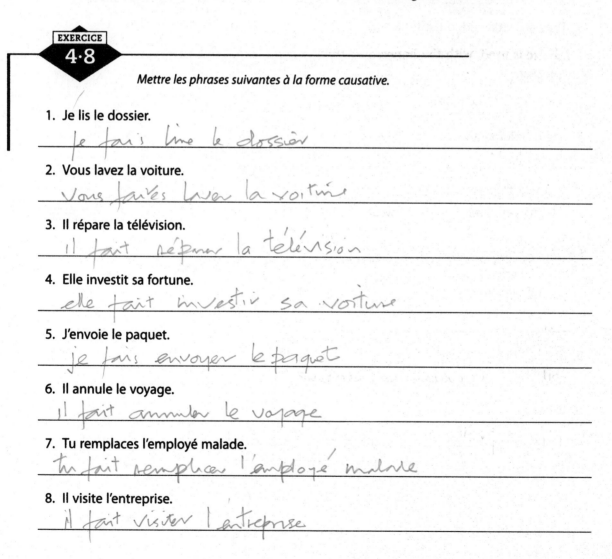

1. Je lis le dossier.

   Je fais lire le dossier

2. Vous lavez la voiture.

   Vous faites laver la voiture

3. Il répare la télévision.

   Il fait réparer la télévision

4. Elle investit sa fortune.

   elle fait investir sa voiture

5. J'envoie le paquet.

   je fais envoyer le paquet

6. Il annule le voyage.

   Il fait annuler le voyage

7. Tu remplaces l'employé malade.

   tu fait remplacer l'employé malade

8. Il visite l'entreprise.

   Il fait visiter l'entreprise

9. Je corrige les copies des étudiants.

Je fais corriga les copies des étudiants

10. Je chante la chanson.

Je fais chanter la chanson.

EXERCICE
4·9

*Traduire les phrases suivantes en utilisant **vous** et la forme **est-ce que** si nécessaire.*

1. They have the letter sent to Paris.

Ils font envoy la lettre à Paris

2. I have been standing in line for ten minutes.

Je fais la queue depuis dix minutes

3. They are attached to their friends.

Ils tiennent a leur amis

4. He really wants to sing this song.

Il tient à chanter cette chanson

5. She is holding a vase.

elle tient un vase.

6. He looks like his father.

il tient de son père

7. It's raining.

il pleut

8. Can you cook? *vous savez fair*

est-ce que ... la cuisin

9. She has her car washed.

elle fait laver sa voiture

10. It's cold.

il fait froid

Devoir and its many facets

The verb devoir (to have to, must)

The verb **devoir** (*must, to have to*) is an irregular verb with various meanings.

je **dois**	*I must*	nous **devons**	*we must*
tu **dois**	*you must*	vous **devez**	*you must*
il/elle **doit**	*he/she must*	ils/elles **doivent**	*they must*

Let's start with the notion of *debt* in the literal and figurative meanings:

- **Devoir** as a *debt*:

Combien est-ce qu'on vous **doit**?	*How much do we owe you?*
Elle me **doit** mille euros.	*She owes me a thousand euros.*
Je vous **dois** quelque chose?	*Do I owe you anything?*
Il **doit** sa vie à son chirurgien.	*He owes his life to his surgeon.*

- **Devoir** as an *obligation*:

Vous **devez assister** à la réunion demain matin.	*You must attend the meeting tomorrow morning.*
L'enfant **doit obéir** à ses parents.	*The child must obey his parents.*
Vous **ne devez pas** y **aller**.	*You must not go there.*

- **Devoir** as a *probability*:

L'avion **doit atterrir** à dix heures.	*The plane is supposed to land at ten o'clock.*
Son livre **doit sortir** la semaine prochaine.	*Her book is supposed to be published next week.*

The voice intonation will often determine if **devoir** implies an obligation or a probability. For example, **il doit venir ce soir**, may mean *he is supposed to come tonight* or *he must come tonight*. Pay attention to intonation and gestures.

- **Devoir** as a *warning* and *suggestion*. When used in the conditional or the past conditional, **devoir** takes on the meaning of *should* or *should have*. We'll cover this aspect in depth in Chapter 12.

Tu **ne devrais pas** lui **prêter** d'argent.	*You should not lend him any money.*
Elles **devraient apprendre** une langue étrangère.	*They should learn a foreign language.*

VOCABULAIRE

une voiture	*a car*	atterrir	*to land*
un autobus	*a bus*	décoller	*to take off (plane)*
un taxi	*a cab*	manquer le train	*to miss the train*
un train	*a train*	conduire	*to drive*
un avion	*a plane*	tomber en panne	*to break down*
une navette	*a shuttle*	faire le plein	*to fill up*
la circulation	*traffic*	monter, descendre	*to get on, to get off*
embarquer	*to go on board*	voyager	*to travel*
débarquer	*to get off*		

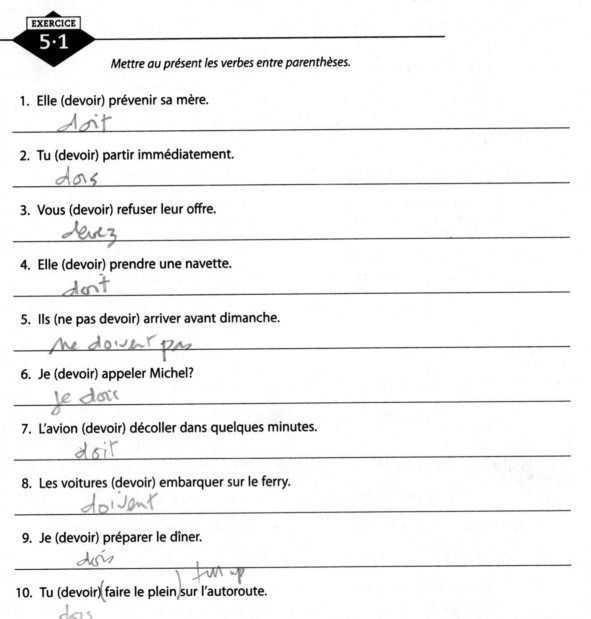

EXERCICE
5·1

Mettre au présent les verbes entre parenthèses.

1. Elle (devoir) prévenir sa mère.

   doit

2. Tu (devoir) partir immédiatement.

   dois

3. Vous (devoir) refuser leur offre.

   devez

4. Elle (devoir) prendre une navette.

   doit

5. Ils (ne pas devoir) arriver avant dimanche.

   ne doivent pas

6. Je (devoir) appeler Michel?

   Je dois

7. L'avion (devoir) décoller dans quelques minutes.

   doit

8. Les voitures (devoir) embarquer sur le ferry.

   doivent

9. Je (devoir) préparer le dîner.

   dois

10. Tu (devoir) (faire le plein) fill up sur l'autoroute.

    dois

*Traduire les phrases suivantes en utilisant **vous** et la forme **est-ce que** si nécessaire.*

1. You must cook tonight.

   tu dois faire la cuisine ce soir

2. She must not work today. _travailler_

   elle ne doit pas aujourd'hui

3. At what time is he supposed to arrive?

   à quelle heure doit-il arriver

4. How much do I owe you?

   combien est-ce que je vous dois

5. Why must he sell his car?

   pourquoi est-ce qu'il doit vendre sa voiture

6. She owes an excuse to Carole.

   elle doit un excuse à Carole

7. Are we supposed to know these verbs?

   est-ce que nous devons connaître ces verbes

8. He owes two thousand dollars to the bank.

   il doit deux milles dollars à la banque

9. You should call Vincent.

   Vous devriez appeler Vincent

10. You should not invite Pierre.

    Vous ne devriez pas inviter Pierre

Faire correspondre les deux colonnes.

_____	1. Elle a des dettes.	a.	Elle doit la vie à son médecin.
_____	2. Elle n'est pas morte.	b.	Elle doit être prudente.
_____	3. Elle va peut-être voyager.	c.	Elle doit faire la cuisine.
_____	4. Elle a des invités.	d.	Elle doit partir en vacances.
_____	5. Elle hésite encore.	e.	Elle doit de l'argent.

Il y a (there is, there are)

Il y a is an impersonal expression that means both *there is* and *there are*.

Il y a un chat sur le canapé.	*There is a cat on the sofa.*
Il n'y a plus rien dans le frigo.	*There is nothing left in the fridge.*

Il y a is used in a variety of expressions.

Qu'est-ce qu'il y a?	*What's the matter?*
Il n'y a qu'à leur dire.	*Just tell them.*
Il y avait une fois...	*Once upon a time . . .*
Il y a cinquante kilomètres d'ici à Paris.	*It's fifty kilometers from here to Paris.*
Il y en a qui feraient mieux de se taire.	*Some people would do better to keep quiet.*

Il s'agit de (it is *a matter of, it's about*)

Il s'agit de (*it is a matter of, it's about*) is a fixed expression that introduces the subject of a work (book, film, etc.) or of a situation.

De quoi s'agit-il?	*What is it about?*
Dans ce film, il s'agit d'un crime.	*This film is about a crime.*
Dans ce roman, il s'agit d'une princesse.	*This novel is about a princess.*
Il s'agit de ton avenir.	*Your future is at stake.*
Il ne s'agit pas de plaisanter.	*This is no time for jokes.*
Il s'agit de faire vite.	*We must act quickly.*
Il ne s'agit pas de dettes.	*It is not a question of debts.*
Il s'agit d'amour.	*It is a matter of love.*

Verbs ending in -eindre and -aindre

Among the -re verbs, some verbs ending in -eindre or -aindre can be grouped together.

Verbs like peindre (*to paint*) include teindre (*to dye*), ceindre (*to encircle*), feindre (*to feign*), craindre (*to fear*), plaindre (*to pity*), and se plaindre (*to complain*).

Let's conjugate the verb peindre:

je peins	*I paint*	nous peignons	*we paint*
tu peins	*you paint*	vous peignez	*you paint*
il/elle peint	*he/she paints*	ils/elles peignent	*they paint*

Le peintre peint le plafond de l'opéra.	*The painter is painting the ceiling of the opera.*
Vous peignez un tableau abstrait.	*You are painting an abstract painting.*

Craindre follows a similar pattern.

je crains	*I fear*	nous craignons	*we fear*
tu crains	*you fear*	vous craignez	*you fear*
il/elle craint	*he/she fears*	ils/elles craignent	*they fear*

Ils craignent le pire.	*They fear the worst.*
Il ne craint pas la douleur.	*He is not afraid of pain.*

EXERCICE 5·4

Conjuguer au présent les verbes entre parenthèses.

1. Elle (craindre) _craint_ de profonds changements.

2. Il (feindre) _feint_ la tristesse.

3. Ils (plaindre) _plaignent_ la pauvre femme.

4. La muraille (ceindre) _ceint_ la ville.

5. Vous (feindre) _feignez_ l'indifférence.

6. Nous (craindre) _craignons_ le ridicule.

7. Vous (peindre) _peignez_ le mur en bleu.

8. Ils (craindre) _craignent_ le froid.

9. Elle (teindre) _teint_ en blond les moustaches de l'acteur.

10. Elle (se plaindre) _se plaint_ tout le temps.

EXERCICE 5·5

*Traduire les phrases suivantes en utilisant **tu** et la forme **est-ce que** si nécessaire.*

1. She is painting the kitchen.

   elle peint la cuisine

2. There is a dog in the car.

   il y a un chien dans le voiture

3. They pity the poor child.

   ils plaignent le pauvre enfant

4. This book is about the French president.

   dans ce livre il s'agit du président français

5. What is it about?

   De quoi s'agit-il?

6. He fears the worst.

   il craint le pire

7. There are books on the table.

   il y a des livres sur la table

8. Is there a computer?

est-ce qu'il y a un ordinateur (.

9. Are you painting the flowers?

~~peignez-vous les fleurs~~ est-ce que j'ai peigne les fleurs

10. It's a matter of passion.

il s'agit de passion

Pronominal verbs

Several different types of verbs are included in the pronominals: the *reflexive*, the *reciprocal*, the *passive*, and the *subjective*. Too many? Not at all! As you study the different types, you'll discover the subtleties of each. How to identify pronominal verbs? Pronominal verbs are verbs that are preceded in the infinitive and in conjugated forms by the pronouns **me, te, se, nous, vous, se**. Let's start with the reflexive verbs.

Reflexive verbs

The action of a reflexive verb is, for the most part, reflected back on the subject, the action being done to oneself. The pronouns **me, te, se** drop the **e** before mute **h** or a vowel.

je **me lève**	*I get up*	nous **nous levons**	*we get up*
tu **te lèves**	*you get up*	vous **vous levez**	*you get up*
il/elle **se lève**	*he/she gets up*	ils/elles **se lèvent**	*they get up*

Il **se lève** à sept heures.	*He gets up at seven.*
Je **me couche** à onze heures.	*I go to bed at eleven.*
Il **s'assoit** sur un banc.	*He sits down on a bench.*

In the negative form, the **ne** follows the subject pronoun and the **pas** follows the conjugated verb.

Elle **ne se réveille pas** avant huit heures.	*She does not wake up until eight o'clock.*
Tu **ne te reposes pas** assez.	*You do not rest enough.*

In the interrogative form, there are three ways of asking questions. You can always make a question with rising intonation (**Tu te couches déjà?**). When inversion is used, the reflexive pronoun remains in front of the verb.

Se rase-t-il tous les matins?	*Does he shave every morning?*
S'occupent-elles de ce dossier?	*Are they taking care of this case (file)?*
Vous maquillez-vous pour monter sur scène?	*Do you put on makeup to go on stage?*

Don't forget the simple interrogative with **est-ce que**:

Est-ce que vous vous préparez à partir?	*Are you getting ready to leave?*
Est-ce que tu t'habilles pour la soirée?	*Are you getting dressed for the party?*

la peau	skin	le coude	elbow
le visage	face	la main	hand
la tête	head	le doigt	finger
les cheveux (*m.pl.*)	hair	l'ongle (*m.*)	nail
les yeux (*m.pl.*)	eyes	la hanche	hip
le nez	nose	la taille	waist
la bouche	mouth	la jambe	leg
les lèvres (*f. pl.*)	lips	le genou	knee
l'oreille (*f.*)	ear	la cheville	ankle
le dos	back	le pied	foot
le bras	arm		

EXERCICE 6·1

Mettre au présent les verbes réfléchis entre parenthèses.

1. Je (s'habiller) _m'habille_ avant de prendre le petit déjeuner.

2. Nous (se lever) _nous levons_ tôt le matin.

3. Elle (se couper) _se coupe_ les cheveux elle-même.

4. Tu (se coucher) _te couches_ trop tard tous les soirs.

5. Ils (se laver) _se lavent_ les mains.

6. Tu (se peigner) _te peignes_ avant de sortir.

7. Vous (se balader) _vous baladez_ dans le parc.

8. Ils (se reposer) _se reposent_ le week-end.

9. Nous (s'amuser) _nous amusons_ à la fête.

10. Elle (se détendre) _se détend_ les jambes sur le canapé.

Reciprocal verbs

The second type of pronominal verb is called *reciprocal*. It describes an action two or more people perform with or for each other. Since two or more people are involved, reciprocal verbs can only be used in the plural (with **se**, **nous**, **vous**).

Ils **s'aiment** beaucoup.	*They love each other a lot.*
Nous **nous parlons** tous les jours.	*We talk to each other every day.*

Mettre au présent les verbes réciproques entre parenthèses.

1. Ils (se marier) _se marien_ la semaine prochaine.

2. Vous (s'embrasser) _vous embrassez_ sur le balcon.

3. Nous (s'écrire) _nous écrivons_ une fois par an.

4. Ils (se retrouver) _se retrouvent_ devant la brasserie.

5. Elles (se voir) _se voyent_ rarement.

6. Nous (se téléphoner) _nous téléphona_ chaque jour.

7. Vous (se quitter) _vous quittez_ sur le quai de la gare.

8. Nous (se disputer) _nous disputa_ assez souvent.

9. Ils (se détester) _se détesvent_ depuis toujours.

10. Nous (se rencontrer) _nous rencontra_ toujours par hasard dans la rue.

Passive pronominals

A third type of pronominal verb is called *passive*. With the passive pronominal verbs, the subject is not a person or an animal. The subject does not perform the action of the verb but rather is subjected to it. It is in the third-person singular, with **se**.

Ça ne **se dit** pas.	*This is not said.*
Ça ne **se fait** pas.	*This is not done.*
Comment ça **se traduit**?	*How is it (that) translated?*
Ça **se voit**.	*It shows.*
Le vin rouge **se boit** chambré.	*Red wine is drunk at room temperature.*

Subjective pronominals

The last type of pronominal verb is called *subjective*. These verbs are neither reflexive nor reciprocal. For idiomatic or historical reasons, they just happen to use the pronominal forms. Try to learn their infinitives with the pronoun **se**.

Elle **s'en va**. (s'en aller)	*She is leaving.*
Il **se doute de** quelque chose. (se douter de)	*He suspects something.*
Ils **s'entendent** très bien. (s'entendre [avec])	*They get along very well.*

Here's a list of commonly used subjective verbs:

s'apercevoir	*to realize*	**je m'aperçois**	*I realize*
s'écrouler	*to collapse*	**je m'écroule**	*I am collapsing*
s'emparer	*to seize*	**je m'empare**	*I am seizing*
s'évanouir	*to faint*	**je m'évanouis**	*I am fainting*
se moquer	*to make fun*	**je me moque**	*I am making fun*

se souvenir	to remember	je me souviens	I remember
s'en aller	to leave	je m'en vais	I am leaving
s'envoler	to vanish	je m'envole	I am vanishing
s'enfuir	to run away	je m'enfuis	I am running away

EXERCICE
6·3

Mettre au présent les verbes subjectifs entre parenthèses.

1. Elle (s'apercevoir) _s'aperçoit_ de sa gaffe. (blunder)
2. Ils (se dépêcher) _se dépêchent_ pour arriver à l'heure.
3. Tu (s'attendre) _t'attends_ à sa visite.
4. Qu'est-ce qui (se passer) _se passe_ ?
5. Vous (se servir) _vous servez_ d'un nouvel appareil.
6. Je (se rendre compte) _me rends compte_ de mon erreur.
7. Tu (se demander) _te demandes_ ce qui va se passer.
8. Elle (se dépêcher) _se dépêche_ car elle est en retard.
9. Tu (se tromper) _te trompes_ de chemin.
10. L'oiseau (s'envoler) _s'envole_ dans le ciel.

Pronominals in the imperative and the infinitive

The pronominal verbs are often used in the imperative, to give commands (*Hurry up! Get up! Let's go!*). We'll study the imperative form in Chapter 19, but in the meantime, note how the imperative form is used with pronominal verbs. For the affirmative imperative, add the stressed pronoun **toi, nous,** or **vous** after the verb, connected with a hyphen.

Réveille-toi!	*Wake up!*
Reposons-nous sur un banc.	*Let's rest on a bench.*
Habillez-vous!	*Get dressed!*

For the negative imperative of pronominal verbs, use **ne** in front of the pronoun and **pas** after the verb. Note that in the negative the reflexive pronoun precedes the verb, as it would in a normal sentence.

Ne te couche pas si tard!	*Do not go to bed so late!*
Ne nous servons pas de cette machine!	*Let's not use this machine!*
Ne vous installez pas dans cette région!	*Do not settle in this region!*

When pronominal verbs are used in the infinitive, the reflexive pronoun is always in the same person and number as the subject, and it precedes the infinitive.

Vous allez **vous apercevoir** de votre erreur.	*You are going to realize your mistake.*
Tu viens de **te marier?**	*Did you just get married?*

EXERCICE

6·4

Conjuguer les verbes entre parenthèses.

1. J'aime (se promener) _me promener_ le long de la Seine.

2. À quelle heure est-ce que tu vas (se lever) _te lever_ ?

3. Nous venons de (se rendre compte) _nous rendre compte_ des conséquences.

4. Elle ne peut pas (se souvenir) _se souvenir_ de son nom.

5. Ils doivent (se marier) _se marier_ au printemps.

6. Vous allez (se demander) _vous demander_ pourquoi il quitte Paris.

7. Nous voulons (s'écrire) _nous écrire_ plus souvent.

8. Je dois (s'habiller) _m'habiller_ pour aller au bal.

9. Vous allez (se voir) _____ pendant les vacances?

10. Nous ne pouvons pas (se plaindre) _nous plaindre_ de la situation.

EXERCICE

6·5

Faire correspondre les deux colonnes.

_e_ 1. Ils sont toujours ensemble.   a. Ils s'écrivent.

_a_ 2. Ils communiquent sans cesse.   b. Ils se détestent.

_d_ 3. Ils s'attendent au pire.   c. Ils aiment marcher.

_c_ 4. Ils se promènent.   d. Ils sont pessimistes.

_b_ 5. Ils ne se parlent jamais.   e. Ils s'aiment. ✓

EXERCICE

6·6

*Traduire les phrases suivantes en utilisant **tu** et l'inversion si nécessaire.*

1. Get up!

Lève-toi

2. She is getting dressed for the party.

elle s'abille pour la soirée

3. She cuts her hair.

elle se coupe les cheveux

4. We are walking in the park.

Nous nous promenons dans le parc.

5. They rest because their legs are tired.

Ils se reposent car leurs les jambes sont fatigué.

6. He is shaving.

il se rase

7. They just got married.

ils viennent de se marier

8. They write to each other.

Ils s'écrivent

9. He is tired. He sits on a bench.

il est fatigué. Il s'assoit sur un banc

10. They love each other.

Ils s'aiment

The passé composé

There are several forms that can be used to talk about the past in French. The most common is the **passé composé**, called in English the compound past or the present perfect. The **passé composé** is one of the tenses colloquially used in French to talk about past events. It refers to a single action in the past. It is built of two parts: the auxiliary or helping verb, **avoir** or **être**, + a past participle.

The past participle of regular verbs

The past participle is formed by adding an ending to the verb stem. Regular past participles take the following endings:

-er verbs take **-é: parler** (*to speak*)	→	**parlé** (*spoken*)
-ir verbs take **-i: choisir** (*to choose*)	→	**choisi** (*chosen*)
-re verbs take **-u: entendre** (*to hear*)	→	**entendu** (*heard*)

Note that the **passé composé** can be translated into English in different ways. Its English equivalent depends on the context.

Elle **a pris** une décision.
> *She made a decision.*
> *She has made a decision.*
> *She did make a decision.*

In the negative form, **ne (n')** is placed in front of **avoir** or **être**, and **pas** after **avoir** or **être**.

Il **a vendu** sa voiture.	*He sold his car.*
Il **n'a pas vendu** sa voiture.	*He did not sell his car.*
Ils **ont dîné** au restaurant.	*They had dinner at the restaurant.*
Ils **n'ont pas dîné** au restaurant.	*They did not have dinner at the restaurant.*

As in the present tense, there are three ways to make a question.

Rising intonation:	Vous avez aimé la pièce?	*Did you like the play?*
Inversion:	**Avez-vous** aimé la pièce?	*Did you like the play?*
With **est-ce que**:	**Est-ce que** vous avez aimé la pièce?	*Did you like the play?*

le cinéma	cinema, movies	la vedette	star (film, sports)
le film	film	les coulisses (f.pl.)	backstage, wings
le documentaire	documentary (film)	les feux de la rampe (m.pl.)	footlights
le metteur en scène	director (film, theater)	l'éclairage (m.)	lighting
tourner un film	to shoot a movie	les décors (m.pl.)	sets
le tournage	shooting (film)	les accessoires (m.pl.)	props
le théâtre	theater	jouer	to play
la pièce de théâtre	play (theater)	un rôle	a part, a role
l'intrigue (f.)	plot	sous-titré(e)	subtitled
l'acteur, l'actrice	actor, actress	doublé(e)	dubbed
le comédien, la comédienne	actor, actress (theater)		

The passé composé with avoir

Most verbs in the **passé composé** are conjugated with **avoir**. Let's review the verb **avoir**:

j'**ai**	*I have*	nous **avons**	*we have*
tu **as**	*you have*	vous **avez**	*you have*
il/elle **a**	*he/she has*	ils/elles **ont**	*they have*

When **avoir** is used with the **passé composé**, with a few exceptions, the past participle *does not* agree in gender and number with the subject of the verb.

Let's briefly review the **passé composé** for -er verbs. It is formed with a conjugated form of **avoir** (or **être**) + the past participle. Drop the infinitive ending (**-er**) and add the participle ending -**é**.

voyager	*to travel*	j'ai (tu as...) voyagé	*I (you . . .) traveled*
marcher	*to walk*	j'ai (tu as...) marché	*I (you . . .) walked*
demander	*to ask*	j'ai (tu as...) demandé	*I (you . . .) asked*

EXERCICE
7·1

Mettre les verbes entre parenthèses au passé composé.

1. Il (inviter) _a invité_ beaucoup de monde.

2. Nous (refuser) _avons refusé_ leur invitation.

3. Tu (travailler) _as travaillé_ hier matin?

4. Il (comprendre) _il a compris_ l'intrigue. (plot)

5. Elle (apporter) _a apporté_ un joli cadeau.

6. Je (voyager) _j'ai voyagé_ avec Rémi.

7. Vous (louer) _avez loué_ une voiture?

8. Elle (sous-titrer) *as-sous-titré* le film.

9. Vous (téléphoner) *avez téléphoné* à vos cousins.

10. Tu (assister) *as assisté* à la pièce de théâtre.

Remember that the past participle of regular -**ir** and -**re** verbs is formed by dropping the infinitive endings -**ir** and -**re** and adding the appropriate ending -**i** or -**u**.

finir	*to finish*	**fini**	*finished*
choisir	*to choose*	**choisi**	*chosen*
vendre	*to sell*	**vendu**	*sold*
perdre	*to lose*	**perdu**	*lost*

In the **passé composé** of verbs conjugated with **avoir**, the past participle agrees with the *direct object* of the verb, but only in sentences where the direct object noun or pronoun *precedes* the verb. For example:

Il a pris **la bonne décision**.	*He made the right decision.*
Il **l'**a prise.	*He made it.*
Elle a compris **ses erreurs**.	*She understood her mistakes.*
Elle **les** a comprises.	*She understood them.*

EXERCICE
7·2

Mettre les verbes entre parenthèses au passé composé.

1. Ils (investir) _____ une grosse somme.

2. Le public (applaudir) _____ les comédiens.

3. Elles (réfléchir) _____ toute la journée.

4. La voiture (ralentir) _____ au carrefour.

5. Ils (attendre) _____ le train une demi-heure.

6. Nous (réussir) _____ à les convaincre.

7. Elle (perdre) _____ ses bijoux en vacances.

8. Tu (grandir) _____ en Europe?

9. Elle (sentir) _____ une bonne odeur venant de la cuisine.

10. Le théâtre (vendre) _____ beaucoup de billets.

Traduire les phrases suivantes.

1. They sold the house in France.

_____

2. I waited ten minutes.

_____

3. He finished the novel.

_____

4. She lost her dictionary.

_____

5. I called Marc.

_____

6. They served an elegant dinner.

_____

7. He bought a car.

_____

8. I chose a very good cheese.

_____

9. We watched the film.

_____

10. They applauded the actor.

_____

Irregular past participles

Many verbs conjugated with **avoir** in the **passé composé** have irregular past participles that you simply have to learn by heart.

Il **a appris** le français à Strasbourg.	*He learned French in Strasbourg.*
Nous **avons compris** la situation.	*We understood the situation.*
Elle m'**a dit** bonjour.	*She said hello to me.*

Here is a sample list of irregular past participles:

acquérir	*to acquire*	**acquis**	*acquired*
apprendre	*to learn*	**appris**	*learned*
avoir	*to have*	**eu**	*had*

boire	to drink	bu	drunk
comprendre	to understand	compris	understood
conduire	to drive	conduit	driven
craindre	to fear	craint	feared
devoir	must, to have to	dû	had to
dire	to say	dit	said
écrire	to write	écrit	written
être	to be	été	been, was
faire	to do, to make	fait	done, made
falloir	to have to	fallu	had to
lire	to read	lu	read
mettre	to put	mis	put
mourir	to die	mort	dead
naître	to be born	né	born
offrir	to offer	offert	offered
ouvrir	to open	ouvert	opened
peindre	to paint	peint	painted
plaire	to please	plu	pleased
pleuvoir	to rain	plu	rained
pouvoir	can, to be able to	pu	could
prendre	to take	pris	taken
recevoir	to receive	reçu	received
rire	to laugh	ri	laughed
savoir	to know	su	known
suivre	to follow	suivi	followed
vivre	to live	vécu	lived
voir	to see	vu	seen
vouloir	to want	voulu	wanted

EXERCICE
7·4

Mettre les verbes entre parenthèses au passé composé.

1. Je (prendre) _____ le train à Lille.

2. Nous (ne pas pouvoir) _____ joindre les Quentin.

3. Ils (suivre) _____ un cours d'anglais en Angleterre.

4. Elle (peindre) _____ un paysage breton.

5. Il (pleuvoir) _____ tout l'après-midi.

6. Vous (recevoir) _____ beaucoup de compliments.

7. Nous (lire) _____ un roman de Zola.

8. Je (faire) _____ la cuisine pour toute la famille.

9. Il (mettre) _____ son chapeau gris.

10. Elle (ouvrir) _____ les fenêtres.

Faire correspondre les deux colonnes.

_____	1. Elle a conduit	a. le journal
_____	2. Tu as compris	b. un accident
_____	3. Vous avez lu	c. une promenade
_____	4. Il a eu	d. les explications
_____	5. Nous avons fait	e. à toute vitesse

The **passé composé** with **être**

Some verbs use **être** instead of **avoir** in the **passé composé**. It is very important to memorize the (finite) list of verbs conjugated with **être**. Many of these are intransitive verbs of movement (**aller, venir, monter**…). In addition, all pronominal (reflexive) verbs (see Chapter 6) are conjugated with **être** in the **passé composé**.

The past participle of verbs conjugated with **être** agrees in gender and number with the subject.

Il est arrivé en retard.	*He arrived late.*
Elle est arrivée en retard.	*She arrived late.*
Ils sont nés en Belgique.	*They (m.) were born in Belgium.*
Elles sont nées en Belgique.	*They (f.) were born in Belgium.*

Here are the verbs conjugated with **être** in the **passé composé**:

aller	*to go*
arriver	*to arrive*
descendre	*to go down*
devenir	*to become*
entrer	*to enter*
monter	*to go up, to climb*
mourir	*to die*
naître	*to be born*
partir	*to leave*
rentrer	*to return*
rester	*to stay*
retourner	*to return, to go back*
revenir	*to return*
sortir	*to go out*
tomber	*to fall*
venir	*to come, to arrive*

Mettre les verbes entre parenthèses au passé composé en utilisant l'inversion si nécessaire.

1. À quel âge ce comédien (monter) _____ sur scène?

2. Nous (rentrer) _____ du théâtre à minuit.

3. La voiture (tomber) _____ en panne près de Madrid.

4. Ils (descendre) _____ par l'escalier.

5. Elles (revenir) _____ de vacances mardi.

6. Quel jour (partir) _____?

7. Elle (aller) _____ à l'opéra hier soir.

8. Luc (aller) _____ au Mexique l'hiver dernier.

9. Molière (mourir) _____ en 1673.

10. Le metteur en scène (rester) _____ dans les coulisses.

Traduire les phrases suivantes.

1. She read the newspaper.

_____

2. We went to Paris.

_____

3. They left last night.

_____

4. He had to leave at five o'clock.

_____

5. They lived in Italy.

_____

6. Zola died in 1902.

_____

7. I wrote a long letter.

_____

8. She has painted the wall white.

_____

9. She stayed at home.

_____

10. He took some vacation.

_____

Pronominal verbs in the passé composé

As we mentioned earlier, all pronominal verbs are conjugated with **être**. The reflexive pronouns precede the auxiliary verb (**être**). In most cases, the past participle agrees in gender and number with the subject of the pronominal verb.

se réveiller to wake up			
je **me suis réveillé(e)**	_I woke up_	nous **nous sommes réveillé(e)s**	_we woke up_
tu **t'es réveillé(e)**	_you woke up_	vous **vous êtes réveillé(e)(s)**	_you woke up_
il/elle **s'est réveillé(e)**	_he/she woke up_	ils/elles **se sont réveillé(e)s**	_they woke up_

Elle **s'est promenée** sur la plage.	_She walked on the beach._
Ils **se sont ennuyés** à la réception.	_They were (got) bored at the reception._
Il **s'est évanoui** à cause de la chaleur.	_He fainted because of the heat._

In the negative, the negation is placed around the auxiliary verb **être**.

Ils **ne** se sont **pas** couchés de bonne heure.	_They did not get up early._
Elle **ne** s'est **pas** promenée le long du canal.	_She did not take a walk along the canal._

In the interrogative form, the reflexive pronoun is placed before **être**.

S'est-il rendu compte de son erreur?	_Did he realize his mistake?_
Vous êtes-vous bien amusés à la fête?	_Did you have a good time at the party?_

Note that the past participle does not agree with the subject of the pronominal verb when the verb is followed by a direct object or by another verb.

Elle s'est offert **une nouvelle moto**.	_She treated herself to a new motorbike._
Elle s'est coupé **les ongles**.	_She trimmed her nails._
Elle s'est fait **arracher** une dent.	_She had a tooth pulled._

When reciprocal verbs take a _direct object_, the past participle agrees with the subject.

Ils **se sont rencontrés** à Venise.	_They met in Venice._
Ils **se sont embrassés**.	_They kissed each other._
Ils **se sont mariés** en mars.	_They got married in March._

When reciprocal verbs take an *indirect object* in French, the past participle *does not* agree.

Ils **se sont téléphoné**.	*They called each other.*
Vous **vous êtes parlé** au téléphone.	*You talked to each other on the phone.*
Ils **se sont écrit** de longues lettres.	*They wrote each other long letters.*

Verbs conjugated with avoir or être

Six verbs among those conjugated with **être** in the **passé composé** (**sortir, rentrer, monter, descendre, passer, retourner**) are conjugated with **avoir** and follow the **avoir** agreement *when a direct object follows the verb*. In these cases, the meaning of the verb has changed.

Ils **sont montés** en haut de la Tour Eiffel.	*They went to the top of the Eiffel Tower.*
Ils **ont monté les malles** au grenier.	*They took the trunks up to the attic.*

Note above that **les malles** is the direct object of **monter**, thus it is conjugated with **avoir**.

Elle **est descendue** au rez-de-chaussée.	*She went down to the ground floor.*
Elle **a descendu les poubelles**.	*She took down the garbage cans.*
Elle **est sortie** avec des amis.	*She went out with some friends.*
Elle **a sorti la voiture** du garage.	*She took the car out of the garage.*
Elle **est rentrée** de vacances hier.	*She came back from vacation yesterday.*
Elle **a rentré les géraniums** dans le salon.	*She brought the geraniums into the living room.*
Je **suis passée** devant les Galeries Lafayette.	*I passed by the Galeries Lafayette.*
J'**ai passé trois semaines** à Tokyo.	*I spent three weeks in Tokyo.*
Je **suis retournée** à Venise pour la troisième fois.	*I went back to Venice for the third time.*
Elle **a retourné l'omelette**.	*She turned over the omelette.*

EXERCICE
7·8

Mettre au passé composé les verbes entre parenthèses.

1. Ils (se promener) _____ le long de la rivière.

2. Il (se douter) _____ de quelque chose.

3. Elles (se maquiller) _____ pour aller au bal.

4. Ils (s'écrire) _____ régulièrement.

5. Nous (s'arrêter) _____ au bord de la route.

6. Ils (s'occuper) _____ de tout.

7. Elles (se balader) _____ à la campagne.

8. Ils (se rencontrer) _____ à une conférence.

9. Tu (se couper) _____ le doigt.

10. Nous (se demander) _____ pourquoi il était absent.

Faire correspondre les deux colonnes.

_____ 1. Elle a sorti   a. le bifteck

_____ 2. Il a retourné   b. devant le boulanger

_____ 3. Elle est rentrée   c. pour la cinquième fois

_____ 4. Je suis passée   d. très tard

_____ 5. Elle est retourné à Rome   e. les chaises de jardin

Traduire les phrases suivantes.

1. They spent a month in China.

_____

2. She fainted.

_____

3. They kissed each other.

_____

4. They had fun at the party.

_____

5. She took the suitcases down.

_____

6. He brushed his teeth.

_____

7. He woke up tired.

_____

8. They wrote each other regularly.

_____

9. Anna stopped for ten minutes.

_____

10. He flipped the omelette.

_____

The imparfait

The imparfait

The uses of the **imparfait** (*imperfect*) are some of the most difficult aspects of French grammar to master. While the **passé composé** is used to talk about an action that took place on a specific occasion in the past, the **imparfait** plays a different role. It is used to describe a state of mind and being in the past as well as continuous, repeated, or habitual past actions.

To form the imperfect, take the **nous** form of the present tense and remove the **-ons** ending, which gives you the stem. Then add the **imparfait** endings (**-ais, -ais, -ait, -ions, -iez, -aient**) to this stem. For example:

parler *to speak*			
nous parlons	→	**parl-**	
je parl**ais**	*I spoke*	nous parl**ions**	*we spoke*
tu parl**ais**	*you spoke*	vous parl**iez**	*you spoke*
il/elle parl**ait**	*he/she spoke*	ils/elles parl**aient**	*they spoke*

Note that the **-ais, -ait, -aient** endings are pronounced alike. Verbs with spelling changes in the present tense **nous** form, such as **manger** and **commencer** (see Chapter 1), retain the spelling change only for the **je, tu, il, elle, ils,** and **elles** subject pronouns.

j'**encourageais**	*I encouraged*
elle **exigeait**	*she demanded*
ils **partageaient**	*they shared*
il **avançait**	*he moved forward*
elle **remplaçait**	*she replaced*
elles **annonçaient**	*they announced*

The extra **e** or the **ç** are not needed in the **nous** and **vous** forms of the **imparfait**.

nous **nagions**	*we swam*
nous **protégions**	*we protected*
nous **commencions**	*we started*
vous **effaciez**	*you erased*

Depending on the context, the **imparfait** can be the equivalent of several past equivalents in English.

Elle **faisait...**	*She was doing . . .*
	She used to do . . .
	She did . . .

Note that the verb **être** has an irregular stem in the **imparfait**.

j'**étais**	*I was*	nous **étions**	*we were*
tu **étais**	*you were*	vous **étiez**	*you were*
il/elle **était**	*he/she was*	ils/elles **étaient**	*they were*

VOCABULAIRE

les vacances (*f.pl.*)	*vacation*	escalader	*to climb*
faire un voyage	*to go on a trip*	une étape	*a stopover (car travel)*
un voyage d'agrément	*a pleasure trip*	explorer	*to explore*
un voyage d'affaires	*a business trip*	une expédition	*an expedition*
un pèlerinage	*a pilgrimage*	une visite guidée	*a guided tour*
à la mer	*by the sea*	visiter	*to visit (a place)*
à la plage	*at the beach*	rendre visite à	*to visit (someone)*
à la campagne	*in the country*	accueillir	*to welcome*
à la montagne	*in the mountains*	un festival	*a festival*
le paysage	*landscape, countryside*	un divertissement	*an entertainment, an*
dans le parc	*in the park*		*amusement*
randonner	*to go hiking*	les loisirs (*m.pl.*)	*leisure time*

EXERCICE
8·1

Mettre les verbes entre parenthèses à l'imparfait.

1. Il (voyager) _____ chaque année en Australie.

2. Tu (faire) _____ du sport à l'école?

3. Nous (être) _____ enchantés de notre expédition.

4. Ils (boire) _____ du café noir le matin.

5. Je (être) _____ champion de tennis.

6. Nous (aimer) _____ faire la cuisine.

7. Elles (partager) _____ une chambre à l'université.

8. Il (prendre) _____ toujours une semaine de vacances en février.

9. Le guide (encourager) _____ les marcheurs.

10. Vous (aller) _____ au bord de la mer en été.

Let's look at the different uses of the **imparfait**. It is used for background and description. It describes a situation that existed in the past, a state of mind or being.

Les rues **étaient** embouteillées.	*The streets were jammed.*
La circulation **était** fluide.	*The traffic was flowing.*
Il **faisait** trop chaud.	*It was too hot.*

| Il **avait** faim. | He was hungry. |
| Elle ne **savait** pas quoi faire. | She did not know what to do. |

The **imparfait** versus the **passé composé**

As they express a mental or physical state of being, some verbs tend to be used more often in the **imparfait** than in the **passé composé**. Among these verbs are: **être** (*to be*), **avoir** (*to have*), **penser** (*to think*), **croire** (*to believe*), **savoir** (*to know*), **espérer** (*to hope*), **sembler** (*to seem*), **paraître** (*to appear*). However, when these verbs are used in the **passé composé**, they may take on a different meaning.

Il **semblait** déprimé.	He looked depressed.
Tout à coup il **a semblé** comprendre la situation.	Suddenly he seemed to understand the situation.
Je **savais** qu'il avait raison.	I knew he was right.
Immédiatement, j'**ai su** qu'il était innocent.	Immediately, I realized he was innocent.

EXERCICE
8·2

Mettre les verbes entre parenthèses à l'imparfait.

1. Il (croire) _____ que tu ne voulais pas venir.

2. Je (être) _____ à la montagne.

3. Elle (penser) _____ à ses prochaines vacances.

4. Ils (espérer) _____ un miracle.

5. Elle (avoir) _____ très faim.

6. Je (savoir) _____ qu'il avait raison.

7. Nous (être) _____ réalistes.

8. Vous (paraître) _____ sceptique.

9. L'exposition (être) _____ fascinante.

10. Il (faire) _____ un temps glacial.

Another use of the **imparfait** is to express habitual, repetitive action. It describes past events that were repeated. *Used to* and *would* (meaning *habitually*) are translated into French by the **imparfait**.

Autrefois, elle **faisait** partie de la chorale.	In the past, she used to belong to the choir.
Ils **allaient** en Inde chaque année.	They used to go (would go) to India every year.
Il **jouait** au tennis le mardi.	He used to (would) play tennis on Tuesdays.

As you can see in the previous examples, some expressions of time or repetition may be an indication of the **imparfait**:

| **souvent** | *often* |
| **fréquemment** | *frequently* |

toujours	*always*
le mardi	*on Tuesdays*
le vendredi	*on Fridays*
chaque jour	*every day*
tous les jours	*every day*
chaque semaine	*every week*
chaque mois	*every month*
chaque année	*every year*
d'ordinaire	*ordinarily*
d'habitude	*usually*
habituellement	*usually*
régulièrement	*regularly*
comme à l'accoutumée	*as usual*
autrefois	*formerly*
jadis	*in times past*

EXERCICE
8·3

Mettre les verbes entre parenthèses à l'imparfait.

1. Nous (suivre) _____ des cours de danse tous les mardis.

2. Je (faire) _____ de la natation tous les jours.

3. La vie (être) _____ plus facile.

4. Nous (faire) _____ la grasse matinée tous les dimanches.

5. À cette époque, ils (habiter) _____ en banlieue.

6. Nous (boire) _____ du café.

7. Autrefois, ils (assister) _____ à tous les concerts.

8. Dans son enfance, elle (faire) _____ de l'équitation.

9. Dans le passé, vous (se voir) _____ plus souvent.

10. Elle (travailler) _____ chez Guerlain.

The **imparfait** is also used to describe a continuous action that was going on in the past when another action (expressed in the **passé composé**) interrupted it.

Elle **regardait** la télévision quand soudain elle **a entendu** un grand bruit.	*She was watching television when suddenly she heard a loud noise.*
Il **faisait** ses devoirs quand son frère **est arrivé**.	*He was doing his homework when his brother arrived.*

To express the idea that an action had been going on for a period of time before being interrupted, use the **imparfait** with **depuis**. This is the equivalent to the past of **depuis** + present tense you studied in Chapter 1.

Ils **étaient** à la montagne **depuis une semaine** quand ils **ont décidé** d'aller au bord de la mer.
Il **randonnait depuis trois jours** quand il **a trouvé** cette belle auberge.

They had been in the mountains for a week when they decided to go to the seashore.
He had been hiking for three days when he found this beautiful inn.

Mettre les verbes entre parenthèses à l'imparfait.

1. Il (faire) _____ un discours quand quelqu'un dans l'assistance l'a interrompu.

2. Je (dormir) _____ quand le chat a sauté sur mon lit.

3. Nous (bavarder) _____ depuis une heure quand il est arrivé.

4. Ils (se reposer) _____ quand une alarme a retenti.

5. Vous (parler) _____ depuis un moment quand soudain il s'est levé.

6. Elle (étudier) _____ l'architecture depuis un an quand elle a décidé de

   changer de filière.

7. Ils (danser) _____ quand la musique s'est arrêtée.

8. Il (réfléchir) _____ quand une idée lui a traversé l'esprit.

9. Elle (travailler) _____ dans son bureau quand ils ont frappé à la porte.

10. Je (attendre) _____ Roland depuis dix minutes quand enfin il est arrivé.

*Traduire les phrases suivantes en utilisant la forme **tu** si nécessaire.*

1. I used to play tennis every Thursday.

_____

2. You were studying when the phone rang.

_____

3. We were sleeping when suddenly we heard a loud noise.

_____

4. The restaurant was crowded.

_____

5. It was cold in the mountains.

_____

6. They looked tired.

_____

7. The play was fascinating.

_____

8. She used to work at the Galeries Lafayette.

_____

9. We were waiting for the bus when it started to rain.

_____

10. She knew they were wrong.

_____

The **imparfait** with special constructions

With a **si** + **on** construction, the **imparfait** is used to make a suggestion or to invite someone to do something. The informal **on** refers to two or more people and is conjugated in the third-person singular.

Si on allait en France cet été?	*What about going to France this summer?*
Si on achetait des billets?	*What about buying tickets?*
Si on allait nager dans le lac?	*What about going swimming in the lake?*
Si on allait rendre visite à Léo?	*What about paying a visit to Léo?*

EXERCICE
8·6

Mettre les verbes entre parenthèses à l'imparfait.

1. Si on (aller) _____ se promener dans la forêt?

2. Si on (déjeuner) _____ ensemble?

3. Si on (apporter) _____ une boîte de chocolats à Julie?

4. Si on (attendre) _____ encore quelques minutes?

5. Si on (commander) _____ un dessert?

6. Si on (faire) _____ un voyage en Grèce?

7. Si on (ouvrir) _____ un restaurant?

8. Si on (investir) _____ dans cette entreprise?

9. Si on (réfléchir) _____ avant de prendre une décision?

10. Si on (choisir) _____ une autre formule?

You will encounter the **imparfait** in other idiomatic constructions, for instance, preceded by **si seulement**, to express a wish or a regret.

Si seulement on pouvait prendre des vacances!	*If only we could take a vacation!*
Si seulement elle était à l'heure!	*If only she were on time!*
Si seulement ils habitaient plus près!	*If only they lived closer!*
Si seulement vous saviez!	*If only you knew!*

In Chapter 4, you studied the immediate past with the verb **venir** + **de** + infinitive. The immediate past can also be used in the **imparfait** to describe an action that *had just happened*.

Elle **vient de téléphoner**.	*She has just called.*
Elle **venait de téléphoner** quand il est entré.	*She had just called when he walked in.*
Il **vient d'accepter** ce poste.	*He just accepted this position.*
Il **venait d'acccepter** ce poste quand on lui en a proposé un autre.	*He had just accepted this position when he was offered another one.*

EXERCICE
8·7

Passé composé ou imparfait?

1. Je (aller) _____ chez le dentiste hier.

2. Quand il (être) _____ adolescent, il (jouer) _____ au football.

3. À cette époque-là, ils (tenir) _____ une brasserie place d'Italie.

4. Ils (randonner) _____ dans les Alpes le week-end passé.

5. Nous (dîner) _____ dans ce restaurant tous les samedis.

6. Si on (prendre) _____ un café?

7. Tu (avoir) _____ l'air fatigué.

8. Chaque jour, il (écrire) _____ une lettre à son amie.

9. Je (regarder) _____ un film quand elle (arriver) _____ .

10. La campagne (être) _____ si belle.

The **futur simple** and the **futur antérieur**

The **futur simple**

You have become acquainted with the future in Chapter 4 when you studied the **futur immédiat**. French has two other future constructions: the **futur simple** and the **futur antérieur**. To form the **futur simple** of most verbs, use the infinitive as the stem and add the endings **-ai, -as, -a, -ons, -ez, -ont**. For **-re** verbs, drop the **e** from the infinitive before adding the endings. Here are some examples:

décider to *decide*

je décider**ai**	*I'll decide*	nous décider**ons**	*we'll decide*
tu décider**as**	*you'll decide*	vous décider**ez**	*you'll decide*
il/elle décider**a**	*he'll/she'll decide*	ils/elles décider**ont**	*they'll decide*

choisir to *choose*

je choisir**ai**	*I'll choose*	nous choisir**ons**	*we'll choose*
tu choisir**as**	*you'll choose*	vous choisir**ez**	*you'll choose*
il/elle choisir**a**	*he'll/she'll choose*	ils/elles choisir**ont**	*they'll choose*

répondre to *answer*

je répondr**ai**	*I'll answer*	nous répondr**ons**	*we'll answer*
tu répondr**as**	*you'll answer*	vous répondr**ez**	*you'll answer*
il/elle répondr**a**	*he'll/she'll answer*	ils/elles répondr**ont**	*they'll answer*

VOCABULAIRE

un(e) élève	a student (elementary school)	un brouillon	a first draft
		passer un examen	to take an exam
		réussir à un examen	to pass an exam
un étudiant, une étudiante	a student (university)	échouer à un examen	to fail an exam
		parler l'anglais couramment	to be fluent in English
un professeur	a teacher, a professor	être rouillé(e)	to be rusty
un cours	a course	un curriculum vitae (C.V.)	a résumé
un examen	an exam		
un stage	training, an internship	analyser	to analyze
		expliquer	to explain
apprendre	to learn	faire l'école buissonnière	to play hooky
enseigner	to teach		
étudier	to study	recevoir son diplôme	to get one's degree
suivre un cours	to take a class		
les devoirs (*m.pl.*)	homework	une note	a grade

Mettre au futur simple les verbes entre parenthèses.

1. Vous (suivre) _____ un cours de français.

2. Nous (dîner) _____ chez Yann la semaine prochaine.

3. Tu (entendre) _____ de la belle musique.

4. Elle (chercher) _____ un autre emploi.

5. Ils (ne jamais oublier) _____ votre générosité.

6. Je (travailler) _____ samedi après-midi.

7. Nous (rendre visite) _____ à notre famille.

8. Il (finir) _____ le livre avant lundi.

9. On (remplacer) _____ tous les meubles.

10. Tu (partir) _____ avant nous.

The endings of the **futur simple** are the same for all verbs. However, some irregular verbs have irregular stems. You simply have to memorize them.

aller	*to go*	**j'irai**	*I'll go*
apercevoir	*to notice*	**j'apercevrai**	*I'll notice*
avoir	*to have*	**j'aurai**	*I'll have*
courir	*to run*	**je courrai**	*I'll run*
devenir	*to become*	**je deviendrai**	*I'll become*
devoir	*must, to have to*	**je devrai**	*I'll have to*
envoyer	*to send*	**j'enverrai**	*I'll send*
être	*to be*	**je serai**	*I'll be*
faire	*to do*	**je ferai**	*I'll do*
falloir	*to have to*	**il faudra**	*one will have to*
mourir	*to die*	**je mourrai**	*I'll die*
pleuvoir	*to rain*	**il pleuvra**	*it'll rain*
pouvoir	*can, to be able to*	**je pourrai**	*I'll be able to*
recevoir	*to receive*	**je recevrai**	*I'll receive*
revenir	*to return, to come back*	**je reviendrai**	*I'll return, I'll come back*
savoir	*to know*	**je saurai**	*I'll know*
tenir	*to hold*	**je tiendrai**	*I'll hold*
valoir	*to be worth*	**il vaudra**	*it will be worth*
venir	*to come*	**je viendrai**	*I'll come*
voir	*to see*	**je verrai**	*I'll see*
vouloir	*to want*	**je voudrai**	*I'll want*

Some slight spelling modifications occur with some verbs. These are seen throughout all persons of the future conjugation.

acheter	*to buy*	**j'achèterai**	*I'll buy*
appeler	*to call*	**j'appellerai**	*I'll call*
employer	*to hire*	**j'emploierai**	*I'll use, I'll hire*
essuyer	*to wipe*	**j'essuierai**	*I'll wipe*
jeter	*to throw*	**je jetterai**	*I'll throw*

nettoyer	*to clean*	**je nettoierai**	*I'll clean*
préférer	*to prefer*	**je préférerai**	*I'll prefer*

Mettre au futur simple les verbes entre parenthèses.

1. Il (être) _____ déçu de ne pas vous voir.

2. L'étudiant (faire) _____ un stage à Nantes.

3. Tu (savoir) _____ demain si tu as réussi à ton examen.

4. Nous (avoir) _____ les résultats demain.

5. Le professeur (aller) _____ à Paris en juin.

6. Il (préférer) _____ suivre le cours d'histoire de l'art.

7. Nous (voir) _____ un bon film au cinéma.

8. Il (falloir) _____ remettre les devoirs jeudi.

9. Elle (pouvoir) _____ aller à la campagne avec nous.

10. Il (pleuvoir) _____ demain.

As in English, the French future tense is used to describe future events.

Les étudiants **passeront** leurs examens en mai.	*Students will take their exams in May.*
Les cours **recommenceront** en décembre.	*Courses will resume in December.*

In a compound sentence in French, if the main clause is in the **futur simple**, the dependent clause, introduced by some conjunctions, will also be in the **futur simple**. Note that in English, such a dependent clause will be in the present tense.

aussitôt que	*as soon as*
dès que	*as soon as*
lorsque	*when*
quand	*when*
tant que	*as long as*

Elle **ira** à Paris quand elle **aura** le temps.	*She'll go to Paris when she **has** time.*
Il nous **dira** lorsqu'il **faudra** parler.	*He'll tell us when we **have** to talk.*
Elle vous **préviendra** dès qu'elle **aura** les résultats.	*She'll inform you as soon as she **gets** the results.*
Aussitôt qu'il **arrivera**, nous **partirons**.	*As soon as he **arrives**, we'll leave.*
Elle vous **téléphonera** aussitôt qu'elle **atterrira** à Londres.	*She'll call you as soon as she **lands** in London.*
Tant qu'il y **aura** du soleil, nous **resterons** sur la terrasse.	*As long as the sun **is** out, we'll stay on the terrace.*

The future tense of **être** and **avoir** is sometimes used to express *probability* in the present, to indicate something that is likely or allegedly true.

| L'étudiant n'est pas en classe. Il **sera** encore endormi. | *The student is not in class. He is probably still asleep.* |
| Le professeur n'a pas demandé nos devoirs. Il **sera** distrait. | *The teacher did not ask for our homework. He's probably distracted.* |

In a narration, the **futur simple** can be used to express a future idea from the standpoint of the past, as shown in the following examples. (Note that English uses a conditional form, *would*, in this case.)

| Malheureusement, ses œuvres ne **seront** reconnues qu'après sa mort. | *Unfortunately, her works would become recognized only after her death.* |
| Un des génies du dix-huitième siècle et il **mourra** dans la misère. | *One of the geniuses of the eighteenth century, and he would die in misery.* |

The **futur simple** can be used instead of an imperative (command form) to achieve a less peremptory tone.

Vous voudrez bien lui envoyer ma réponse.	*Please send him my answer.*
Je vous demanderai de faire preuve de compassion.	*Please show a little compassion.*
Vous voudrez bien nous excuser.	*Please excuse us.*

EXERCICE

9·3

Mettre au futur simple les verbes entre parenthèses.

1. Vous (aller) _____ à l'opéra quand vos amis (être) _____ à Lyon.

2. Nous (prendre) _____ une décision dès que la presse (annoncer) _____ les résultats.

3. L'exposition (avoir lieu) _____ en janvier quand tous les tableaux (être) _____ réunis.

4. Le professeur (emmener) _____ les élèves au musée dès qu'il (pouvoir) _____ .

5. Il (devoir) _____ nous appeler dès qu'il (être) _____ en contact avec M. Clément.

6. Tant qu'il y (avoir) _____ des hommes, il y (avoir) _____ des guerres.

7. Elle (enseigner) _____ le français quand elle (habiter) _____ au Vietnam.

8. Nous (jouer) _____ au bridge quand nous (rendre visite) _____ à nos amis.

9. Elle (se reposer) _____ quand elle (avoir) _____ de longues vacances.

10. Dès qu'il (obtenir) _____ l'accord, il (partir) _____ .

Changer les verbes du futur immédiat au futur simple.

1. L'avion va décoller à onze heures.

_____

2. Tu vas apprendre à conduire.

_____

3. Je vais peindre le salon.

_____

4. Ils vont sortir avec des amis.

_____

5. Vous allez recevoir une invitation.

_____

6. Nous allons débarquer à midi.

_____

7. Elle va écrire une lettre au président.

_____

8. Tu vas mettre ton chapeau gris.

_____

9. Ils vont aller en Bolivie.

_____

10. Il va vivre jusqu'à cent ans.

_____

EXERCICE

9·5

Faire correspondre les deux colonnes.

_____ 1. Elle recevra   a. le français

_____ 2. Tu courras   b. à un âge avancé

_____ 3. Il enseignera   c. son diplôme en juin

_____ 4. Elle mourra   d. pilote de ligne

_____ 5. Il deviendra   e. dans le parc

The **futur antérieur**

The **futur antérieur** (*future perfect*) describes an action that will take place and be completed before another future action. To form this compound tense, use the future tense of **avoir** or **être** + the past participle of the main verb. Agreement rules are the same as for the **passé composé**. Although it is rarely used in English, it must be used in French under certain circumstances.

écrire *to write*			
j'**aurai écrit**	*I'll have written*	nous **aurons écrit**	*we'll have written*
tu **auras écrit**	*you'll have written*	vous **aurez écrit**	*you'll have written*
il/elle **aura écrit**	*he/she will have written*	ils/elles **auront écrit**	*they'll have written*

devenir *to become*			
je **serai devenu(e)**	*I'll have become*	nous **serons devenu(e)s**	*we'll have become*
tu **seras devenu(e)**	*you'll have become*	vous **serez devenu(e)(s)**	*you'll have become*
il/elle **sera devenu(e)**	*he'll/she'll have become*	ils/elles **seront devenu(e)s**	*they'll have become*

Nous **aurons résolu** tous les problèmes d'ici la fin de l'année.	*We'll have solved all the problems by the end of the year.*
Il **aura enseigné** le français toute sa vie.	*He'll have taught French all his life.*

EXERCICE 9·6

Mettre les verbes entre parenthèses au futur antérieur.

1. Elle (apprendre) _____ le français au Laos.

2. Il (finir) _____ son roman avant la fin de l'année.

3. Nous (visiter) _____ tous les sites historiques de la région.

4. Les chercheurs (trouver) _____ un nouveau vaccin.

5. On (découvrir) _____ un remède plus efficace.

6. Je (répondre) _____ à toutes les questions.

7. Elle (se reposer) _____ des semaines au bord du lac.

8. Ils (compléter) _____ leur stage de formation.

9. Il (mourir) _____ depuis longtemps.

10. Je (voir) _____ l'essentiel.

Sometimes you have a choice between the **futur simple** and the **futur antérieur**. When both clauses use the **futur simple**, it is implied that both actions take place simultaneously.

Elle vous **téléphonera** dès qu'elle **finira** son roman.	*She'll call you as soon as she finishes her novel.*

If you want to mark an anteriority, use the **futur antérieur**.

Elle vous **téléphonera** dès qu'elle **aura fini** son roman.	*She'll call you as soon as she finishes (will have finished) her novel.*
Dès que vous **accepterez** cette théorie, on en **discutera** plus longuement.	*As soon as you accept this theory, we'll discuss it at length.*
Dès que vous **aurez accepté** cette théorie, on en **discutera** plus longuement.	*As soon as you accept (will have accepted) this theory, we'll discuss it at length.*

The **futur antérieur** can also express the *probability* of a past action, in the same way that the **futur simple** can be used to express probability in the present.

Elle **aura** encore **échoué** à ses examens!	*She probably failed her exams again!*
Il **aura** encore **brûlé** le gigot d'agneau!	*He probably burnt the leg of lamb again!*
Ils **auront manqué** leur train.	*They probably missed their train.*
Son fils **aura** encore **fait** des bêtises!	*His son probably got in trouble again!*

The **futur antérieur** is also used after **si**, implying a completed action. **Si** means *whether* in this case.

Je me demande s'ils **auront signé** le contrat.	*I wonder whether they'll have signed the contract.*
Je me demande **si** j'**aurai** tout **réglé** avant ce soir.	*I am wondering whether I'll have resolved everything by tonight.*
Il se demande s'il **aura terminé** à temps.	*He wonders whether he'll have finished on time.*

In French, the **futur antérieur** is *never* used after **si** implying a future condition. Use the present instead.

S'il **a** le temps, il passera vous voir.	*If he has time, he'll stop by to see you.*
Si vous **pouvez**, envoyez-moi votre CV avant lundi.	*If you can, send me your résumé before Monday.*

EXERCICE
9·7

*Traduire les phrases suivantes en utilisant **vous** si nécessaire.*

1. We'll play tennis.

_____

2. You'll need to buy a new car.

_____

3. I'll take a history course.

_____

4. We'll visit Venice when we are in Italy.

_____

5. They'll go to Dakar.

_____

6. We'll walk along the beach.

_____

7. He'll study French when he is in Bordeaux.

_____

8. They'll see the Picasso exhibition when they are in Paris.

_____

9. She'll travel to Asia when she gets her degree.

_____

10. He'll become a doctor.

_____

Conjunctions used with the indicative mood

You have just seen examples of conjunctions frequently used with the **futur simple** and the **futur antérieur**. These include:

aussitôt que	*as soon as*
dès que	*as soon as*
lorsque	*when*
quand	*when*
tant que	*as long as*

Let's learn a few more conjunctions followed by the indicative mood. In Chapter 13 we'll study other conjunctions followed by the subjunctive mood.

alors que	*while, whereas*
après que	*after*
comme	*as, since*
étant donné que	*given, in view of*
maintenant que	*now that*
parce que	*because*
pendant que	*while*
puisque	*since*
si	*if*
sous prétexte que	*under the pretext that*
tandis que	*whereas*
vu que	*given, in view of*

As we saw earlier in this chapter, some conjunctions require the future tense in both the main and the dependent clauses. When using another tense, the balance of tenses is the same as with the other conjunctions.

Elle apprendra le russe **quand** elle sera en Russie.	*She'll learn Russian when she is in Russia.*
Je t'écrirai **dès que** je serai à Rio.	*I'll write to you as soon as I am in Rio.*
Dès qu'ils sortaient de l'école, ils allaient au stade.	*As soon as they left school, they used to go to the stadium.*

Il a fondu en larmes **quand** il a appris qu'il avait raté l'examen.	He burst into tears when he found out he had failed the exam.
Puisque tu as le temps, aide-moi à finir mes devoirs.	Since you have time, help me finish my homework.
Il lisait pendant **qu'**elle écrivait.	He was reading while she was writing.
Étant donné que vous avez démissionné, nous ne pouvons rien faire pour vous.	Given that you resigned, we cannot do anything for you.
Il t'a fait ce cadeau **parce que** tu le mérites.	He gave you this present because you deserve it.
Comme il pleuvait, ils sont partis.	Since it was raining, they left.
Le téléphone a sonné **alors que** j'étais dans mon bain.	The phone rang while I was in my bath.
Si tu veux y aller, appelle-moi!	If you want to go there, call me!

EXERCICE 9·8

Mettre au futur simple les verbes entre parenthèses.

1. Puisqu'il a raté son examen, il (ne pas aller) _____ en vacances.

2. Étant donné qu'il est parti, la situation ne (faire) _____ qu'empirer.

3. Il devra trouver une excuse parce qu'elle (ne pas pouvoir) _____ assister à la réunion.

4. Il fera chaud chez elle alors que chez lui, on (geler) _____ .

5. Si nous avons le temps, nous (se promener) _____ au bord du lac.

6. Dès que j'aurai terminé l'enregistrement, je vous (envoyer) _____ un CD.

7. Elle dormira tandis que je (faire) _____ la vaisselle.

8. Tant qu'ils seront là, tout (aller) _____ bien.

9. Quand tu vivras à Paris, tu (découvrir) _____ beaucoup de nouvelles choses.

10. Aussitôt que le paquet sera arrivé, je vous (contacter) _____ .

The plus-que-parfait

The **plus-que-parfait** (*pluperfect*) indicates a past action that happened before another past action started (in English, *had done*). It can be seen as "past" past tense.

Formation of the plus-que-parfait

To form the **plus-que-parfait**, use the forms of **avoir** or **être** in the **imparfait** + the past participle of the main verb.

Let's review the **imparfait** of the auxiliaries **être** and **avoir**:

être *to be*			
j'**étais**	*I was*	nous **étions**	*we were*
tu **étais**	*you were*	vous **étiez**	*you were*
il/elle **était**	*he/she was*	ils/elles **étaient**	*they were*

avoir *to have*			
j'**avais**	*I had*	nous **avions**	*we had*
tu **avais**	*you had*	vous **aviez**	*you had*
il/elle **avait**	*he/she had*	ils/elles **avaient**	*they had*

Il **avait** toujours **fini** avant les autres.	*He had always finished before the others.*
Tu **avais oublié** l'anniversaire de ta meilleure amie.	*You had forgotten your best friend's birthday.*
Il n'**avait** pas **pu** les joindre.	*He had not been able to reach them.*
Elle **était partie** sans laisser d'adresse.	*She had departed without leaving an address.*

EXERCICE
10·1

Mettre au plus-que-parfait les verbes entre parenthèses.

1. Je (dîner) _____ place d'Italie.

2. Elle (expliquer) _____ la situation en détail.

3. Vous (investir) _____ dans leur entreprise.

4. Elles (arriver) _____ à la réception en retard.

5. Tu (décider) _____ d'aller en Russie.

6. Nous (rouler) _____ toute la nuit.

7. Il (échouer) _____ à son examen.

8. Tu (aller) _____ en vacances tout seul.

9. Je (obtenir) _____ un nouveau poste.

10. Il (boire) _____ un très bon vin.

VOCABULAIRE

une pharmacie	*a pharmacy*	une gélule	*a capsule*
un pharmacien, une pharmacienne	*a pharmacist*	un analgésique	*a painkiller*
		une toux	*a cough*
une ordonnance	*a prescription*	tousser	*to cough*
un médicament	*medicine, a medication*	avoir un rhume	*to have a cold*
		avoir la grippe	*to have the flu*
un remède	*a remedy*	avoir mal à la tête	*to have a headache*
un sirop	*a syrup*	avoir mal au dos	*to have a backache*
un traitement	*a treatment*	avoir mal au ventre	*to have a stomachache*
des contre-indications (*f.pl.*)	*contraindications*		
		être allergique	*to be allergic*
des effets secondaires (*m.pl.*)	*side effects*	une douleur	*a pain, an ache*
		souffrir	*to suffer*
un cachet d'aspirine	*an aspirin tablet*	conseiller	*to advise*

In the **plus-que-parfait**, all pronominal verbs are conjugated with **être** and agree in gender and number with the subject.

Je m'étais évanouie dans la pharmacie.	*I had fainted in the pharmacy.*
Vous vous étiez promenés le long du canal Saint-Martin.	*You had walked along the Saint-Martin canal.*
Nous nous étions embrassés sur le Pont-Neuf.	*We had kissed on the Pont-Neuf.*
Il s'était souvenu de cet incident avant de revoir son ancienne amie.	*He had remembered this incident before seeing his former girlfriend again.*

EXERCICE

10·2

Mettre au plus-que-parfait les verbes entre parenthèses.

1. Il (prendre) _____ un cachet d'aspirine.

2. Nous (se réveiller) _____ à l'aube

3. Tu (se demander) _____ s'il était allergique.

4. Elle (s'habiller) _____ pour la soirée.

5. Ils (se marier) _____ en septembre.

6. Louise et Julie (se coucher) _____ tard.

7. Il (se souvenir) _____ de cet homme.

8. Nous (se promener) _____ dans les jardins du Luxembourg.

9. Elle (se reposer) _____ sur un banc.

10. Elles (s'écrire) _____ pendant des années.

Use of the plus-que-parfait

As we mentioned earlier, the **plus-que-parfait** (*pluperfect*) indicates a past action that happened before another past action started. This anteriority can be implied or stated. Therefore, the **plus-que-parfait** is often combined with a dependent clause that states this clearly.

Je **ne m'étais pas rendu compte** que j'étais malade.	*I had not realized I was sick.*
Elle avait faim parce qu'elle **n'avait pas eu** le temps de déjeuner.	*She was hungry because she had not had time for lunch.*

EXERCICE 10·3

Mettre au plus-que-parfait les verbes entre parenthèses.

1. Il était en retard car sa voiture (tomber) _____ en panne sur l'autoroute.

2. Le médecin lui a demandé si elle (avoir) _____ la grippe.

3. Elle a pensé que je (ne pas expliquer) _____ la situation.

4. Il a refusé de prendre le médicament que le médecin (prescrire) _____ .

5. Elle était furieuse car il (oublier) _____ leur anniversaire de mariage.

6. Lorsque Lucie est arrivée, Paul (partir) _____ .

7. Je ne savais pas que Bertrand (inviter) _____ toute sa famille.

8. Elle ne se souvenait plus où elle (rencontrer) _____ le frère de Lucien.

9. Comme il n'avait pas d'analgésique, il (souffrir) _____ pendant des heures.

10. Il voulait savoir si elle (recevoir) _____ son bouquet de fleurs.

Faire correspondre les deux colonnes.

_____ 1. Il avait commandé un sandwich

_____ 2. Il était arrivé en retard

_____ 3. Il avait perdu son carnet d'adresses

_____ 4. Il avait échoué à son examen

_____ 5. Il avait beaucoup souffert

a. car il avait mal au dos

b. car il n'avait pas assez étudié

c. en raison d'une panne

d. parce qu'il avait faim

e. et il n'avait pas pu nous téléphoner

Beware of the English language

Sometimes in English the French **plus-que-parfait** is translated as a simple tense. However, if there is any anteriority in a series of actions, the **plus-que-parfait** must be used in French.

Léa a dû prendre le médicament que le médecin lui **avait prescrit**.	*Léa had to take the medicine the doctor (had) **prescribed** for her.*
Elle a eu une réaction allergique au médicament qu'elle **avait pris**.	*She had an allergic reaction to the medicine she **took** (had taken).*

In Chapter 1, you studied **depuis** with the present tense. In Chapter 8, you studied **depuis** with the **imparfait** (where English uses the **plus-que-parfait**). Let's review a few examples.

Ils **dînent** dans ce restaurant thaïlandais **depuis des années**.	*They have been dining at this Thai restaurant for years.*
Ils **dînaient** dans ce restaurant thaïlandais **depuis des années** quand ils **ont décidé** d'essayer le restaurant d'en face.	*They had been dining at this Thai restaurant for years when they decided to try the restaurant across the street.*
Elle **prend** de la vitamine C **depuis des mois**.	*She has been taking vitamin C for months.*
Elle **prenait** de la vitamine C **depuis des mois** quand le médecin lui **a dit** de prendre aussi du calcium.	*She had been taking vitamin C for months when the doctor told her to take calcium also.*

The **plus-que-parfait**, when used with **si seulement**, expresses a wish or regret about past events.

Si seulement il n'avait pas attrapé un rhume!	*If only he had not caught a cold!*
Si seulement il était allé chez le médecin plus tôt!	*If only he had gone to the doctor's earlier!*
Si seulement elle n'avait pas raté son examen!	*If only she had not failed her exam!*
Si seulement vous aviez pu être parmi nous!	*If only you had been able to be with us!*

*Commencer les phrases par **si seulement** et mettre au plus-que-parfait les verbes entre parenthèses.*

1. (vous) (ne pas être) en retard

_____

2. (tu) (étudier) le français plus jeune

_____

3. (nous) (savoir) la vérité

_____

4. (elle) (rester) plus longtemps

_____

5. (il) (rendre visite à) sa cousine Flore

_____

6. (je) (prendre) une meilleure décision

_____

7. (elle) (expliquer) la situation plus clairement

_____

8. (vous) (pouvoir venir) à la réception

_____

9. (tu) (comprendre) les problèmes

_____

10. (il) (conseiller) autre chose

_____

Traduire les phrases suivantes.

1. He took the medicine the doctor had prescribed.

_____

2. She knew they had made a mistake.

_____

3. He was sick because he had eaten too much dessert.

_____

4. I wondered why she had stayed three months in Vienna.

_____

5. I thought they had understood the problem.

_____

6. If only he had not been late!

_____

7. She was tired because she had only slept five hours.

_____

8. He was hungry because he had not eaten since seven A.M.

_____

9. We thought he had seen this film.

_____

10. He thought she had read the book.

_____

The present conditional and the past conditional

·11·

The present conditional

The **présent du conditionnel** (*present conditional*) has many uses we'll explore in this chapter. It is formed by adding the endings of the imperfect to the future stem of the verb. For -**er** and -**ir** verbs, the future stem is the entire infinitive form. For -**re** verbs, drop the final -**e** from the infinitive before adding the conditional endings. As you saw in Chapter 9, a number of irregular verbs have an irregular future stem. This same stem is used to form the present conditional.

mettre *to put*			
je **mettrais**	*I would put*	nous **mettrions**	*we would put*
tu **mettrais**	*you would put*	vous **mettriez**	*you would put*
il/elle **mettrait**	*he/she would put*	ils/elles **mettraient**	*they would put*

faire *to do*			
je **ferais**	*I would do*	nous **ferions**	*we would do*
tu **ferais**	*you would do*	vous **feriez**	*you would do*
il/elle **ferait**	*he/she would do*	ils/elles **feraient**	*they would do*

VOCABULAIRE

un animal	*an animal*	un hippopotame	*a hippopotamus*
un agneau	*a lamb*	un kangourou	*a kangaroo*
un aigle	*an eagle*	un lapin	*a rabbit*
un âne	*a donkey*	un lion	*a lion*
une baleine	*a whale*	un loup	*a wolf*
un bœuf	*an ox*	un mouton	*a sheep*
un canard	*a duck*	un oiseau	*a bird*
un chameau	*a camel*	un ours	*a bear*
un chat	*a cat*	un pingouin	*a penguin*
un chaton	*a kitten*	un poisson	*a fish*
une chauve-souris	*a bat*	un poisson rouge	*a goldfish*
un cheval	*a horse*	une poule	*a hen*
une chèvre	*a goat*	un renard	*a fox*
un chien	*a dog*	un requin	*a shark*
un cochon	*a pig*	un rhinocéros	*a rhinoceros*
une colombe	*a dove*	un serpent	*a snake*
un coq	*a rooster*	un singe	*a monkey*
un crapaud	*a toad*	une souris	*a mouse*
un crocodile	*a crocodile*	un taureau	*a bull*

un dauphin	*a dolphin*	un tigre	*a tiger*
un écureuil	*a squirrel*	une tortue	*a tortoise*
un éléphant	*an elephant*	une vache	*a cow*
une girafe	*a giraffe*	un veau	*a calf*
une grenouille	*a frog*	un zèbre	*a zebra*

Ces animaux **auraient** plus à manger dans cette région.	*These animals would have more to eat in this region.*
Il **aimerait** avoir une tortue.	*He would like to have a turtle.*
Dans un monde idéal, il n'y **aurait** pas de guerres.	*In an ideal world, there would be no war.*
Dans de telles circonstances, que **feriez**-vous?	*In such circumstances, what would you do?*

EXERCICE 11·1

Mettre les verbes au présent du conditionnel.

1. aller (nous) _____

2. voyager (elle) _____

3. dire (nous) _____

4. avoir (je) _____

5. manger (ils) _____

6. prendre (elle) _____

7. être (tu) _____

8. demander (vous) _____

9. écrire (je) _____

10. savoir (tu) _____

Uses of the present conditional

The **présent du conditionnel** is used to express a wish or a suggestion. For example:

Je **voudrais finir** ce projet aussitôt que possible.	*I would like to finish this project as soon as possible.*
À ta place, je **parierais** sur ce cheval.	*If I were you, I would bet on this horse.*
Ce **serait** génial de pouvoir y aller ensemble.	*It would be great to go together.*
Il **aimerait rencontrer** la femme de sa vie.	*He would like to meet the woman of his dreams.*

The **présent du conditionnel** is used to make a statement or a request more polite.

Pourriez-vous nous **donner** votre avis?	*Could you give us your opinion?*
Voudriez-vous **dîner** avec nous ce soir?	*Would you like to have dinner with us this evening?*
Est-ce que tu **pourrais** me **donner** un coup de main?	*Could you give me a hand?*
Est-ce que tu **voudrais assister** à la réunion?	*Would you like to attend the meeting?*

EXERCICE
11·2

*Traduire les verbes entre parenthèses en utilisant **vous** et l'inversion.*

1. (*Would you*) aller au théâtre la semaine prochaine? _____

2. (*Could we*) passer chez vous après le spectacle? _____

3. (*Could you*) changer la date de votre départ? _____

4. (*Would you*) m'acheter le journal pendant mes vacances? _____

5. (*Would he*) signer cette pétition? _____

6. (*Could you*) nourrir mes poissons rouges? _____

7. (*Could she*) prendre un train plus tard? _____

8. (*Would you*) aller avec moi en Tanzanie? _____

9. (*Could we*) finir ce projet la semaine prochaine? _____

10. (*Would they*) accompagner Sonia à la gare? _____

The **présent du conditionnel** is used when a condition is implied. When the main clause is in the **présent du conditionnel**, the **si** clause is in the **imparfait**.

Nous **irions** à Rome **si** nous **pouvions**.	*We would go to Rome if we could.*
Régis **finirait** son roman **s'il pouvait** trouver une maison d'édition.	*Régis would finish his novel if he could find a publisher.*
Nous **aurions** un chien **si** notre appartement **était** plus grand.	*We would have a dog if our apartment were bigger.*
Nous **viendrions si** notre baby-sitter **était** disponible.	*We would come if our babysitter were available.*

The **présent du conditionnel** is also used to express unconfirmed or alleged information. In this case it is called the **conditionnel journalistique**, seen from time to time in the press or heard on news broadcasts.

La reine d'Angleterre **se rendrait** en Australie la semaine prochaine.	*The Queen of England is reportedly going to Australia next week.*
Son beau-frère **serait impliqué** dans une affaire de fraude fiscale.	*His (her) brother-in-law is allegedly involved in tax fraud.*

Le président **signerait** le traité en fin
d'après-midi.

*The president will reportedly sign the treaty
by the end of the afternoon.*

Un sous-marin hollandais **serait** au
large des côtes bretonnes.

*A Dutch submarine is reportedly off the coast
of Brittany.*

In formal French, **savoir** in the **présent du conditionnel** is the equivalent of **pouvoir** (*can,
to be able to*) in the present or the simple future.

Je ne **saurais** vous dire combien
j'apprécie votre geste.

*I shall never be able to tell you how much I
appreciate your gesture.*

Je ne **saurais** vous répondre.

*I am afraid I can't answer. (I wouldn't know
how to answer you.)*

EXERCICE

11·3

*Mettre à l'imparfait les verbes dans la proposition **si**, et au conditionnel ceux de la
proposition principale.*

1. Si je (avoir) moins de travail, je (voyager) plus.

_____

2. S'ils (attendre), ils (obtenir) un meilleur prix pour leur appartement.

_____

3. Si nous (planter) plus de fleurs, nous (avoir) un plus beau jardin.

_____

4. Si je (vendre) mon appartement, je (pouvoir) acheter cette maison.

_____

5. S'il (pouvoir), il (déménager).

_____

6. Si vous les (inviter), nous (être) ravis.

_____

7. Si ma voiture (tomber) en panne, je (piquer) une crise.

_____

8. Si elle (avoir) plus d'argent, elle (venir) avec nous.

_____

9. Si vous (s'organiser) autrement, votre vie (être) plus facile.

_____

10. Si tu (dormir) plus, tu (avoir) de meilleures notes à l'école.

_____

Conjuguer les verbes entre parenthèses en utilisant d'abord le présent du conditionnel, puis l'imparfait.

1. Elle (être) contente si tu (venir) ce soir.

   _____

2. Nous (faire) une promenade dans le parc s'il (faire) beau.

   _____

3. Ils (prendre) leur retraite s'ils (pouvoir).

   _____

4. Il (accompagner) Sophie à l'opéra s'il (ne pas être) occupé.

   _____

5. Il y (avoir) moins de problèmes si vous (suivre) mes conseils.

   _____

6. Elles (aller) au musée s'il (être) ouvert avant onze heures.

   _____

7. Vous (finir) plus tôt si vous (travailler) plus efficacement.

   _____

8. Nous vous (croire) si vous nous (dire) la vérité.

   _____

9. Elle (acheter) cette voiture si elle (être) moins chère.

   _____

10. Tu lui (offrir) ce poste si tu (avoir) confiance en lui.

    _____

*Traduire les phrases suivantes en utilisant **tu** si nécessaire.*

1. He would go to Paris if he had more time.

   _____

2. She would buy this coat if it were less expensive.

   _____

3. We would be delighted if you came on Sunday.

_____

4. I would write a letter if you needed it.

_____

5. The president is reportedly in Brazil today.

_____

6. It would be prettier if there were more flowers.

_____

7. I would invite Chloé if I went to Paris.

_____

8. The director will reportedly sign the contract.

_____

9. She would eat the soup if she were hungry.

_____

10. He would read the paper this morning if he could.

_____

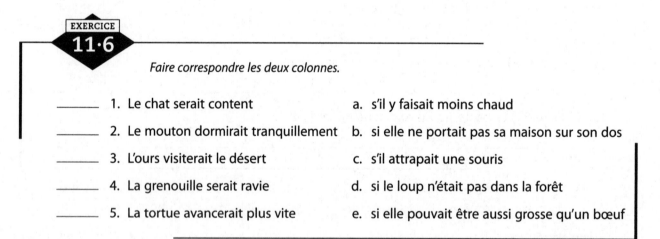

Faire correspondre les deux colonnes.

_____ 1. Le chat serait content   a. s'il y faisait moins chaud

_____ 2. Le mouton dormirait tranquillement   b. si elle ne portait pas sa maison sur son dos

_____ 3. L'ours visiterait le désert   c. s'il attrapait une souris

_____ 4. La grenouille serait ravie   d. si le loup n'était pas dans la forêt

_____ 5. La tortue avancerait plus vite   e. si elle pouvait être aussi grosse qu'un bœuf

The past conditional

The **passé du conditionnel** (*past conditional*) expresses what would have happened if another event had taken place, or if certain conditions had or had not been present. It is formed with the present conditional of **être** or **avoir** and the past participle of the main verb. The rules of agreement common to all compound tenses still apply.

donner to *give*			
j'**aurais donné**	*I would have given*	nous **aurions donné**	*we would have given*
tu **aurais donné**	*you would have given*	vous **auriez donné**	*you would have given*
il/elle **aurait donné**	*he/she would have given*	ils/elles **auraient donné**	*they would have given*

venir to *come*			
je **serais venu(e)**	*I would have come*	nous **serions venu(e)s**	*we would have come*
tu **serais venu(e)**	*you would have come*	vous **seriez venu(e)(s)**	*you would have come*
il/elle **serait venu(e)**	*he/she would have come*	ils/elles **seraient venu(e)s**	*they would have come*

Elle **aurait accepté** votre offre.	*She would have accepted your offer.*
Nous **aurions été** déçus.	*We would have been disappointed.*
Tu **aurais ri**!	*You would have laughed!*
Ils **se seraient mis** en colère.	*They would have gotten angry.*

Uses of the past conditional

The **passé du conditionnel** can express regret or reproach.

Nous **aurions voulu** y assister.	*We would have liked to attend.*
Tu **aurais dû** arriver plus tôt.	*You should have arrived earlier.*
Elle **aurait aimé** le féliciter.	*She would have liked to congratulate him.*
Cela **aurait été** tellement plus facile.	*It would have been so much easier.*

The **passé du conditionnel** is usually found in sentences where the **si** (dependent) clause is in the **plus-que-parfait**.

Elle **aurait fini** plus tôt **si** vous l'**aviez aidée**.	*She would have finished earlier if you had helped her.*
Je **serais arrivé** à l'heure **s'il y avait eu** moins de circulation.	*I would have arrived on time if there had been less traffic.*
Si le patron **n'avait pas voté** la délocalisation, l'usine **serait restée** ouverte.	*If the boss had not opted for a relocation, the factory would have stayed open.*
Il **n'aurait pas** tant **gagné** d'argent **s'il était resté** à Bordeaux.	*He would not have made as much money if he had stayed in Bordeaux.*

The **passé du conditionnel** is used like the **present du conditionnel** as a **conditionnel journalistique** to express a statement not necessarily confirmed by authorities. In most cases that imply the English *allegedly* or *reportedly*, the conditional (past or present) will be used in French. See the following examples:

Le tremblement de terre **aurait fait** des milliers de victimes au Mexique.	*The earthquake reportedly killed thousands of people in Mexico.*
Le président l'**aurait gracié**.	*The president reportedly granted him his pardon.*
Ce célèbre chanteur français **se serait installé** en Suisse.	*This famous French singer reportedly moved to Switzerland.*
Il **aurait volé** la voiture de son voisin.	*He allegedly stole his neighbor's car.*

Conjuguer les verbes entre parenthèses en utilisant d'abord le passé du conditionnel, puis le plus-que-parfait.

1. Nous (dîner) avec vous si nous (pouvoir).

   _____

2. Elle (visiter) ce musée si elle (avoir) plus de temps.

   _____

3. Elle (voir) ce film s'il (être) sous-titré.

   _____

4. Ils (inviter) Charles s'il (ne pas travailler) ce soir-là.

   _____

5. Il (faire) un documentaire sur ce sujet s'il (trouver) le financement.

   _____

6. Ils (vendre) leur maison si leurs enfants (déménager).

   _____

7. Vous (arriver) à temps si votre voiture (ne pas tomber) en panne.

   _____

8. Le directeur (démissionner) si les ouvriers (ne pas faire) pression.

   _____

9. Cette pièce (avoir) du succès s'il y (avoir) plus de temps pour les répétitions.

   _____

10. Nous (venir) si nous (recevoir) votre invitation plus tôt.

    _____

Conjuguer les verbes entre parenthèses en utilisant d'abord le plus-que-parfait, puis le passé du conditionnel.

1. S'il (finir) son projet, il (ne pas devoir) travailler le week-end.

   _____

2. Si je (mettre) mon manteau, je (ne pas avoir) si froid.

   _____

3. Si vous (pouvoir) témoigner au tribunal, la situation (être) différente.

_____

4. Si on (ne pas guillotiner) le roi, l'histoire du pays (prendre) une tournure différente.

_____

5. S'il (apprendre) sa grammaire, il (faire) moins de fautes.

_____

6. Si elle (se présenter) aux élections, elle (être élue).

_____

7. Si nous (commander) un couscous, nous (ne pas avoir) faim plus tard.

_____

8. Si elle (pouvoir), elle (être) danseuse.

_____

9. Si tu (être) plus pratique, nous (voyager) sans bagages.

_____

10. Si je (savoir), je (ne pas engager) Daniel.

_____

The **présent** or **passé du conditionnel** are also used with the expression **au cas où** (*in case*).

Au cas où le projet **ne serait pas fini** cet après-midi, appelez-moi.	*In case the project is not finished by this afternoon, call me.*
Au cas où ce cadeau **ne** vous **plairait pas**, dites-le-moi.	*In case you do not like this present, let me know.*
Au cas où il **aurait échoué** à l'examen, on lui donnera une autre chance.	*In case he failed the exam, we'll give him another chance.*
Au cas où tu **n'aurais pas retrouvé** tes clés, Christian s'occupera de toi.	*In case you did not find your keys, Christian will take care of you.*

EXERCICE
11·9

Traduire les phrases suivantes en utilisant le conditionnel journalistique, présent ou passé.

1. The prime minister reportedly went to China yesterday.

_____

2. The witness allegedly gave the police a different version.

_____

3. The cyclone reportedly killed two hundred people in this town.

_____

4. The director reportedly resigned.

_____

5. The storm has reportedly destroyed a hundred houses.

_____

6. Unemployment is reportedly going to decline next year.

_____

7. The health minister reportedly signed the reform.

_____

8. Penguins are reportedly unable to reproduce because of global warming.

_____

9. His new neighbor allegedly stole his car.

_____

10. A French actor reportedly bought a house in California last week.

_____

EXERCICE
11·10

Faire correspondre les deux colonnes.

_____ 1. Au cas où il pleuvrait   a. viens regarder le film chez moi

_____ 2. Au cas où tu l'aurais oublié   b. elle pourrait se servir des miennes

_____ 3. Au cas où ta télévision serait en panne   c. prends un parapluie

_____ 4. Au cas où elle aurait perdu ses notes   d. prévenez la police

_____ 5. Au cas où quelque chose aurait été volé   e. c'est mon anniversaire demain

Could, should, would?

Could, *should*, and *would* have different meanings in English and are translated in several ways in French. Each time you come across one of these verbs, try to consider its nuance in English.

Could

When *could* refers to a single, unique action in the past, the **passé composé** of **pouvoir** is used.

j'**ai pu**	*I could*	nous **avons pu**	*we could*
tu **as pu**	*you could*	vous **avez pu**	*you could*
il/elle **a pu**	*he/she could*	ils/elles **ont pu**	*they could*

Note the following examples:

Il n'a pas pu lui parler.	*He could not talk to him.*
J'ai pu la convaincre.	*I managed to convince her.*
Nous n'avons pas pu y aller.	*We could not go there.*
Il a pu obtenir les fonds.	*He succeeded in obtaining the funding.*

When *could* refers to a description or a habitual action, the **imparfait** of **pouvoir** is used.

je **pouvais**	*I could*	nous **pouvions**	*we could*
tu **pouvais**	*you could*	vous **pouviez**	*you could*
il/elle **pouvait**	*he/she could*	ils/elles **pouvaient**	*they could*

Note the following examples:

En ce temps-là, les femmes ne **pouvaient** pas voter.	*At that time, women could not vote.*
À cette époque, les voitures ne **pouvaient** pas traverser la ville.	*At that time, cars couldn't drive through the city.*
Si jeune, il **pouvait** quand même prendre une telle décision!	*So young, he was still able to make such a decision!*
Après la mort de sa femme, il ne **pouvait** plus écrire.	*After his wife's death, he could no longer write.*

When *could* refers to an idea of the future, a hypothesis, a suggestion, or a request, the **présent du conditionnel** of **pouvoir** is used.

je **pourrais**	*I could*	nous **pourrions**	*we could*
tu **pourrais**	*you could*	vous **pourriez**	*you could*
il/elle **pourrait**	*he/she could*	ils/elles **pourraient**	*they could*

Note the following examples:

Pourrais-tu me prêter le livre dont tu m'as parlé?	*Could you lend me the book you told me about?*
Pourriez-vous m'expliquer votre méthode de travail?	*Could you explain to me your working method?*
Je **pourrais** vous prêter ma voiture.	*I could lend you my car.*
Ils **pourraient** apprendre à jouer de la clarinette.	*They could learn how to play the clarinet.*

VOCABULAIRE

les instruments (*m.pl.*)	*instruments*	**l'harmonica** (*m.*)	*harmonica*
l'accordéon (*m.*)	*accordion*	**la harpe**	*harp*
l'alto (*m.*)	*viola*	**le hautbois**	*oboe*
la basse	*string bass; bass guitar*	**le piano**	*piano*
la batterie	*drums*	**le saxophone**	*saxophone*
les castagnettes (*f.pl.*)	*castanets*	**le synthétiseur**	*synthesizer*
la clarinette	*clarinet*	**le tambour**	*drum*
le clavecin	*harpsichord*	**le tambourin**	*tambourine*
le cor	*French horn*	**le trombone**	*trombone*
la contrebasse	*double bass (= la basse)*	**la trompette**	*trumpet*
la cymbale	*cymbal*	**le violon**	*violin*
la flûte	*flute*	**le violoncelle**	*cello*
la guitare	*guitar*	**le xylophone**	*xylophone*
la guitare électrique	*electric guitar*		

EXERCICE
12·1

*Traduire les phrases suivantes en utilisant **vous** et l'inversion si nécessaire.*

1. Could you help clean the house after the party?

_____

2. We could not go on vacation.

_____

3. I could buy her a new flute.

_____

4. At that time, they could not understand.

_____

5. Could we start eating?

_____

6. We could go see a movie tonight.

_____

7. Thanks to her rich aunt, she could pay for her studies.

_____

8. I think she could do better.

_____

9. When you were a kid, you would play with your dolls for hours.

_____

10. Could you teach me how to play the guitar?

_____

Should

When *should* means *ought to*, the **conditionnel** (**présent** or **passé**) is used.

je **devrais**	*I should*	j'**aurais dû**	*I should have*
tu **devrais**	*you should*	tu **aurais dû**	*you should have*
il/elle **devrait**	*he/she should*	il/elle **aurait dû**	*he/she should have*
nous **devrions**	*we should*	nous **aurions dû**	*we should have*
vous **devriez**	*you should*	vous **auriez dû**	*you should have*
ils/elles **devraient**	*they should*	ils/elles **auraient dû**	*they should have*

Note the following examples:

Elle **devrait se détendre** un peu.	*She should relax a bit.*
Vous **devriez aller** au concert.	*You should go to the concert.*
Tu **aurais dû** lui **demander** des explications.	*You should have asked him for explanations.*
Vous **auriez dû** l'**emmener** au festival de musique.	*You should have taken him to the music festival.*

EXERCICE
12·2

*Traduire les phrases suivantes en utilisant **vous** et l'inversion si nécessaire.*

1. You should learn to play the guitar.

_____

2. They shouldn't have said that.

_____

3. I should write to Pierre.

_____

4. I should have talked to them.

_____

5. Do you think Julien should have called you before coming?

_____

6. I shouldn't have called so early.

_____

7. We shouldn't take the car, it's too dangerous.

_____

8. I think you should take a vacation.

_____

9. You should rent a piano for the party.

_____

10. Marie thinks her father should be present for this occasion.

_____

Would

When *would* refers to a repeated action in the past, the **imparfait** is used. Note the following examples:

Quand j'étais étudiant, je **lisais** les journaux tous les jours.	*When I was a student, I would read the newspapers every day.*
Quand ils étaient adolescents, ils **jouaient** au volley-ball le jeudi.	*When they were teens, they would play volleyball on Thursdays.*

When *would* refers to a polite request, the **présent du conditionnel** is used. Note the following examples:

Voudrais-tu me **montrer** le chemin?	*Would you mind showing me the way?*
Est-ce que tu **voudrais** bien m'**aider** à résoudre ce problème?	*Could you help me solve that problem?*

When *would* refers to a specific action in the past, the **passé composé** of **vouloir** is used. Note the following examples:

Nous leur avons demandé de nous accorder un peu de temps; ils **n'ont pas voulu** le **faire**.	*We asked them to give us a little time; they would not do it.*
Je lui ai posé la question plusieurs fois; elle **n'a pas voulu répondre**.	*I asked her the question several times; she would not answer.*

When *would* refers to an idea of the future, a hypothesis, or a suggestion, the **présent du conditionnel** of the main verb is used. The **imparfait** is used in the **si** clause.

Je vous le **dirais** si je le **savais**.   *I would tell you if I knew.*
Elle **serait** si heureuse s'il la **demandait**   *She would be so happy if he proposed to her.*
en mariage.

EXERCICE

12·3

Traduire en anglais les phrases suivantes.

1. S'il était moins paresseux, il aurait de meilleures notes à l'école.

_____

2. Quand nous étions enfants, nos parents nous emmenaient en vacances au Maroc tous

les ans.

_____

3. Samuel a demandé un peu plus d'argent. Son patron n'a pas voulu le lui donner.

_____

4. Si Emmanuelle était disponible, elle viendrait.

_____

5. Quand elle était étudiante à Paris, elle allait au cinéma tous les dimanches.

_____

6. Si Sylvie avait plus d'argent, elle s'achèterait de nouvelles chaussures.

_____

7. S'ils avaient le choix, ils ne déménageraient pas.

_____

8. Voudrais-tu me dire ce qui s'est passé à cette réunion?

_____

9. Catherine voulait faire demi-tour, mais son mari n'a pas voulu le faire.

_____

10. Pourriez-vous m'expliquer comment cela marche?

_____

*Traduire en français les phrases suivantes en utilisant **tu** et l'inversion si nécessaire.*

1. Could you read this document?

   _____

2. We should buy tickets for the concert.

   _____

3. Valérie could help you!

   _____

4. At that time, she could not go out very often.

   _____

5. Could you send me a copy of that letter?

   _____

6. I asked her to help me; she would not do it.

   _____

7. Pascal would play the violin if he had more time.

   _____

8. Marie could not tell him the truth.

   _____

9. When we were kids, we would play for hours on the beach.

   _____

10. Don't you think you should change your haircut?

    _____

Could, would ou should? Traduire en anglais les phrases suivantes.

1. Pourrais-tu ouvrir la porte?

   _____

2. À cette heure, il devrait être à la maison.

   _____

3. Ils n'ont pas pu avoir de billets.

   _____

4. Voudriez-vous bien participer à ce projet?

_____

5. Je suis venu le chercher; il n'a pas voulu venir avec moi.

_____

6. Si tu étais moins égoïste, tu aurais plus d'amis.

_____

7. Voudrais-tu bien me montrer comment ça fonctionne?

_____

8. Il n'a pas pu partir à temps.

_____

9. Lorsque nous étions enfants, nous allions à la mer tous les étés.

_____

10. Il devrait réfléchir avant de parler.

_____

Faire correspondre les deux colonnes.

_____ 1. Marie serait ravie   a. venir manger à la maison ce soir.

_____ 2. Vous devriez   b. elle circulait en vélo.

_____ 3. Quand elle habitait à la campagne,   c. si Marc l'invitait à dîner.

_____ 4. Je serais moins inquiet   d. me prévenir que tes parents venaient

                                           aussi.

_____ 5. Tu aurais dû   e. si tu me téléphonais en arrivant.

The present subjunctive and the past subjunctive

The present subjunctive

The subjunctive is a mood, not a tense. The mood of a verb determines how one views an event. You have already studied verb tenses in the indicative mood (**le présent, l'imparfait,** and **le futur**), stating objective facts, and in the conditional mood, relating to possibilities. In Chapter 19 we will study the imperative mood that gives commands. The subjunctive is another mood that refers to someone's opinion or deals with hypothetical actions.

For most verbs, the present of the subjunctive is formed by adding the subjunctive endings (**-e, -es, -e, -ions, -iez, -ent**) to the stem. The stem for **je, tu, il/elle, ils/elles** is found by dropping the **-ent** ending from the third-person plural present indicative form (**ils/elles**). Note that the sound of the verb will be the same for all these persons.

Let's look at the verb **penser** (*to think*). The third-person plural: **ils/elles pensent**. The stem: **pens-**

je pens**e**	*I speak*
tu pens**es**	*you speak*
il/elle pens**e**	*he/she speaks*
ils/elles pens**ent**	*they speak*

The stem for the **nous** and **vous** subjunctive forms is found by dropping the **-ons** from the first-person plural of the present indicative. For **nous** and **vous**, the present subjunctive is identical to the forms of the **imparfait**. The first-person plural: **nous pensons**. The stem: **pens-**

nous pens**ions**	*we speak*
vous pens**iez**	*you speak*

Let's conjugate the verb **dire** (*to say*) in the present subjunctive:

je **dise**	*I say*	nous **disions**	*we say*
tu **dises**	*you say*	vous **disiez**	*you say*
il/elle **dise**	*he/she says*	ils/elles **disent**	*they say*

And **mettre** (*to put*):

je **mette**	*I put*	nous **mettions**	*we put*
tu **mettes**	*you put*	vous **mettiez**	*you put*
il/elle **mette**	*he/she puts*	ils/elles **mettent**	*they put*

Some verbs have irregular forms in the present subjunctive. **Être** (*to be*) and **avoir** (*to have*) have both irregular stems and endings.

être			
je **sois**	*I am*	nous **soyons**	*we are*
tu **sois**	*you are*	vous **soyez**	*you are*
il/elle **soit**	*he/she is*	ils/elles **soient**	*they are*

avoir			
j'**aie**	*I have*	nous **ayons**	*we have*
tu **aies**	*you have*	vous **ayez**	*you have*
il/elle **ait**	*he/she has*	ils/elles **aient**	*they have*

The following three verbs have an irregular subjunctive stem but regular endings.

pouvoir *can, to be able to*			
je **puisse**	*I can*	nous **puissions**	*we can*
tu **puisses**	*you can*	vous **puissiez**	*you can*
il/elle **puisse**	*he/she can*	ils/elles **puissent**	*they can*

savoir *to know*			
je **sache**	*I know*	nous **sachions**	*we know*
tu **saches**	*you know*	vous **sachiez**	*you know*
il/elle **sache**	*he/she knows*	ils/elles **sachent**	*they know*

faire *to do, to make*			
je **fasse**	*I do*	nous **fassions**	*we do*
tu **fasses**	*you do*	vous **fassiez**	*you do*
il/elle **fasse**	*he/she does*	ils/elles **fassent**	*they do*

Aller (*to go*) and **vouloir** (*to want*) have an irregular stem in the **je, tu, il/elle, ils/elles** forms and are partially irregular in the **nous** and **vous** forms.

aller *to go*			
j'**aille**	*I go*	nous **allions**	*we go*
tu **ailles**	*you go*	vous **alliez**	*you go*
il/elle **aille**	*he/she goes*	ils/elles **aillent**	*they go*

vouloir *to want*			
je **veuille**	*I want*	nous **voulions**	*we want*
tu **veuilles**	*you want*	vous **vouliez**	*you want*
il/elle **veuille**	*he/she wants*	ils/elles **veuillent**	*they want*

VOCABULAIRE

un ordinateur	*a computer*	**l'informatique** (*f.*)	*computer science*
une souris	*a mouse*	**un(e) internaute**	*a Internet surfer*
une touche	*a key (on keyboard)*	**une banque de données**	*a data bank*
un clavier	*a keyboard*	**une base de données**	*a data base*
un écran	*a screen*	**une disquette**	*a floppy disk*
cliquer	*to click*	**une page d'accueil**	*a home page*
imprimer	*to print*	**la Toile**	*the Web*
une imprimante	*a printer*	**un disque dur**	*a hard drive*

un logiciel	a software program	se connecter	to log on
numérique	digital	surfer sur Internet	to surf the Net
numériser	to digitize	télécharger	to download
sauvegarder	to save	un site Web	a website

Uses of the subjunctive

There are three main concepts that require the use of the subjunctive: wish, emotion, and doubt.

The subjunctive is used after verbs expressing the notion of *wish* and *desire*. It is used when the subject of the main clause is different from the subject of the dependent clause. Compare:

Je veux acheter cet ordinateur.	*I want to buy this computer.*
Je veux que tu achètes cet ordinateur.	*I want you to buy this computer.*

Compare:

Vous désirez suivre un cours d'informatique.	*You want to take a computer science class.*
Vous désirez que nous suivions un cours d'informatique.	*You want us to take a computer science course.*
Elle souhaite que tu ailles en France.	*She wishes you would go to France.*
J'exige que vous arriviez à l'heure.	*I demand that you arrive on time.*
Il demande que nous soyons plus efficaces.	*He is asking us to be more efficient.*

The subjunctive is used after expressions of *emotion*.

Je regrette qu'il ne puisse pas être ici.	*I am sorry he can't be here.*
Nous sommes ravis que tu prennes tes vacances ici.	*We are delighted you are vacationing here.*
Ils sont déçus que le cours soit annulé.	*They are disappointed that the class is canceled.*
Je suis content que tu viennes dimanche.	*I am happy you are coming on Sunday.*

The subjunctive is also used after expressions of *doubt*.

Je ne suis pas convaincu qu'il ait raison.	*I am not convinced he is right.*
Je doute qu'il comprenne vos questions.	*I doubt he understands your questions.*
Elle ne croit pas que vous trouviez leur projet intéressant.	*She does not think you find their project interesting.*
Je ne pense pas qu'il sache ce qu'il fait.	*I doubt he knows what he is doing.*

The verbs **penser** (*to think*) and **croire** (*to believe*) in the affirmative are followed by the indicative mood. However, in the negative and interrogative, the subjunctive can be used to underline the uncertainty of the event.

Je ne crois pas que Daniel est coupable.	*I don't think Daniel is guilty.*
Je ne crois pas que Daniel soit coupable.	*I don't think Daniel is guilty.*

The first sentence above means "I am actually sure Daniel is innocent." In the second example, there is some doubt about his guilt (or innocence). The difference will be detected in context and with the intonation of the voice or through gestures.

Mettre les verbes au subjonctif.

1. Elle préfère que tout le monde (être) _____ là avant de commencer.

2. Je doute que vous (comprendre) _____ l'importance de cet événement.

3. Sa mère aimerait mieux qu'elle (ne pas sortir) _____ ce soir.

4. A-t-il fini le projet? Non. Mais je tiens à ce qu'il le (finir) _____ aujourd'hui.

5. Je doute qu'ils (gérer) _____ cette affaire correctement.

6. J'ai peur que ces logiciels (ne pas être) _____ compatibles.

7. Ils souhaitent que cette aventure (avoir) _____ une fin heureuse.

8. Il craint que ce projet (être) _____ un échec.

9. Elle est contente qu'il (pouvoir) _____ acheter la maison de ses rêves.

10. Le juge ne croit pas qu'il (dire) _____ la vérité.

The subjunctive is also used after certain impersonal expressions, in the same way that some verbs are followed by the indicative and others by the subjunctive. In most cases, the impersonal expressions followed by the subjunctive express will, obligation, necessity, emotion, and doubt. Here are some impersonal expressions that are followed by the *indicative*:

il est certain	*it is certain*	**il est sûr**	*it is sure*
il est évident	*it is obvious*	**il est vrai**	*it is true*
il est probable	*it is probable*	**il me semble**	*it seems to me*

And here are some impersonal expressions that are followed by the *subjunctive*:

il faut	*one must*	**il est possible**	*it is possible*
il est essentiel	*it is essential*	**il est indispensable**	*it is essential*
il est juste	*it is fair*	**il se peut**	*it may be*
il est important	*it is important*	**il vaut mieux**	*it is better*
il est préférable	*it is preferable*	**il est souhaitable**	*it is desirable*
il est naturel	*it is natural*	**il est normal**	*it is normal*
il est rare	*it is rare*	**il est utile**	*it is useful*
il est étrange	*it is strange*	**il est bizarre**	*it is odd*
il est étonnant	*it is amazing*	**il est surprenant**	*it is surprising*
il est triste	*it is sad*	**il est dommage**	*it is a shame*
il est regrettable	*it is unfortunate*	**cela ne vaut pas la peine**	*it is not worth it*

Let's compare the use of the indicative and the subjunctive with some impersonal expressions:

Il est **certain** qu'il **viendra** ce soir.	*It is certain he'll come tonight.*
Il est **possible** qu'il **vienne** ce soir.	*It is possible he'll come tonight.*

Look at these example sentences with impersonal expressions.

Il faut que vous commenciez vos recherches dès que possible.	*You have to begin your research as soon as possible.*

Il est étonnant que vous demandiez un salaire si élevé.	*It is surprising that you're asking for such a high salary.*
Il est rare qu'ils finissent leurs rapports à temps.	*It is rare for them to finish their reports on time.*
Il est regrettable que ce logiciel coûte si cher.	*It is unfortunate this software is so expensive.*
Il se peut que cette imprimante soit incompatible.	*It is possible this printer is not compatible.*
Il est triste que vous démissionniez cette semaine.	*It is sad you are resigning this week.*
Il faut que vous refassiez la page d'accueil de votre site.	*You must redo the home page of your website.*
Il est étrange qu'il télécharge tous vos documents.	*It is strange that he downloads all your documents.*
Il est possible que leurs dossiers soient numériques.	*Their files may be digital.*

Mettre les propositions subordonnées au subjonctif.

1. Il faut que vous (aller) _____ voir ce film.

2. Il est essentiel que vous (arriver) _____ avant la fin de la semaine.

3. Il est impensable que nous (accepter) _____ ces conditions.

4. Il est possible que nous (voyager) _____ cet été.

5. Il est important qu'il (être) _____ à l'heure.

6. Il vaut mieux que nous (ne rien dire) _____ .

7. Il est regrettable que ses enfants (habiter) _____ si loin.

8. Il est dommage que vous (vendre) _____ votre maison de campagne.

9. Il est indispensable qu'elle (suivre) _____ un cours d'informatique.

10. Il est rare que nous (emporter) _____ du travail à la maison.

When you use conjunctions, you will also have to decide whether to use the indicative or the subjunctive in the following clause.

afin que	*so that, in order to*	**pour que**	*so that, in order to*
de peur que	*for fear that*	**de crainte que**	*for fear that*
avant que	*before*	**jusqu'à ce que**	*until*
bien que	*although*	**quoique**	*although*
sans que	*without*	**à moins que**	*unless*
pourvu que	*provided that*	**à condition que**	*on the condition that*
en attendant que	*waiting for*		

Nous partirons demain **à moins qu'**il y **ait** une grève.	*We'll leave tomorrow unless there is a strike.*
Il viendra avec nous **à condition que** son patron lui **donne** un jour de congé.	*He'll come with us on the condition that his boss gives him a day off.*
Tout sera fini **avant qu'**ils **arrivent**.	*Everything will be done before they arrive.*
Je sauvegarde toutes ses données **de peur qu'**il les **perde**.	*I save all his data for fear he loses (he'll lose) it.*
Ils ont pris la décision **sans qu'**elle le **sache**.	*They made the decision without her knowing it.*
Il est tolérant **pourvu qu'**on **respecte** ses idées.	*He is tolerant provided one respects his ideas.*
Quoiqu'il **fasse** froid, ils se promènent dans la forêt.	*Although it is cold, they take a walk in the forest.*

Refer to Chapter 9 for the list of conjunctions that are followed by the indicative mood.

EXERCICE

13·3

Mettre les verbes entre parenthèses au subjonctif.

1. Il ne commencera pas son discours avant que vous (donner) _____ le signal.

2. Elle est généreuse quoiqu'elle (ne pas être) _____ riche.

3. Je t'aiderai à condition que tu me (faire) _____ une faveur.

4. Nous les inviterons pour qu'ils (ne pas se sentir) _____ délaissés.

5. Elle déposera un brevet de peur qu'on lui (voler) _____ son idée.

6. J'achèterai leur appartement pour qu'ils (pouvoir) _____ s'installer à la campagne.

7. Il téléchargera le dossier bien qu'il (ne pas répondre) _____ exactement à ses besoins.

8. Elle a un blog pour que ses lecteurs (donner) _____ leurs réactions.

9. Nous donnerons nos opinions pourvu qu'elles (rester) _____ anonymes.

10. Elle achètera un appareil numérique pour que sa fille (pouvoir) _____ lui envoyer des photos au cours de son voyage.

Pourvu que

Pourvu que has the sense of *provided that*.

Il ne démissionnera pas **pourvu que** le directeur lui **donne** une augmentation de salaire.	*He won't resign provided the director gives him a raise.*

When used in a single clause, **pourvu que** takes a different meaning. It is a handy expression, also followed by the subjunctive, that expresses hopes and desires.

Pourvu qu'il y ait un cybercafé!	*Let's hope there is a cybercafé!*
Pourvu qu'ils aient l'adresse!	*Let's hope they have the address!*
Pourvu qu'il réussisse!	*Let's hope he succeeds!*
Pourvu que leur base de données **soit** à jour!	*Let's hope their database is up to date!*

The subjunctive is also used after a superlative or an adjective conveying a superlative idea, such as: **premier** (*first*), **dernier** (*last*), **seul** (*only*), **unique** (*unique*), etc.

C'est **le meilleur** ordinateur **que** je **connaisse**.	*It's the best computer I know.*
C'est **le seul** logiciel **qui puisse** vous être utile.	*It's the only software that can be of use to you.*
C'est **la pire** chose **qui puisse** lui arriver.	*It's the worst thing that could happen to him.*
C'est la personne **la plus** sympathique **qu'il connaisse**.	*He's/She's the friendliest person he knows.*

The relative pronouns **qui** and **que** can sometimes be followed by the subjunctive. If there is some doubt about the existence of someone or the possible realization of something, the subjunctive may be used after the relative pronoun.

Connaîtriez-vous **quelqu'un qui sache** parler le chinois couramment?	*Would you know someone who can speak Chinese fluently?*
Il cherche **quelqu'un qui puisse** créer un logiciel pour son entreprise.	*He is looking for someone who can create a piece of software for his company.*

EXERCICE
13·4

Indicatif ou subjonctif?

1. Il dit que leur page d'accueil (être) _____ attrayante.

2. Elle doute qu'il (faire) _____ chaud demain.

3. Ils sont heureux que leurs enfants (pouvoir) _____ aller en Europe cet été.

4. Je pense que Maud (avoir) _____ raison.

5. Je veux que tu (faire) _____ la présentation jeudi.

6. Tu ne crois pas qu'ils (avoir) _____ assez d'expérience.

7. Vous savez qu'ils (être) _____ toujours en retard.

8. Nous souhaitons que vous (obtenir) _____ ce poste.

9. Ils exigent que vous (parler) _____ une langue étrangère.

10. Vous savez que cet ordinateur (être) _____ obsolète.

EXERCICE

13·5

Mettre les propositions subordonnées suivantes au subjonctif.

1. Il est rare que nous (voyager) _____ dans cette région.

2. Il me semble que vous (se tromper) _____ souvent.

3. Il faut que nous (trouver) _____ un bon restaurant.

4. Il est naturel que je (connaître) _____ cette ville. C'est ma ville natale!

5. Il est essentiel que nous (acheter) _____ un nouvel ordinateur.

6. Il est dommage que ce logiciel (ne pas être) _____ plus performant.

7. Elle reste chez elle de peur qu'il y (avoir) _____ une tempête de neige.

8. Nous vous contacterons avant que vous (envoyer) _____ la rédaction du contrat.

9. Vérifiez les chiffres afin qu'on (pouvoir) _____ communiquer le rapport.

10. Bien que son livre (être) _____ bien écrit, il ne trouvera guère de lecteurs.

EXERCICE

13·6

*Traduire les phrases suivantes en utilisant **vous** si nécessaire.*

1. Let's hope he is right!

_____

2. She is happy he can study French.

_____

3. It is possible you can buy this software here.

_____

4. Call us before we go to France!

_____

5. It is strange he is late.

_____

6. Let's hope he can come!

_____

7. She wants you to buy this computer.

_____

8. Although he is tired, he reads the newspaper.

_____

9. Although he makes a few mistakes, his French is very good.

_____

10. It is the most beautiful city I know.

_____

The past subjunctive

The past subjunctive is used in the same way as the present subjunctive. In such sentences, the action of the dependent clause is *anterior* to the action of the main clause. To form the past subjunctive, use the present subjunctive of **avoir** or **être** + the past participle of the verb.

penser *to think*			
j'**aie pensé**	*I have thought*	nous **ayons pensé**	*we have thought*
tu **aies pensé**	*you have thought*	vous **ayez pensé**	*you have thought*
il/elle **ait pensé**	*he/she has thought*	ils/elles **aient pensé**	*they have thought*

venir *to come*			
je **sois venu(e)**	*I have come*	nous **soyons venu(e)s**	*we have come*
tu **sois venu(e)**	*you have come*	vous **soyez venu(e)(s)**	*you have come*
il/elle **soit venu(e)**	*he/she has come*	ils/elles **soient venu(e)s**	*they have come*

Je suis désolé **que tu n'aies pas pu travailler** avec nous.	*I am sorry you were not able to work with us.*
Nous sommes ravis **qu'elle ait gagné** la médaille d'or.	*We are delighted she won the gold medal.*

EXERCICE

13·7

Mettre les verbes entre parenthèses au passé du subjonctif.

1. Je doute que tu (lire) _____ tout le livre.

2. Nous sommes ravis que vous (pouvoir) _____ être parmi nous.

3. Il est possible que le logiciel (être) _____ défectueux.

4. Je suis surpris que vous (ne pas voir) _____ ce film.

5. Il a peur que Charles (manquer) _____ le train.

6. Il n'est pas certain qu'il (réussir) _____ à son examen.

7. Je crains qu'il (plagier) _____ mes idées.

8. Il a envoyé le courriel avant que je (pouvoir) _____ ajouter un mot.

9. Il est douteux qu'ils (lire) _____ tous les dossiers.

10. Je suis content que vous (dire) _____ la vérité.

Changer du présent au passé du subjonctif.

1. Il est content que nous partions.

_____

2. Nous sommes ravis que tu puisses venir avec nous.

_____

3. Je ne crois pas qu'il aille à l'exposition.

_____

4. Il doute qu'elle réussisse.

_____

5. Elle a peur qu'il ait un accident de moto.

_____

6. Ils sont contents que Laurent se marie.

_____

7. Nous sommes désolés que votre sœur soit malade.

_____

8. Il est douteux qu'ils aillent en Patagonie.

_____

9. Il est regrettable que leurs enfants soient si peu reconnaissants.

_____

10. Il est incroyable que vous ne sachiez pas la réponse.

_____

EXERCICE
13·9

Faire correspondre les deux colonnes.

_____ 1. Je pense

_____ 2. Il est bizarre

_____ 3. Marie! J'ai bien peur

_____ 4. Il est essentiel pour l'entreprise

_____ 5. Ils sont ravis

a. que nous ayons raté le dernier métro.

b. que leur fille ait obtenu son diplôme.

c. que Jean ait refusé une telle offre!

d. qu'il pleuvra demain.

e. que vous assistiez à la conférence de presse.

The infinitive mood

The **infinitif présent**

You will come across the **infinitif**, the infinitive mood, on many occasions. It is used more frequently in French than in English. The **infinitif** can be used as the subject of a verb. (Note that the present participle is used in English instead.)

Faire la cuisine est son passe-temps favori.	*Cooking is his favorite pastime.*
Suivre des cours de cuisine est amusant.	*Taking cooking classes is fun.*
Voyager par le train est rapide.	*Traveling by train is fast.*
Apprendre une langue étrangère est très utile.	*Learning a foreign language is very useful.*

The **infinitif** is also used for general instructions, prescriptions, public notices, and proverbs (where the imperative is often used in English).

Prendre une fois par jour.	*Take once a day.*
Ne pas se pencher par la fenêtre.	*Do not lean out of the window.*
Ne pas marcher sur la pelouse.	*Keep off the lawn.*
Lire le mode d'emploi avant utilisation.	*Read the instructions before using.*

Since a verb in the infinitive mood is not conjugated, the negation (**ne... pas**) does not surround the verb but rather precedes it, and is not separated.

Il a promis de **ne pas ajouter** trop d'ail.	*He promised not to add too much garlic.*
Je lui ai demandé de **ne pas faire frire** le poisson.	*I asked her not to fry the fish.*
Elle m'a dit de **ne pas mettre** d'huile.	*She told me not to put any oil in.*
Je lui ai conseillé de **ne pas mettre** le gâteau au four avant midi.	*I advised her not to put the cake in the oven before noon.*

VOCABULAIRE

ajouter	*to add*	**broyer**	*to grind, to crush*
assaisonner	*to season*	**caraméliser**	*to caramelize*
bouillir	*to boil*	**couper**	*to cut*
braiser	*to braise*	**cuire**	*to cook*

▶

décortiquer	to shell, to husk	griller	to grill, to toast
écailler	to scale (fish)	hacher	to chop, to mince
écraser	to crush, to squash	macérer	to macerate, to soak
écumer	to skim (soup)	mariner	to marinate
émincer	to slice thinly	mettre au four	to put in the oven
épicer	to spice	mijoter	to simmer
éplucher	to peel (vegetables)	paner	to coat with bread crumbs
faire la cuisine	to cook	pétrir	to knead
faire revenir	to brown	piler	to crush
faire sauter	to sauté	pocher	to poach
farcir	to stuff	râper	to grate
flamber	to flambé	réduire	to reduce (by boiling)
frire	to fry	rôtir	to roast
garnir	to garnish	tremper	to soak
glacer	to glaze	verser	to pour
gratiner	to brown, to cook au gratin		

Although nowadays French household magazines tend to use the imperative mood in recipes and other instructions, the **infinitif présent** is often used in professional cookbooks and other instruction manuals.

Hacher le persil.	*Chop the parsley.*
Farcir la dinde.	*Stuff the turkey.*
Râper une demi-livre de fromage.	*Grate half a pound of cheese.*
Pocher le poisson.	*Poach the fish.*

EXERCICE
14·1

Traduire les phrases suivantes en utilisant l'infinitif présent.

1. Writing this book was a challenge.

   _____

2. Studying French is fun.

   _____

3. Working four days a week is ideal.

   _____

4. Finding a new job will be difficult.

   _____

5. Walking along the Seine is pleasant.

   _____

6. Waking up at five A.M. is too early.

   _____

7. Cooking takes a lot of time.

_____

8. Take this medicine twice a day.

_____

9. Add some pepper.

_____

10. Do not put in any garlic.

_____

The infinitive is used after *verbs of perception* (where the present participle is used in English).

J'**ai vu** les moutons **traverser** la route.	*I saw the sheep crossing (cross) the road.*
Elle **a entendu** le coq **chanter**.	*She heard the rooster crowing (crow).*
On **entendait** le chef **fredonner** une chanson.	*We could hear the chef humming (hum) a song.*
Elle **a vu** la biche **sauter** par-dessus la clôture.	*She saw the doe jumping (jump) over the fence.*

The infinitive is used in the *interrogative infinitive*.

Que **répondre**?	*What can I (can we) answer?*
Comment le lui **expliquer**?	*How to explain it to him?*
Pourquoi **protester**?	*Why protest?*
Que **dire**?	*What is there to say?*
Quoi **faire**?	*What can we do?*

You learned **faire** in Chapter 4. This causative form with **faire** is used to express the idea of *having something done by someone* or of *causing something to happen.*

Il a **fait macérer** la viande vingt-quatre heures.	*He macerated the meat twenty-four hours.*
Elle **a fait rôtir** le poulet.	*She roasted the chicken.*
J'**ai fait griller** le pain.	*I toasted the bread.*
J'**ai fait tremper** les pruneaux.	*I soaked the prunes.*

The infinitive is used after expressions of *spending time.*

Elle **passe son temps à créer** de nouvelles recettes.	*She spends her time creating new recipes.*
Il **passe ses vacances à lire** des livres de cuisine.	*He spends his vacation reading cookbooks.*
Il **a gaspillé sa vie à ne rien faire**.	*He wasted his life doing nothing.*
Je **passe mon temps à chercher** de nouvelles épices.	*I spend my time looking for new spices.*

The infinitive is used after expressions of *position*. The preposition **à** precedes the infinitive. (Note the present participle equivalents in English.)

Il **est debout à éplucher** des carottes.	*He is standing peeling carrots.*
Elle **est assise à écosser** des petits pois.	*She is sitting shelling peas.*

| Il **est accroupi** dans le jardin **à cueillir** des fraises. | He is squatting in the garden picking strawberries. |
| Elle **est à genoux à arracher** les mauvaises herbes. | She is kneeling pulling out weeds. |

EXERCICE 14·2

Réécrire les phrases suivantes en traduisant les expressions entre parenthèses.

1. Elle passe ses après-midi (*cooking*).

_____

2. Ils passent leurs nuits (*dancing*).

_____

3. Ils sont accoudés au comptoir (*talking*).

_____

4. Elle est assise (*peeling vegetables*).

_____

5. Il a gaspillé sa vie (*working for them*).

_____

6. Tu as perdu ton temps (*looking for another job*).

_____

7. Je suis allongée sur la plage (*reading*).

_____

8. Elle est debout dans le jardin (*picking some flowers*).

_____

9. Il passe son temps (*dreaming*).

_____

10. Ils passent leurs journées (*shopping*).

_____

The **infinitif passé**

The **infinitif passé** (*past infinitive*) is used to mark anteriority. It is formed with the infinitive of **avoir** or **être** and the past participle of the main verb. (Note that, for verbs conjugated with **être**, the past participle of the **infinitif passé** agrees with the subject of the sentence.)

Les hôtes ont remercié le chef d'**avoir préparé** un si bon repas.	*The guests thanked the chef for having prepared such a good meal.*
Nous nous sommes excusés d'**être partis** avant le dessert.	*We apologized for leaving before dessert.*
Il a regretté d'**avoir oublié** l'anniversaire de Clara.	*He regretted having forgotten Clara's birthday.*
Comment pouvait-il **avoir brûlé** tout le dîner?	*How could he have burnt the whole dinner?*

EXERCICE 14·3

Mettre les verbes suivants à l'infinitif passé, au masculin singulier.

1. dormir _____

2. aller _____

3. manger _____

4. se promener _____

5. regarder _____

6. tomber _____

7. se lever _____

8. préparer _____

9. partir _____

10. allumer _____

One common occurrence of the **infinitif passé** is after the preposition **après** (*after*), while the **infinitif présent** follows **avant de** (*before*).

Gérard fait mariner la viande **avant d'éplucher** un oignon.	*Gérard marinates the meat before peeling an onion.*
Gérard fait mariner la viande **après avoir épluché** un oignon.	*Gérard marinates the meat after peeling an onion.*
Elle se lave les mains **avant de décortiquer** les crevettes.	*She washes her hands before shelling the shrimp.*
Elle se lave les mains **après avoir décortiqué** les crevettes.	*She washes her hands after shelling the shrimp.*
Je fais la cuisine **avant d'aller** au cinéma.	*I cook before going to the movies.*
Je fais la cuisine **après être allé** au cinéma.	*I cook after going to the movies.*
Elle lit le journal **avant de se lever**.	*She reads the paper before getting up.*
Elle lit le journal **après s'être levée**.	*She reads the paper after getting up.*

*Changer **avant de** en **après** en utilisant l'infinitif passé.*

1. Elle prend des vacances avant de compléter son projet.

_____

2. Il écrit la lettre avant de consulter son ami.

_____

3. Je prépare un thé avant de cueillir des fruits.

_____

4. Ils rendent visite à leurs amis avant d'aller au théâtre.

_____

5. Il verse le vin avant de servir le dîner.

_____

6. Elle se maquille avant de s'habiller.

_____

7. Nous dînons avant de regarder le film à la télévision.

_____

8. Ils se promènent avant de travailler.

_____

9. Je réfléchis avant de téléphoner.

_____

10. Nous allons chez Julien avant de choisir un cadeau.

_____

Verbs with their prepositions

When a verb is followed by another verb in the infinitive (**j'aime danser**), the first thing to ask is whether or not it is followed by a preposition. There is no magic recipe, you need to learn them by heart as you go along. Some verbs are not followed by a preposition, others are followed by **à**, **de**, **sur**, etc., before an infinitive, and sometimes before a noun or pronoun.

Verbs not followed by a preposition

Let's start with verbs that are *not* followed by a preposition:

aimer	*to like, to love*
aller	*to go*
avouer	*to admit*

compter	*to intend, to plan*
désirer	*to desire, to wish*
détester	*to hate (to)*
devoir	*must, to have to*
écouter	*to listen to*
espérer	*to hope to*
faire	*to do*
falloir	*must, to be necessary to*
laisser	*to let, to allow*
oser	*to dare (to)*
paraître	*to appear, to seem*
penser	*to think*
pouvoir	*can, to be able to*
préférer	*to prefer*
prétendre	*to claim*
savoir	*to know (how to)*
sembler	*to seem to*
sentir	*to feel, to think*
souhaiter	*to wish to*
venir	*to come*
voir	*to see*
vouloir	*to want to*

Les Corbin **aiment manger** au restaurant.	*The Corbins love to eat out.*
Elle **voudrait devenir** traiteur.	*She would like to become a caterer.*
J'**avoue ne pas comprendre** son but.	*I admit I do not understand his goal.*
Il **sait faire** la sauce béchamel.	*He knows how to make béchamel sauce.*

In the above examples, the subject of the first verb is the same as the one for the second verb; that's why the infinitive form is used. When the subjects are different, a dependent clause introduced by **que** is required. Depending on the verb in the main clause, the dependent clause can be in the indicative or the subjunctive.

J'espère obtenir ce poste.	*I am hoping to get this position.*
J'espère **qu'elle obtiendra** ce poste.	*I am hoping she'll get this position.*
Tu veux apprendre ce métier.	*You want to learn this craft.*
Tu veux **qu'il apprenne** ce métier.	*You want him to learn this craft.*

In some cases, a French verb does not need a preposition even though its English equivalent requires one.

Elle **attend** le train.	*She is waiting **for** the train.*
Il **a abandonné** le projet.	*He gave **up** the project.*
Nous **écoutons** la conférence.	*We are listening **to** the lecture.*
Soudain, ils **sont entrés**.	*Suddenly they walked **in**.*

EXERCICE 14·5

Mettre au présent les verbes entre parenthèses.

1. Il (détester) _____ attendre.

2. Ils (vouloir) _____ acheter un nouvel ordinateur.

3. Nous (devoir) _____ partir dans une heure.

The infinitive mood **121**

4. Je (pouvoir) _____ vous aider.

5. Nous (désirer) _____ renouveler notre abonnement.

6. Tu (vouloir) _____ goûter ces plats.

7. Elle (sembler) _____ comprendre les conséquences.

8. Tu (penser) _____ pouvoir réussir?

9. Il (falloir) _____ faire mariner le poisson.

10. Vous (aller) _____ passer une bonne soirée.

Verbs followed by the preposition à

Many verbs are followed by the preposition **à** when they precede an infinitive. You have already encountered quite a few in previous chapters. These will also need to be memorized.

s'accoutumer à	*to get accustomed to*
aider à	*to help to*
s'amuser à	*to enjoy*
apprendre à	*to learn to, to show how to*
arriver à	*to manage to*
aspirer à	*to aspire to*
s'attendre à	*to expect to*
autoriser à	*to authorize to*
chercher à	*to try to, to attempt to*
commencer à	*to start to*
consentir à	*to agree to, to consent to*
continuer à	*to continue to, to keep on*
se décider à	*to make up one's mind to*
encourager à	*to encourage to*
se faire à	*to get used to*
faire attention à	*to pay attention to*
s'habituer à	*to get used to*
hésiter à	*to hesitate to*
inciter à	*to encourage to*
s'intéresser à	*to get interested in*
inviter à	*to invite to*
se mettre à	*to start to, to begin to*
parvenir à	*to manage to*
préparer à	*to get ready to*
renoncer à	*to give up*
se résigner à	*to resign oneself to*
réussir à	*to succeed in*
songer à	*to think about*
tenir à	*to insist on, to be eager to*
viser à	*to aim at*

Il **commence à travailler** à huit heures.	*He starts to work at eight o'clock.*
Ils **se préparent à partir**.	*They are getting ready to leave.*
Elle l'**a encouragé à s'inscrire**.	*She encouraged him to sign up.*
Tu **as réussi à obtenir** un prix.	*You managed to get an award.*

Verbs followed by the preposition de

Now that you have memorized some of the **à** verbs, let's look at some verbs followed by the preposition **de** when they precede an infinitive.

accepter de	*to accept, to agree to*
accuser de	*to accuse (of)*
s'arrêter de	*to stop*
avoir besoin de	*to need to*
avoir envie de	*to feel like, to want*
avoir l'intention de	*to intend to*
avoir peur de	*to be afraid of*
cesser de	*to stop, to cease*
choisir de	*to choose to*
conseiller de	*to advise (to)*
se contenter de	*to content oneself with*
convaincre de	*to convince (to)*
craindre de	*to fear (to)*
défendre de	*to forbid (to)*
demander de	*to ask (to)*
se dépêcher de	*to hurry to*
s'efforcer de	*to try hard to*
empêcher de	*to prevent (from)*
s'empêcher de	*to refrain from*
envisager de	*to contemplate*
essayer de	*to try to*
éviter de	*to avoid*
s'excuser de	*to apologize for*
faire semblant de	*to pretend to*
feindre de	*to feign to, to pretend to*
finir de	*to finish, to end up*
interdire de	*to forbid (to)*
menacer de	*to threaten to*
mériter de	*to deserve to*
offrir de	*to offer to*
oublier de	*to forget to*
permettre de	*to allow (to), to permit (to)*
persuader de	*to persuade (to), to convince (to)*
se plaindre de	*to complain of*
projeter de	*to plan to/on*
promettre de	*to promise to*
refuser de	*to refuse to*
regretter de	*to regret*
remercier de	*to thank (for)*
reprocher de	*to reproach for*
soupçonner de	*to suspect of*
se souvenir de	*to remember to*
tâcher de	*to try to*

Il **a essayé de faire** un soufflé.	*He tried to make a soufflé.*
Elle **a refusé de** nous **donner** sa recette.	*She refused to give us her recipe.*
Ils **ont promis de** l'**envoyer** au Cordon Bleu.	*They promised to send him to the Cordon Bleu cooking school.*
J'**ai fini de lire** le roman.	*I finished reading the novel.*

EXERCICE

14·6

À ou de? Mettre la préposition.

1. J'ai appris _____ faire une mousse au chocolat.

2. Ils ont choisi _____ s'installer dans une région gastronomique.

3. Il s'habitue _____ vivre dans une grande ville.

4. Elle nous reproche _____ ne jamais lui rendre visite.

5. Tu as renoncé _____ faire ce voyage.

6. Elle se souvient _____ la cuisine de sa grand-mère.

7. Il tient _____ sa voiture.

8. Tu lui as conseillé _____ suivre des cours de cuisine.

9. Ils se plaignent _____ tout.

10. Son grand-père a promis _____ faire des gâteaux.

EXERCICE

14·7

*Traduire les phrases suivantes en utilisant la forme **vous** si nécessaire.*

1. They want to travel to France.

_____

2. He spent hours peeling potatoes.

_____

3. Cooking is her favorite pastime.

_____

4. Do not forget to add some salt!

_____

5. He is afraid of burning the meat.

_____

6. They feel like eating a chocolate soufflé.

_____

7. He stopped smoking.

_____

8. They refused to go out.

9. She is learning how to cook.

_____

10. Try to understand the situation!

_____

Chapter 27 will have other tricky, capricious verbs that use different prepositions.

The present participle and the gerund

The present participle

You have used the **participe passé** (*past participle*) many times with the compound tenses. Another participle is the **participe présent** (*present participle*). It is formed by dropping the **-ons** ending from the present tense **nous** form and adding **-ant**.

chanter to sing			
nous chantons	*we sing*	**chantant**	*singing*

partir to leave			
nous partons	*we leave*	**partant**	*leaving*

choisir to choose			
nous choisissons	*we choose*	**choisissant**	*choosing*

boire to drink			
nous buvons	*we drink*	**buvant**	*drinking*

voir to see			
nous voyons	*we see*	**voyant**	*seeing*

répondre to answer			
nous répondons	*we answer*	**répondant**	*answering*

Some spelling changes occur with some **-cer** and **-ger** verbs:

commencer to start			
nous commençons	*we start*	**commençant**	*starting*

influencer to influence			
nous influençons	*we influence*	**influençant**	*influencing*

manger to eat			
nous mangeons	*we eat*	**mangeant**	*eating*

nager to swim			
nous nageons	*we swim*	**nageant**	*swimming*

Pronominal verbs follow the same pattern. Do not forget the pronoun corresponding to the subject. Let's look at the present participle of **se promener** (*to take a walk*):

me promenant	*walking*	**nous** promenant	*walking*
te promenant	*walking*	**vous** promenant	*walking*
se promenant	*walking*	**se** promenant	*walking*

Three verbs have an irregular present participle:

être	*to be*	**étant**	*being*
avoir	*to have*	**ayant**	*having*
savoir	*to know*	**sachant**	*knowing*

VOCABULAIRE

jouer	*to play*	**la boxe**	*boxing*
un joueur, une joueuse	*a player*	**le cyclisme**	*biking, cycling*
un(e) adversaire	*an opponent*	**le football**	*soccer*
une équipe	*a team*	**le football américain**	*football*
gagner	*to win*	**le golf**	*golf*
remporter une victoire	*to win*	**le jogging**	*jogging*
battre	*to beat*	**la lutte**	*wrestling*
un vainqueur	*a winner*	**la natation**	*swimming*
un(e) gagnant(e)	*a winner*	**le patinage**	*ice skating*
un(e) perdant(e)	*a loser*	**la plongée**	*diving*
un match	*a game*	**le ski**	*skiing*
manquer	*to miss*	**la descente**	*downhill skiing*
courir	*to run*	**le ski de fond**	*cross-country skiing*
sauter	*to jump*	**le ski nautique**	*waterskiing*
lancer	*to throw*	**le tennis**	*tennis*
s'entraîner	*to train*	**la voile**	*sailing*
un entraîneur	*a trainer*	**un stade**	*a stadium*
le base-ball	*baseball*	**une raquette**	*a racket*
le basket-ball	*basketball*	**un ballon**	*a ball*

Some **participes présents** can be used as nouns. When used as a noun, the present participle changes according to gender and number. For example:

un gagnant	*a winner (masculine)*	**une gagnante**	*a winner (feminine)*
un perdant	*a loser (masculine)*	**une perdante**	*a loser (feminine)*

Many **participes présents** can be used as adjectives. When used as an adjective, the **participe présent** agrees with the noun it modifies. For example:

des matchs épuisants	*exhausting games*
un commentateur fascinant	*a fascinating commentator*
un sport exigeant	*a demanding sport*
une pièce amusante	*an amusing play*

The **participe présent** can also be used as a verb. Note that when used as a verb, the present participle is invariable.

La police l'a aperçu **entrant** dans un laboratoire médical.	*The police saw him entering (as he was entering) a medical lab.*
Étant blessé au genou, il n'a pas pu jouer.	*Since he has a knee injury, he was not able to play.*

The present participle and the gerund   **127**

| Ne **sachant** pas comment nous excuser, nous lui avons offert des fleurs. | *Not knowing how to apologize, we gave her some flowers.* |
| **Traversant** la rue, elle a perdu son chapeau. | *Crossing (As she crossed) the street, she lost her hat.* |

When an action precedes another one, **avoir** and **être** in the **participe présent** can be combined with a **participe passé**. Note that the past participle agrees with the subject of the sentence if the verb is conjugated with **être**.

ayant vu	*having seen*
ayant compris	*having understood*
ayant joué	*having played*
ayant traversé	*having crossed*
étant allé(e)(s)	*having gone*
étant parti(e)(s)	*having left*
nous étant promené(e)s	*having walked*
nous étant retrouvé(e)s	*having met*

Ayant accepté la défaite, les joueurs **sont rentrés** chez eux.	*Having accepted the defeat, the players went home.*
Étant partis très tôt, nous **sommes arrivés** les premiers.	*Having left very early, we were the first to arrive.*
Nous étant promenés toute la journée, nous **étions** fatigués.	*Having walked all day, we were tired.*
M'étant couchée à l'aube, j'**ai fait** la grasse matinée.	*Having gone to bed at dawn, I slept late.*
N'ayant pas dormi de la nuit, il **était** de mauvaise humeur.	*Not having slept all night, he was in a bad mood.*

EXERCICE

15·1

Mettre au participe présent les verbes suivants.

1. finir _____

2. savoir _____

3. donner _____

4. protéger _____

5. faire _____

6. avoir _____

7. avancer _____

8. être _____

9. prononcer _____

10. vendre _____

The gerund

When the present participle is introduced by **en**, it is referred to as the **gérondif** (*gerund*). It is formed with **en** + the present participle. It describes the relationship between two actions. It can express simultaneity, manner, condition, or causality.

Il s'est foulé la cheville **en jouant** au foot.	*He sprained his ankle while playing football.*
Elle écoute de la musique **en conduisant**.	*She listens to music while driving.*
M. Vincent a gagné beaucoup d'argent **en achetant** ces toiles.	*Mr. Vincent made a lot of money buying (when he bought) these paintings.*
En renvoyant ce joueur, vous feriez une grosse erreur.	*If you fired this player, you would make a big mistake.*

When **tout** precedes the gerund, it underscores a tension, a contradiction between two actions. For example:

Tout en étant un bon joueur, il ne marquait jamais de but.	*While being (Even though he was) a good player, he never scored a goal.*
Tout en faisant semblant d'écouter le professeur, il jouait avec son iPod.	*While pretending to listen to the teacher, he was playing with his iPod.*
Tout en pleurant, il riait.	*While crying, he was laughing.*
Tout en prétendant le contraire, elle voulait être élue.	*While claiming otherwise, she wanted to be elected.*

EXERCICE
15·2

Mettre au gérondif les verbes suivants.

1. C'est en (faire) _____ de l'exercice que vous serez en forme.

2. Elle chante en (prendre) _____ une douche.

3. Il s'est tordu la cheville en (jouer) _____ au volley.

4. Ils ont bronzé en (faire) _____ du ski de fond.

5. Il l'a invitée à dîner en (savoir) _____ que cela lui ferait plaisir.

6. En (aller) _____ en Inde, il a fait escale en Allemagne.

7. Tout en (se plaindre) _____, elle avait l'air satisfaite.

8. Ils ont découvert la basilique de Lisieux en (visiter) _____ la Normandie.

9. J'ai rencontré un ami en (arriver) _____ à Paris.

10. Il a tout perdu en (parier) _____ tous les jours au casino.

Traduire les phrases suivantes.

1. He lost his keys while walking in the park.

_____

2. Not having seen the film, I can't make any comment.

_____

3. They saw Paul while crossing the street.

_____

4. Knowing the truth, she could not stay silent.

_____

5. He made money selling paintings.

_____

6. It was a fascinating game.

_____

7. Having finished the book, he left.

_____

8. They listen to music while working.

_____

9. I knit while watching television.

_____

10. He fell while jumping over the wall.

_____

The passé simple

The **passé simple** (*simple past, historical past*) is a verb tense used mainly in written French, for literary and historical material. It may also be heard during a formal speech. It is the equivalent of the **passé composé**, used to recount a specific action in the past. When relating events, quality newspapers use the **passé simple** for refinement. Scandal sheets will often use it to convey a sense of drama. When reading French literature of all periods, you will need to recognize the **passé simple** to get a full appreciation of the text.

Formation of the passé simple

The **passé simple** of regular -**er** verbs is formed by adding the endings -**ai**, -**as**, -**a**, -**âmes**, -**âtes**, -**èrent** to the infinitive stem.

répéter *to repeat*			
je répét**ai**	*I repeated*	nous répét**âmes**	*we repeated*
tu répét**as**	*you repeated*	vous répét**âtes**	*you repeated*
il/elle répét**a**	*he/she repeated*	ils/elles répét**èrent**	*they repeated*

Verbs like **commencer** and **manger** have a spelling change. When the **passé simple** ending starts with -**a**, use the cedilla (ç) for verbs ending in -**cer** and add an extra -**e**- for verbs ending in -**ger**.

Elle prononça un discours.	*She made a speech.*
Je remplaçai le comédien malade.	*I replaced the sick actor.*
Il partagea sa fortune.	*He shared his fortune.*
Nous déménageâmes de nombreuses fois.	*We moved many times.*

The **passé simple** of regular -**ir** and -**re** verbs like **partir** (*to leave*) and **répondre** (*to answer*) is formed by adding the endings -**is**, -**is**, **it**, -**îmes**, -**îtes**, -**irent** to the infinitive stem.

partir *to leave*			
je part**is**	*I left*	nous part**îmes**	*we left*
tu part**is**	*you left*	vous part**îtes**	*you left*
il/elle part**it**	*he/she left*	ils/elles part**irent**	*they left*

répondre *to answer*			
je répond**is**	*I answered*	nous répond**îmes**	*we answered*
tu répond**is**	*you answered*	vous répond**îtes**	*you answered*
il/elle répond**it**	*he/she answered*	ils/elles répond**irent**	*they answered*

Avoir (*to have*) and **être** (*to be*) are irregular in the **passé simple**.

avoir *to have*			
j'**eus**	*I had*	nous **eûmes**	*we had*
tu **eus**	*you had*	vous **eûtes**	*you had*
il/elle **eut**	*he/she had*	ils/elles **eurent**	*they had*

être *to be*			
je **fus**	*I was*	nous **fûmes**	*we were*
tu **fus**	*you were*	vous **fûtes**	*you were*
il/elle **fut**	*he/she was*	ils/elles **furent**	*they were*

On **frappa** à la porte et il **se leva**.	*Someone knocked on the door and he got up.*
Il **fut** surpris par notre réaction.	*He was surprised by our reaction.*
Ils **répondirent** immédiatement à notre lettre.	*They answered our letter immediately.*
Elles **partirent** aussitôt après le discours.	*They left right after the speech.*

VOCABULAIRE

l'art (*m.*)	*art*	une statue	*a statue*
un musée	*a museum*	une nature morte	*a still life*
une collection	*a collection*	un chef-d'œuvre	*a masterpiece*
collectionner	*to collect*	une photographie	*a photograph*
un collectionneur,	*a collector*	un vernissage	*an opening (art show)*
une collectionneuse		peindre	*to paint*
une galerie	*a gallery*	dessiner	*to draw*
une visite guidée	*a guided tour*	sculpter	*to sculpt*
un conservateur,	*a curator*	un peintre	*a painter*
une conservatrice		un(e) paysagiste	*a landscape painter*
une exposition	*an exhibition*	un(e) portraitiste	*a portrait painter*
les beaux-arts (*m.pl.*)	*fine arts*	une palette	*a palette*
une toile	*a canvas, a painting*	un pinceau	*a paintbrush*
une peinture	*a painting*	un chevalet	*an easel*
un tableau	*a painting*	un dessinateur,	*a designer, a sketcher*
une aquarelle	*a watercolor (painting)*	une dessinatrice	
une gravure	*an etching*	un sculpteur	*a sculptor*
un dessin	*a drawing*	un(e) photographe	*a photographer*
une sculpture	*a sculpture*	un atelier	*a studio, a workshop*

The **passé simple** of irregular verbs

Other verbs have an irregular **passé simple**. For some verbs the stem of the **passé simple** is based on the past participle, but this is not a fixed rule.

Here are some of the irregular verbs in the **passé simple** that will let you start right in reading French newspapers or novels. It is especially useful to learn the third-person singular and plural forms.

boire (*to drink*)	il/elle **but**	*he/she drank*	ils/elles **burent**	*they drank*
conduire (*to drive*)	il/elle **conduisit**	*he/she drove*	ils/elles **conduisirent**	*they drove*
connaître (*to know*)	il/elle **connut**	*he/she knew*	ils/elles **connurent**	*they knew*

convaincre (*to convince*)	il/elle **convainquit**	*he/she convinced*	ils/elles **convainquirent**	*they convinced*
courir (*to run*)	il/elle **courut**	*he/she ran*	ils/elles **coururent**	*they ran*
couvrir (*to cover*)	il/elle **couvrit**	*he/she covered*	ils/elles **couvrirent**	*they covered*
craindre (*to fear*)	il/elle **craignit**	*he/she feared*	ils/elles **craignirent**	*they feared*
croire (*to believe*)	il/elle **crut**	*he/she believed*	ils/elles **crurent**	*they believed*
devoir (*to have to*)	il/elle **dut**	*he/she had to*	ils/elles **durent**	*they had to*
écrire (*to write*)	il/elle **écrivit**	*he/she wrote*	ils/elles **écrivirent**	*they wrote*
éteindre (*to turn off [the light]*)	il/elle **éteignit**	*he/she turned off*	ils/elles **éteignirent**	*they turned off*
faire (*to do*)	il/elle **fit**	*he/she did*	ils/elles **firent**	*they did*
falloir (*to have to*)	il **fallut**	*one had to, it was necessary to*		
introduire (*to introduce*)	il/elle **introduisit**	*he/she introduced*	ils/elles **introduisirent**	*they introduced*
lire (*to read*)	il/elle **lut**	*he/she read*	ils/elles **lurent**	*they read*
mettre (*to put*)	il/elle **mit**	*he/she put*	ils/elles **mirent**	*they put*
mourir (*to die*)	il/elle **mourut**	*he/she died*	ils/elles **moururent**	*they died*
naître (*to be born*)	il/elle **naquit**	*he/she was born*	ils/elles **naquirent**	*they were born*
obtenir (*to obtain*)	il/elle **obtint**	*he/she obtained*	ils/elles **obtinrent**	*they obtained*
offrir (*to offer*)	il/elle **offrit**	*he/she offered*	ils/elles **offrirent**	*they offered*
peindre (*to paint*)	il/elle **peignit**	*he/she painted*	ils/elles **peignirent**	*they painted*
plaire (*to please*)	il/elle **plut**	*he/she pleased*	ils/elles **plurent**	*they pleased*
pleuvoir (*to rain*)	il **plut**	*it rained*		
pouvoir (*can*)	il/elle **put**	*he/she could*	ils/elles **purent**	*they could*
prendre (*to take*)	il/elle **prit**	*he/she took*	ils/elles **prirent**	*they took*
recevoir (*to receive*)	il/elle **reçut**	*he/she received*	ils/elles **reçurent**	*they received*
rire (*to laugh*)	il/elle **rit**	*he/she laughed*	ils/elles **rirent**	*they laughed*
savoir (*to know*)	il/elle **sut**	*he/she knew*	ils/elles **surent**	*they knew*
sourire (*to smile*)	il/elle **sourit**	*he/she smiled*	ils/elles **sourirent**	*they smiled*
tenir (*to hold*)	il/elle **tint**	*he/she held*	ils/elles **tinrent**	*they held*
valoir (*to be worth*)	il/elle **valut**	*it was worth*	ils/elles **valurent**	*they were worth*
venir (*to come*)	il/elle **vint**	*he/she came*	ils/elles **vinrent**	*they came*
vivre (*to live*)	il/elle **vécut**	*he/she lived*	ils/elles **vécurent**	*they lived*
vouloir (*to want*)	il/elle **voulut**	*he/she wanted*	ils/elles **voulurent**	*they wanted*

EXERCICE

16·1

Mettre l'infinitif des verbes suivants.

1. Ils furent de grands collectionneurs. _____

2. J'eus un profond respect pour cet artiste. _____

3. Elles peignirent des natures mortes. _____

4. Nous fîmes un tour de son atelier. _____

5. Il vint nous rejoindre au vernissage. _____

6. Tu lus toutes ses œuvres. _____

7. Vous voulûtes lui faire un compliment. _____

8. Elle sut tout de suite que c'était un chef-d'œuvre. _____

9. Il plut à tout le monde. _____

10. J'éteignis la lumière. _____

EXERCICE
16·2

Mettre au passé simple les verbes entre parenthèses.

1. *Le Rouge et le noir* (être) _____ publié en 1830.

2. En France, les femmes (obtenir) _____ le droit de vote en 1944.

3. Jacques Cartier (explorer) _____ la région de Montréal en 1535.

4. Charles de Gaulle (mourir) _____ en 1970.

5. Édouard Manet (peindre) _____ *Le déjeuner sur l'herbe* en 1863.

6. La terre (trembler) _____ au Japon en 1923.

7. Catherine de Médicis (introduire) _____ l'usage de la fourchette en France.

8. Le voyage inaugural du TGV (avoir lieu) _____ en 1981.

9. Johnny Hallyday (faire) _____ son premier concert à l'Olympia en 1961.

10. La Côte-d'Ivoire (devenir) _____ indépendante en 1960.

EXERCICE
16·3

Traduire les phrases suivantes en utilisant le passé simple.

1. He lived ten years in Amsterdam.

_____

2. She introduced this new method.

_____

3. They read all his books.

_____

4. He died in Italy.

_____

5. He was surprised.

_____

6. I wanted to thank him.

_____

7. She was born in Rouen.

_____

8. They bought a new easel.

_____

9. She became a portrait painter.

_____

10. He smiled and left.

_____

The passive voice

A sentence can either be in the active or the passive voice. In the active voice, the subject performs the action, while in the **voix passive** (*passive voice*), the subject is acted upon. That is, in the passive voice, the subject and the object exchange roles. Be aware that the passive voice is much more common in English than in French. In French, one tends to use the active voice.

Compare the active and the passive voices.

The active voice:

Les croisés **envahissent** le pays.	*The crusaders are invading the country.*
La souris **mange** le fromage.	*The mouse eats the cheese.*

The passive voice:

Le pays **est envahi** par les croisés.	*The country is being invaded by the crusaders.*
Le fromage **est mangé** par la souris.	*The cheese is being eaten by the mouse.*

Formation of the passive voice

The passive voice is formed with **être** in the tense required + the past participle of the main verb.

il **est** construit	*it is (being) built*
il **a été** construit	*it has been built*
il **était** construit	*it was built*
il **fut** construit	*it was built*
il **sera** construit	*it will be built*
il **serait** construit	*it would be built*

VOCABULAIRE

la police	*police*	**prendre la fuite,**	*to flee*
le policier	*police officer*	**s'enfuir**	
arriver sur les lieux	*to arrive at the*	**poursuivre**	*to chase,*
du crime	*crime scene*		*to pursue*
une fusillade	*a shoot-out,*	**attraper**	*to catch*
	a gun battle	**arrêter**	*to arrest*

passer les menottes à quelqu'un	to handcuff someone	un attentat	a terrorist attack
voler	to steal	un détournement d'avion	a hijacking
un vol	a theft	un témoin	a witness
cambrioler	to burglarize	un témoignage	a testimony, a piece of evidence
un cambriolage	a burglary		
un vol à l'étalage	(a case of) shoplifting	témoigner	to testify
une agression	a mugging, an assault	prévenir la police	to call the police
le harcèlement	harassment	les empreintes digitales (f. pl.)	fingerprints
le blanchiment d'argent	money laundering		
le chantage	blackmail	l'ADN (m.)	DNA
l'escroquerie (f.)	swindle, fraud	l'accusé(e)	the accused
un escroc	a crook	être condamné(e) à	to be sentenced to
un meurtre	a murder	une amende	a fine
un assassin	a murderer	une peine	a sentence
un meurtrier, une meurtrière	a murderer		

EXERCICE 17·1

Mettre les phrases suivantes à la voix passive. Attention aux temps de verbe!

1. Le policier a attrapé le voleur.

_____

2. Le roi a signé le traité.

_____

3. Le médecin prescrit un nouveau traitement.

_____

4. Le cambrioleur a volé le tableau.

_____

5. Le chien a mordu l'homme au chapeau gris.

_____

6. L'ennemi a pris l'otage.

_____

7. L'enfant a déchiré le canapé.

_____

8. Le marchand d'art vendra un célèbre tableau.

_____

9. Les envahisseurs prennent la forteresse.

_____

10. Le professeur félicite les étudiants.

_____

Mettre les phrases suivantes à la voix active. Attention aux temps de verbe!

1. Le gâteau a été fait par le chef.

_____

2. L'objet a été conçu par l'artisan.

_____

3. Le château a été érigé par le roi.

_____

4. Le document sera signé par l'ambassadeur.

_____

5. Le tableau a été vendu par le propriétaire.

_____

6. Le fauteuil est griffé par le chat.

_____

7. L'amende a été payée par le malfaiteur.

_____

8. Le vase a été volé par l'antiquaire.

_____

9. Le livre sera écrit par un journaliste.

_____

10. Les élèves sont punis par le professeur.

_____

The agent with **par** and with **de** in the passive voice

In most cases, the agent is introduced by **par**.

Ce rapport **a été fait par** un consultant américain.	*This report was written by an American consultant.*
Cette bague **a été retrouvée par** la police.	*This ring was found by the police.*
Ce manoir **a été construit par** une famille fortunée.	*This mansion was built by a wealthy family.*
Ces éditoriaux **seront écrits par** notre rédacteur en chef.	*These editorials will be written by our editor in chief.*

However, the preposition **de** is commonly used after verbs expressing emotion or opinion.

Ce professeur **est apprécié de** ses étudiants.	*This teacher is appreciated by his students.*
Ce gérant **est estimé de** ses employés.	*This manager is respected by his employees.*

That is, when the **voix passive** is followed by the preposition **de** (rather than **par**), the agent plays a less active role.

Le voleur **est suivi de** ses complices.	*The thief is followed by his accomplices.*
Le voleur **est suivi par** la police.	*The thief is followed by the police.*
Le château **est entouré de** douves.	*The castle is surrounded by a moat.*
Le château **est entouré par** les envahisseurs.	*The castle is surrounded by the invaders.*

Uses of the passive voice

The **voix passive** is used to emphasize the subject.

Une écharpe blanche **a été retrouvée** sur les lieux du crime.	*A white scarf was found on the crime scene.*
Le témoignage de M. Baulieu **a été entendu** ce matin.	*Mr. Baulieu's testimony was heard this morning.*

The **voix passive** is also used to avoid specifying the agent of the action.

Aucune décision ne **sera prise** avant l'arrivée du nouveau directeur.	*No decision will be made before the new director's arrival.*
Son incompétence **a été** très **remarquée**.	*His incompetence was clearly noticed.*
Aucun rapport n'**a été envoyé**.	*No report was sent.*

Avoiding the passive voice in French

The **voix passive** can be replaced by the active voice in French with the following reflexive verbs: **se laisser, se faire, se voir, s'entendre dire**. Note the passive voice forms in the English translations.

Elle **s'est fait faire** un robe pour son mariage.	*She had a dress made for her wedding.*
Il **s'est vu contraint** d'accepter.	*He found himself forced to accept.*
Ils **se sont laissés influencer** très facilement.	*They let themselves be influenced very easily.*

In Chapter 6, you studied one type of pronominal verb called the passive pronominal. This construction is another example of the **voix passive**.

Ça ne **se dit** pas.	*That isn't said.*
Comment ça **se traduit**?	*How is it translated?*
Ça **se voit**.	*It shows.*
Le vin blanc **se boit** frais.	*White wine is to be drunk chilled.*

French often prefers to use the third-person singular form **on** rather than the passive voice construction.

Ici, **on parle anglais**.	*English is spoken here.*
On vous demande au téléphone.	*You are wanted on the phone.*

EXERCICE 17·3

Traduire les phrases suivantes en utilisant la voix passive.

1. The castle is being built by the queen.

_____

2. The painting was stolen by an art dealer.

_____

3. A pink hat was found in the park yesterday.

_____

4. This verb is followed by the indicative (mood).

_____

5. The house is surrounded by the police.

_____

6. A new remedy will be invented before 2050.

_____

7. This vaccine was invented in 1885.

_____

8. The decision was made on Monday.

_____

9. The letter was read by a witness.

_____

10. The house is surrounded by trees.

_____

Indirect speech

Indirect speech is used, both in English and in French, to relate conversational exchanges or information in the third person.

Direct speech versus indirect speech

In direct speech (**le discours direct**), one says something or asks a question directly.

Quentin demande:
  « Où allez-vous? »
Pierre dit:
  « Le président est à Milan. »

Quentin asks:
  "Where are you going?"
Pierre says:
  "The president is in Milan."

In indirect speech (**le discours indirect**), the words of one or more people are reported or a question is asked indirectly. There are no quotation marks.

Quentin demande **où vous allez**.

Pierre dit **que le président est à Milan**.

Quentin is asking where you are going.

Pierre is saying that the president is in Milan.

Verbs in the main clause of indirect speech are followed by **que** (**où**, **si**, etc.); the verb in the dependent clause is usually in the indicative. Here are some typical main clause verbs:

affirmer	*to say, to claim*
annoncer	*to announce*
assurer	*to ensure, to maintain*
avouer	*to confess*
confier	*to confide*
constater	*to note, to notice*
crier	*to shout*
déclarer	*to state*
dire	*to say*
expliquer	*to explain*
observer	*to notice, to observe*
prétendre	*to claim*
promettre	*to promise*
remarquer	*to notice, to observe*
répondre	*to answer*
révéler	*to reveal*

s'apercevoir	*to realize*
savoir	*to know*
se rendre compte	*to realize*

Balancing tenses: la concordance des temps

If the verb in the main clause is in the present tense, the verb in the dependent clause remains in the same tense as it is in the direct speech.

Paul dit: « Ce n'**est** pas important. »	*Paul says: "It's not important."*
Paul dit que ce n'**est** pas important.	*Paul says it is not important.*
Je lui avoue: « Je **ne suis jamais allé** en Argentine. »	*I admit to him: "I have never been to Argentina."*
Je lui avoue que je **ne suis jamais allé** en Argentine.	*I admit to him that I have never been to Argentina.*
Il répond: « J'**avais** toujours faim quand j'étais jeune. »	*He answers: "I was always hungry when I was young."*
Il répond qu'il **avait** toujours faim quand il était jeune.	*He answers that he was always hungry when he was young.*

VOCABULAIRE

la politique	*politics*	le droit de vote	*right to vote*
le pouvoir	*power*	l'électeur, l'électrice	*voter*
le gouvernement	*government*	le scrutin	*ballot*
gouverner	*to govern*	le bulletin de vote	*(paper) ballot*
le/la politique	*politician*	le suffrage universel	*universal suffrage*
la gauche	*the left*	la réforme	*reform*
la droite	*the right*	gagner les élections	*to win the elections*
le centre	*the center*	perdre les élections	*to lose the elections*
le parti	*(political) party*	le sondage	*poll*
la coalition	*coalition*	la démocratie	*democracy*
l'élection (*f.*)	*election*	la monarchie	*monarchy*
la voix	*vote*	le multipartisme	*multiparty system*
le premier tour	*first round*	la parité	*equality between men and women*
le deuxième tour	*second round*		
élire	*to elect*	l'abstention (*f.*)	*abstention*
être élu(e)	*to be elected*	boycotter	*to boycott*
voter	*to vote*		

EXERCICE
18·1

*Mettre les phrases suivantes au discours indirect en commençant la phrase par **Il veut savoir si**.*

1. Le programme du parti est bien défini.

_____

2. Nous allons boycotter les prochaines élections.

_____

3. Tu vas voter dimanche.

_____

4. Le ministre de l'éducation a proposé des réformes.

_____

5. Elle acceptera notre proposition.

_____

6. Le parti a choisi son candidat.

_____

7. Les femmes peuvent voter dans ce pays.

_____

8. Vous viendrez samedi soir.

_____

9. Elle a fini ses recherches.

_____

10. La parité sera jamais réalisée.

_____

EXERCICE
18·2

Relier les deux membres de phrase.

1. Elle sera absente mardi. (Elle annonce que)

_____

2. Paul s'est trompé. (Ils avouent que)

_____

3. Ses produits sont les meilleurs. (La marchande dit)

_____

4. Elles avaient tort. (Tu sais bien que)

_____

5. Le candidat a peu de chance de gagner. (On se rend compte que)

_____

6. Le musée est ouvert. (Ils ne savent pas si)

_____

7. Tu n'avais rien entendu. (Tu réponds que)

_____

8. Il n'est jamais allé en France. (Elle nous apprend que)

_____

9. Ils avaient dilapidé leur fortune. (Il nous déclare que)

_____

10. Le peintre habite. (Il ignore où)

_____

Learning **la concordance des temps**, that is, balancing tenses, is one of the most difficult tasks of a French learner. When switching from direct to indirect speech, some changes of tense occur when the main clause verb is in the **passé composé**. Here are the three main scenarios:

Present recounted in the imparfait

If the direct speech is in the present tense, the dependent clause verb is changed into the **imparfait**.

Elle **est** en Inde.	_She is in India._
J'**ai entendu dire** qu'elle **était** en Inde.	_I heard she was in India._
Tu **travailles** pour France 2.	_You are working for France 2._
J'**ai entendu dire** que tu **travaillais** pour France 2.	_I heard you were working for France 2._
Il **pleut** à Londres.	_It is raining in London._
J'**ai entendu dire** qu'il **pleuvait** à Londres.	_I heard it was raining in London._
Ce candidat **a** une chance de gagner.	_This candidate has a chance of winning._
On m'**a dit** que ce candidat **avait** une chance de gagner.	_I heard this candidate has (had) a chance of winning._

Passé composé recounted in the plus-que-parfait

If the direct speech is in the **passé composé**, the verb in the dependent clause is changed into the **plus-que-parfait**.

Ils **ont élu** le candidat de gauche.	_They elected the candidate from the left._
On m'**a dit** qu'ils **avaient élu** le candidat de gauche.	_I heard they had elected the candidate from the left._
Elle **a expliqué** son programme.	_She explained her program._
On m'**a dit** qu'elle **avait expliqué** son programme.	_I heard she (had) explained her program._
Il **a démissionné**.	_He resigned._
On nous **a dit** qu'il **avait démissionné**.	_We heard he had resigned._
Vous **avez voté** pour moi.	_You voted for me._
J'**ai entendu dire** que vous **aviez voté** pour moi.	_I heard you had voted for me._

Future recounted in the present conditional

If the direct speech is in the future, the dependent clause verb is changed into the **conditionnel** in the indirect speech.

Vous **vous présenterez** aux élections.	*You'll run for election.*
J'ai entendu dire que vous **vous présenteriez** aux élections.	*I heard you would run for election.*
Tu **iras** en France.	*You'll go to France.*
J'ai entendu dire que tu **irais** en France.	*I heard you would go to France.*
Ils **achèteront** une maison.	*They'll buy a house.*
J'ai entendu dire qu'ils **achèteraient** une maison.	*I heard they would buy a house.*
Ils **se retrouveront** à Lyon.	*They'll meet in Lyon.*
J'ai entendu dire qu'ils **se retrouveraient** à Lyon.	*I heard they would meet in Lyon.*

EXERCICE
18·3

*Commencer les phrases par **J'ai entendu dire que**. Attention à la concordance des temps.*

1. Tu as accepté leur offre la semaine dernière.

_____

2. Elle a vendu sa voiture hier.

_____

3. Tu travailleras à Chicago l'an prochain.

_____

4. Elle ira en Asie demain.

_____

5. Ils se sont mariés le mois dernier.

_____

6. Il fait froid à Moscou aujourd'hui.

_____

7. Ils s'installeront au Canada l'an prochain.

_____

8. Il a quitté son poste vendredi dernier.

_____

9. Elle est la candidate favorite en ce moment.

_____

10. Tu as pris beaucoup de photos hier soir.

_____

Traduire les phrases suivantes en utilisant **vous** si nécessaire.

1. They know you are living in Paris.

_____

2. I have heard you are living in Paris.

_____

3. I heard you lived in Paris in 1995.

_____

4. I heard you'll go to Paris next year.

_____

5. He says his cat is adorable.

_____

6. I heard you had a cat.

_____

7. I heard you had a cat when you lived on the Victor Hugo Boulevard.

_____

8. I heard your sister will give you her cat.

_____

9. I was told you voted for me.

_____

10. We realize she has a chance to win.

_____

The imperative mood

The imperative mood (**l'impératif**) is used to give orders, make suggestions, or give advice.

Formation of the imperative

To make the three forms of the imperative, take the **tu**, **nous**, and **vous** forms of the present tense. For the **-er** verbs, drop the **-s** of the present tense **tu** form.

parler *to speak*	
Parle!	*Speak!*
Parlons!	*Let's speak!*
Parlez!	*Speak!*

choisir *to choose*	
Choisis!	*Choose!*
Choisissons!	*Let's choose!*
Choisissez!	*Choose!*

répondre *to answer*	
Réponds!	*Answer!*
Répondons!	*Let's answer!*
Répondez!	*Answer!*

boire *to drink*	
Bois!	*Drink!*
Buvons!	*Let's drink!*
Buvez!	*Drink!*

Prends un café avant de partir!	*Have a coffee before you leave!*
Signez votre nom ici!	*Sign your name here!*
Allons leur rendre visite!	*Let's go visit them!*
Épelez votre nom, s'il vous plaît.	*Please spell your name.*
Faites un effort!	*Make an effort!*
Téléphone à Jérôme immédiatement!	*Call Jérôme immediately!*

In the negative form, the negation is placed around the verb. Note that object pronouns immediately precede the verb (following **ne** [**n'**]) in the negative imperative.

N'oubliez pas son anniversaire!	*Don't forget her birthday!*
Ne l'appelle pas dimanche!	*Don't call him on Sunday!*
N'y allons pas avant midi.	*Let's not go there before noon.*

147

Ne parle pas si fort!	*Don't talk so loud!*
Ne prends pas ma voiture!	*Don't take my car!*
Ne signez pas ce document avant de l'avoir lu.	*Do not sign this document before reading it.*

EXERCICE 19·1

Mettre à l'impératif les phrases suivantes.

1. Prendre le train de neuf heures. (tu)

2. Regarder le film à la télé ce soir. (vous)

3. Dîner sur la terrasse. (nous)

4. Acheter le journal. (tu)

5. Boire à sa santé. (nous)

6. Expliquer les conditions. (vous)

7. Ne pas courir si vite. (tu)

8. Épeler ton nom. (tu)

9. Prêter votre dictionnaire à Marie. (vous)

10. Ne pas inviter Denis. (tu)

VOCABULAIRE

un nom	*a name*	**Comment épelez-**	*How do you spell*
un prénom	*a first name*	**vous votre nom?**	*your name?*
un surnom	*a nickname*	**s'appeler**	*to call oneself,*
épeler	*to spell*		*to be named*

Comment vous appelez-vous?	*What is your name?*	**un permis de conduire**	*a driver's license*
Je m'appelle…	*My name is . . .*	**un certificat de vaccination**	*a vaccination certificate*
l'état civil (*m.*)	*civil status*	**célibataire**	*single*
la date de naissance	*birth date*	**marié(e)**	*married*
le lieu de naissance	*place of birth*	**séparé(e)**	*separated*
Où êtes-vous né(e)?	*Where were you born?*	**divorcé(e)**	*divorced*
Je suis né(e) à…	*I was born in . . .*	**veuf, veuve**	*widow, widower*
une naissance	*a birth*	**une parenté**	*a kinship*
un extrait de naissance	*a birth certificate*	**un lien de parenté**	*a family tie*
un mariage	*a marriage, a wedding*	**un arbre généalogique**	*a family tree*
un décès	*a death*	**un(e) ancêtre**	*an ancestor*
une adresse	*an address*	**signer**	*to sign*
une carte d'identité	*an identity card*	**cocher**	*to check off*
un passeport	*a passport*		

Irregular imperative forms

Some imperatives are irregular. Let's take a look at **être**, **avoir**, and **savoir**.

être to be	
sois	*be*
soyons	*let's be*
soyez	*be*

avoir to have	
aie	*have*
ayons	*let's have*
ayez	*have*

savoir to know	
sache	*know*
sachons	*let's know*
sachez	*know*

The irregular verb **vouloir** (*to want*) is used only in the **vous** imperative form.

Veuillez accepter mes excuses!	*Please accept my excuses!*
Sois sage!	*Be good!*
Aie plus de patience!	*Have more patience!*
Sachez que je suis avec vous!	*Be aware (Know that) I am with you!*
Ne soyez pas si rigide!	*Don't be so rigid!*
Veuillez signer le contrat.	*Please sign the contract.*

The imperative of pronominal verbs

When putting pronominal verbs in the imperative, watch for the pronoun and its position. The pronoun *follows* the verb form in the affirmative imperative; **me (m')** and **te (t')** become **moi** and **toi**. However, the pronoun *precedes* the verb in the negative imperative. For a review of pronominal verbs, see Chapter 6.

Tu te lèves.	You get up.
Lève-toi!	Get up!
Ne te lève pas!	Do not get up!
Nous nous promenons.	We take a walk.
Promenons-nous!	Let's take a walk!
Ne nous promenons pas!	Let's not take a walk!
Vous vous reposez.	You are resting.
Reposez-vous!	Take a rest!
Ne vous reposez pas!	Do not rest!

EXERCICE
19·2

Mettre à l'impératif les phrases suivantes.

1. Se laver les mains. (tu)

_____

2. Se balader dans la forêt. (vous)

_____

3. S'écrire plus souvent. (nous)

_____

4. Ne pas se coucher trop tard. (tu)

_____

5. Se réveiller à cinq heures. (vous)

_____

6. S'habiller vite. (tu)

_____

7. Ne pas se tromper de route. (vous)

_____

8. Se retrouver devant la Brasserie Lipp. (nous)

_____

9. Se dépêcher. (tu)

_____

10. Se rencontrer un jour à Paris. (nous)

_____

Traduire les phrases suivantes en utilisant l'impératif.

1. Don't forget your passport! (tu)

_____

2. Let's rest on the bench! (nous)

_____

3. Bring your identification card! (vous)

_____

4. Tell us his first name! (tu)

_____

5. Take this medicine! (tu)

_____

6. Don't be late! (vous)

_____

7. Let's go to Italy! (nous)

_____

8. Close the door! (tu)

_____

9. Wait for me! (vous)

_____

10. Write your address on the envelope! (vous)

_____

Articles and nouns

The definite article with nouns

Let's first look at the definite article. All nouns in French have a gender: masculine or feminine, whether they refer to a person, an animal, a thing, or an abstract notion. While English has only one definite article *the*, French uses **le** for masculine nouns and **la** for feminine nouns. **Le** and **la** are shortened to **l'** before a singular noun or adjective that begins with a vowel sound. The plural **les** is used for both masculine and feminine.

Masculine

le village	*the village*
le pont	*the bridge*

Feminine

la ville	*the city*
la région	*the region*

Plural

les villages (*m.pl.*)	*the villages*
les villes (*f.pl.*)	*the cities*

Le and **la** become **l'** in front of singular nouns starting with a vowel or a mute **h**.

Masculine

l'océan	*the ocean*
l'ami	*the friend*

Feminine

l'île	*the island*
l'autoroute	*the highway*

Où se trouve **le pont** Alexandre III?	*Where is the Alexandre III bridge?*
La ville principale est à cent kilomètres d'ici.	*The main town is a hundred kilometers away.*
Prenez **le chemin** sur **la droite**.	*Take the path on the (your) right.*
Le réchauffement de **la planète** est **le sujet** de sa conférence.	*Global warming is the topic of his lecture.*
Les enfants jouent dans **le jardin**.	*The children are playing in the garden.*
L'ami de Sonia est japonais.	*Sonia's friend is Japanese.*

la terre	*Earth*	une plaine	*a plain*
une planète	*a planet*	une vallée	*a valley*
un pays	*a country*	une montagne	*a mountain*
un continent	*a continent*	une colline	*a hill*
une capitale	*a capital*	une île	*an island*
une ville	*a city*	un pont	*a bridge*
un village	*a village*	la mer	*a sea*
une rue	*a street*	un océan	*an ocean*
une ruelle	*an alley, a lane*	une rivière	*a river (tributary)*
une impasse	*a dead end*	un fleuve	*a river (flowing into the sea)*
un plan de la ville	*a city map*		
un arrondissement	*a (city) district*	un ruisseau	*a brook, a stream*
une région	*a region*	le nord	*north*
une province	*a province*	le sud	*south*
un état	*a state*	l'est (*m.*)	*east*
un royaume	*a kingdom*	l'ouest (*m.*)	*west*
le désert	*the desert*	un peuple	*a people, a nation*
une frontière	*a border*	une tribu	*a tribe*
une carte	*a map*	autochtone	*native*
une route	*a road*	étranger, étrangère	*foreign*
une autoroute	*a highway*	inconnu(e)	*foreign, unknown*
une côte	*a coast(line)*		

The indefinite and partitive articles with nouns

The indefinite articles are **un** (masculine singular) (*a*), **une** (feminine singular) (*a*), and **des** (both masculine and feminine plural) (*some*).

Masculine

un projet	*a project, a plan*
un bâtiment	*a building*
un immeuble	*an apartment building*

Feminine

une maison	*a house*
une lampe	*a lamp*
une avalanche	*an avalanche*
une aubergine	*an eggplant*

Masculine or feminine

un(e) architecte	*an architect*
un(e) artiste	*an artist*
un(e) journaliste	*a journalist*

Masculine and feminine plural

des murs (*m.pl.*)	*(some) walls*
des balcons (*m.pl.*)	*(some) balconies*
des fenêtres (*f.pl.*)	*(some) windows*
des amis (*m.pl.*)	*(some) friends (m.)*
des amies (*f.pl.*)	*(some) friends (f.)*

Est-ce qu'il y a **une piscine**?	*Is there a swimming pool?*
Elle a acheté **un vélo**.	*She bought a bike.*
Nous avons vu **des lapins** dans le jardin.	*We saw (some) rabbits in the garden.*
Il a acheté **des rideaux** pour le salon.	*He bought (some) curtains for the living room.*
Il a **un nouveau chien**.	*He has a new dog.*
Tu veux emprunter **un de mes livres**?	*Do you want to borrow one of my books?*

The partitive article

The partitive article is used when the exact quantity of an item is unknown. In English, the partitive article is often omitted. We say, "I want bread" or "I want some bread." However, the partitive article is always required in French. It is formed by combining **de** and the definite article.

de + le = du
de + l' = de l'
de + la = de la
de + les = des

Je voudrais **du** pain.	*I would like some bread.*
Elle mange **du** chocolat.	*She eats chocolate.*
Nous buvons **de l'**eau minérale.	*We drink mineral water.*
Il achète **de la** viande.	*He is buying meat.*
Elle fait pousser **des** haricots verts.	*She grows green beans.*

When used in the negative, the **du**, **de la**, and **des** all become **de**, since the quantity of the item doesn't exist any longer.

Ce village a **du** charme.	*This village has charm.*
Ce village n'a pas **de** charme.	*This village has no charm.*
Il prête **de** l'argent à son ami.	*He lends money to his friend.*
Il ne prête pas **d'**argent à son ami.	*He does not lend any money to his friend.*
Elle a **des** amis à Paris.	*She has friends in Paris.*
Elle n'a pas **d'**amis à Paris.	*She does not have any friends in Paris.*
Nous avons **des** cartes routières.	*We have road maps.*
Nous n'avons pas **de** cartes routières.	*We do not have any road maps.*

One exception to this rule is when using the verb **être** (*to be*). In the negative, the partitive article is always used with **être**.

C'est **du** fromage de chèvre.	*It's goat cheese.*
Ce n'est pas **du** fromage de chèvre.	*It's not goat cheese.*
C'est **de la** porcelaine.	*It's porcelain.*
Ce n'est pas **de la** porcelaine.	*It's not porcelain.*
C'est **de** l'eau potable.	*It's drinkable water.*
Ce n'est pas **de** l'eau potable.	*It's not drinking water.*

EXERCICE
20·1

Compléter avec l'article partitif approprié.

1. Il prend _____ vacances.

2. Nous mangeons _____ pain.

3. Elle visite _____ monuments.

4. Elle a _____ chance.

5. Il met _____ ail dans la salade.

6. Vous choisissez _____ cadeaux pour vos amis.

7. Il boit _____ lait.

8. Nous envoyons _____ cartes postales en vacances.

9. Tu plantes _____ légumes.

10. Elle veut _____ crème fraîche.

The gender of nouns

The noun endings very often indicate their gender. However, you cannot rely solely on these patterns, as there are exceptions. We'll look at few of them at the end of this section.

Nouns ending in **-age**, **-eau**, and **-ment** tend to be masculine.

le fromage	*cheese*
le barrage	*dam*
le courage	*courage*
le voyage	*trip*
le gâteau	*cake*
le plateau	*tray*
le tableau	*painting*
le château	*castle*
le compliment	*compliment*
le monument	*monument*
le sentiment	*feeling*
le paravent	*screen (furniture)*

Nouns ending in **-t**, **-al**, **-ail**, **-eil**, **-isme** also tend to be masculine.

le chocolat	*chocolate*
le contrat	*contract*
l'état	*state*
le résultat	*result*
le journal	*newspaper*
le métal	*metal*
l'hôpital	*hospital*
le capital	*capital*
l'éventail	*fan (for ventilation)*
le bétail	*cattle, livestock*
le travail	*work*
le détail	*detail*
l'appareil	*apparatus, (still) camera*
le sommeil	*sleep*
le soleil	*sun*
le conseil	*advice*
le tourisme	*tourism*
le colonialisme	*colonialism*
l'idéalisme	*idealism*
l'alpinisme	*mountain climbing*

Nouns ending in **-ure**, **-ence**, **-ance**, **-sion**, **-tion**, **-té**, **-ouille**, **-eille**, **-ie**, **-ette**, **-eur** tend to be feminine.

la sculpture	*sculpture*
la nature	*nature*
la couverture	*cover, blanket*
l'écriture	*writing*
l'intelligence	*intelligence*
l'urgence	*emergency*
la violence	*violence*
la concurrence	*competition*
la croyance	*belief*
l'enfance	*childhood*
la naissance	*birth*
l'ordonnance	*prescription*
la dimension	*dimension*
la profession	*profession*
la tension	*tension*
la télévision	*television*
l'invention	*invention*
la solution	*solution*
l'exposition	*exhibition*
la traduction	*translation*
la qualité	*quality*
l'éternité	*eternity*
la publicité	*advertising*
la nationalité	*nationality*
la grenouille	*frog*
la rouille	*rust*
la ratatouille	*ratatouille (summer vegetable stew)*
la citrouille	*pumpkin*
la bouteille	*bottle*
l'abeille	*bee*
la corbeille	*basket*
la veille	*the day (or evening) before*
la folie	*madness*
la boulangerie	*bakery*
la chimie	*chemistry*
la gastronomie	*gastronomy*
la cigarette	*cigarette*
la cassette	*cassette tape*
la noisette	*hazelnut*
l'omelette	*omelette*
la chaleur	*heat*
la douceur	*softness, gentleness*
la hauteur	*height*
la froideur	*coldness*

For the most part, you can go by these rules and learn the exceptions as you move along. Here are a few exceptions:

la page	*page*
la plage	*beach*
la nuit	*night*
le silence	*silence*
la forêt	*forest*

le traité	treaty
le comité	committee
le parapluie	umbrella
le génie	genius
le bonheur	happiness

Many nouns can be changed from masculine to feminine by adding an **-e** to the masculine form:

l'ami	l'amie	friend
l'étudiant	l'étudiante	student
l'avocat	l'avocate	lawyer
l'Anglais	l'Anglaise	Englishman/woman

Nouns with certain endings form the feminine in other ways:

-eur → -euse

le danseur	la danseuse	dancer
le coiffeur	la coiffeuse	hairdresser
le menteur	la menteuse	liar
le vendeur	la vendeuse	salesperson

-(i)er → (i)ère

l'épicier	l'épicière	grocer
le boulanger	la boulangère	baker
l'ouvrier	l'ouvrière	worker
l'infirmier	l'infirmière	nurse

-teur → -trice

l'instituteur	l'institutrice	teacher (primary school)
le lecteur	la lectrice	reader
l'explorateur	l'exploratrice	explorer
le directeur	la directrice	director, manager

-ien → -ienne

le citoyen	la citoyenne	citizen
le pharmacien	la pharmacienne	pharmacist
l'académicien	l'académicienne	member of the Académie Française
le Vietnamien	la Vietnamienne	Vietnamese man/woman

The feminine of some nouns ends in **-esse**.

le prince	prince	la princesse	princess
le comte	count	la comtesse	countess
le duc	duke	la duchesse	duchess
le dieu	god	la déesse	goddess

Some nouns referring to persons or animals, as in English, have different words for masculine and for feminine.

le roi	king	la reine	queen
le garçon	boy	la fille	girl
l'homme	man	la femme	woman
le cheval	horse	la jument	mare
le cochon	pig	la truie	sow
le taureau	bull	la vache	cow
le mouton	sheep	la brebis	ewe

le père	father	la mère	mother
le fils	son	la fille	daughter
le frère	brother	la sœur	sister
le grand-père	grandfather	la grand-mère	grandmother
l'oncle	uncle	la tante	aunt
le neveu	nephew	la nièce	niece
le cousin	cousin (male)	la cousine	cousin (female)

A few nouns have different meanings in the masculine and feminine.

le livre	book	la livre	pound (weight, currency)
le tour	trip, ride	la tour	tower
le page	page (boy)	la page	page (book)
le poste	job, television set	la poste	post office
le moule	mold, form	la moule	mussel
le rose	pink, rose (color)	la rose	rose
le poêle	stove	la poêle	frying pan
le manche	handle	la manche; la Manche	sleeve; English Channel

The plural of nouns

In most cases, an -**s** is added to a noun to make it plural.

une maison	a house	des maisons	houses
un livre	a book	des livres	books

If a noun in the plural begins with a vowel or a mute **h**, the -**s** of **les** or **des** is pronounced **z** (liaison).

une île	an island	des îles	islands
un inconnu	a stranger	des inconnus	strangers
un hôpital	a hospital	des hôpitaux	hospitals
un homme	a man	des hommes	men

Nouns ending in -**s**, -**x**, or -**z** do not change in the plural.

un pas	a step	des pas	steps
une voix	a voice	des voix	voices
un nez	a nose	des nez	noses

Nouns ending in -**eu**, -**eau** usually take an -**x** in the plural.

un château	a castle	des châteaux	castles
un gâteau	a cake	des gâteaux	cakes
un neveu	a nephew	des neveux	nephews
un jeu	a game	des jeux	games

Nouns ending in -**al** usually change to -**aux**.

un cheval	a horse	des chevaux	horses
un journal	a newspaper	des journaux	newspapers

Here again, you'll find exceptions, such as:

un bal	a ball (dance)	des bals	balls
un genou	a knee	des genoux	knees
un pneu	a tire	des pneus	tires

un festival	*a festival*	**des festivals**	*festivals*
un œil	*an eye*	**des yeux**	*eyes*
un bijou	*a jewel*	**des bijoux**	*jewels*

In French, no -s is added to a family name used in the plural. You'll refer to **Monsieur et Madame Renaud** as **les Renaud**.

EXERCICE 20·2

Masculin ou féminin? **Le** *ou* **la**?

1. _____ réveil

2. _____ chanteur

3. _____ culture

4. _____ propriété

5. _____ courage

6. _____ chance

7. _____ document

8. _____ restaurant

9. _____ beauté

10. _____ gouvernement

EXERCICE 20·3

Mettre au masculin les noms suivants. Ne pas oublier l'article défini.

1. reine _____

2. sœur _____

3. grand-mère _____

4. vendeuse _____

5. décoratrice _____

6. nièce _____

7. fille _____

8. rédactrice _____

9. Brésilienne _____

10. princesse _____

Mettre au féminin les noms suivants.

1. C'est le directeur. _____

2. C'est mon coiffeur. _____

3. C'est le pharmacien. _____

4. C'est l'oncle de Paul. _____

5. C'est mon frère. _____

6. C'est son instituteur. _____

7. C'est le roi. _____

8. C'est mon cousin. _____

9. C'est un homme. _____

10. C'est le boucher. _____

The gender of countries

Countries, continents, states, provinces, and regions also have a gender. For geographical nouns, an **-e** ending usually indicates the feminine. Other endings tend to be masculine. Here are some examples of feminine countries:

la France	*France*
l'Italie	*Italy*
l'Espagne	*Spain*
l'Argentine	*Argentina*
la Chine	*China*
la Grèce	*Greece*
la Turquie	*Turkey*
l'Algérie	*Algeria*
la Tanzanie	*Tanzania*
la Côte-d'Ivoire	*Ivory Coast*

And some masculine countries:

le Portugal	*Portugal*
le Pérou	*Peru*
le Kenya	*Kenya*
le Maroc	*Morocco*
le Canada	*Canada*
le Japon	*Japan*
le Vietnam	*Vietnam*
le Laos	*Laos*
le Venezuela	*Venezuela*
le Luxembourg	*Luxemburg*

Note that some countries and states ending in **-e** are masculine:

le Mexique	*Mexico*
le Cambodge	*Cambodia*
le Maine	*Maine*
le Mozambique	Mozambique

EXERCICE
20·5

Masculin ou féminin? Mettre l'article défini.

1. _____ Belgique

2. _____ Californie

3. _____ Canada

4. _____ Angleterre

5. _____ Colorado

6. _____ Russie

7. _____ Égypte

8. _____ Irlande

9. _____ Guatemala

10. _____ Hongrie

Geographical names with prepositions

To express *in* or *to* with a geographical name, the preposition varies.

Cities

With cities, the preposition **à** is used.

Nous irons **à Tokyo** la semaine prochaine.	*We'll go to Tokyo next week.*
Elle habite **à Hanoi**.	*She lives in Hanoi.*

Cities are usually *not* preceded by an article. Note the following exceptions: **Le Caire, La Nouvelle-Orléans, La Havane, Le Havre, La Rochelle, Le Touquet**.

Il vivait à **La Havane**.	*He lived in Havana.*
Le Touquet est sa station balnéaire préférée.	*Le Touquet is his favorite beach resort.*

Countries and states

With countries, regions, states, and provinces, the article and/or the preposition change according to gender and number.

en	before feminine countries and regions
en	before masculine countries beginning with a vowel
au	before singular masculine countries
aux	before plural countries

Ils ont acheté une maison **en Sicile**.	*They bought a house in Sicily.*
Ces médecins travaillent **en Afghanistan**.	*These doctors work in Afghanistan.*
Ils sont allés **au Liban**.	*They went to Lebanon.*
Il investira **aux États-Unis**.	*He'll invest in the United States.*

However, with provinces, departments, or states, the preposition may vary. Before feminine nouns or masculine nouns starting with a vowel, use **en**.

la Pennsylvanie	**en** Pennsylvanie
la Provence	**en** Provence
l'Alsace (*f.*)	**en** Alsace
l'Arizona (*m.*)	**en** Arizona

Au is used in front of masculine states.

le Texas	**au** Texas
le Tennessee	**au** Tennessee

In front of masculine nouns starting with a consonant, **dans le** often replaces **au**. Try to be aware of examples as you hear or read them.

le Midi	**dans le** Midi
le Languedoc	**dans le** Languedoc
le Poitou	**dans le** Poitou

We sometimes need to differentiate between U.S. or Canadian cities and states or provinces that have the same name.

Le siège est **à New York**.	*The main office is in New York (City).*
Leur cabane se trouve **dans l'État de New York**.	*Their cabin is in New York State.*
Il a ouvert un restaurant **à Washington**.	*He opened a restaurant in Washington, D.C.*
Ce parc se trouve **dans l'État de Washington**.	*This park is located in Washington State.*

Islands

Although usage may vary, the preposition **à** (**aux** in the plural) is often used for islands.

à Tahiti
à Hawaii
à Cuba
à Madagascar
à La Réunion
aux Maldives
aux Seychelles

Some exceptions:

en Haïti
en Martinique
en Guadeloupe

Compléter avec la préposition appropriée.

1. Jean habite _____ Italie.

2. Maud s'est installée _____ Virginie.

3. Alex a des amis _____ Normandie.

4. Il envisage d'acheter une maison _____ Maroc.

5. Renée est en voyage d'affaires _____ Canada.

6. Ils passent leurs vacances _____ Bolivie.

7. Sandrine a de la famille _____ Espagne.

8. Laurent a accepté un poste _____ Norvège.

9. Nous aimerions aller _____ Japon.

10. Voudriez-vous aller _____ Inde avec nous?

*Formuler une phrase complète en utilisant le verbe **habiter** et les prépositions appropriées.*

1. Marie/Lyon/France

_____

2. Christina/Istanbul/Turquie

_____

3. Fatima/Tunis/Tunisie

_____

4. Laurent/Varsovie/Pologne

_____

5. Vincent/Caracas/Venezuela

_____

6. Nancy/Toronto/Canada

_____

7. Xavier/Mexico/Mexique

_____

8. Patrick/Boston/États-Unis

_____

9. Henri/Sydney/Australie

_____

10. Martha/Berlin/Allemagne

_____

How to say *from*

From is expressed by **de (d')** for continents, feminine countries, provinces, regions, and states. For masculine and plural entities, the definite article is retained (**du, des**).

Elle est rentrée **de Suède** hier soir.	*She came back from Sweden last night.*
Il n'est pas encore revenu **d'Italie**.	*He is not yet back from Italy.*
Elle est originaire **du Brésil**.	*She comes from Brazil.*
Je reviens **du Sénégal**.	*I am back from Senegal.*
Le vol arrive **des États-Unis**.	*The flight is arriving from the United States.*

EXERCICE
20·8

Compléter les phrases suivantes.

1. Cet objet vient _____ Égypte.

2. Ces bijoux en provenance _____ Inde sont en argent.

3. Marc vient _____ Normandie.

4. Rapporte-moi un pull _____ Écosse.

5. Ils sont natifs _____ Chili.

6. Ces épices viennent _____ Maroc.

7. Ce paquet est arrivé ce matin _____ États-Unis.

8. Ces épices proviennent _____ Asie.

9. Ces produits en provenance _____ Colombie sont vendus dans les supermarchés.

10. Il est tout juste revenu _____ Mexique.

Traduire les phrases suivantes.

1. She lives in a village in Ireland.

_____

2. Her brother lives in Russia.

_____

3. He studied in France.

_____

4. She went to Normandy last summer.

_____

5. They traveled to Greece in May.

_____

6. They import products from Argentina.

_____

7. Their son works in California.

_____

8. She took this picture in Japan.

_____

9. They are building a bridge in a village in Senegal.

_____

10. Let's go to China!

_____

All the pronouns

Subject pronouns

There are many types of pronouns in French. Let's start with the *subject pronouns* you have already used when conjugating verbs.

je	*I*
tu	*you* (singular familiar)
il	*he, it* (masculine)
elle	*she, it* (feminine)
on	*one, we, they, people*
nous	*we*
vous	*you* (singular formal and all plurals)
ils	*they* (masculine, or mixed masculine and feminine)
elles	*they* (feminine)

The third-person pronouns apply to people, animals, or things.

Bertrand est chirurgien.	*Bertrand is a surgeon.*
Il est chirurgien.	*He is a surgeon.*
Les trois sœurs jouent dans le salon.	*The three sisters are playing in the living room.*
Elles jouent dans le salon.	*They are playing in the living room.*
Le chat est assis sur la chaise.	*The cat is sitting on the chair.*
Il est assis sur la chaise.	*It is sitting on the chair.*
La ville est très polluée.	*The city is very polluted.*
Elle est très polluée.	*It is very polluted.*

Remember that there are two ways of saying *you* in French. Use **tu** and its verb forms to talk to friends, family members, children, and animals. Use **vous** when you are addressing a stranger or someone you don't know well, or to maintain a certain degree of distance or respect. Note, however, that the contemporary trend is toward familiarity, especially among peers. It all depends on the setting and the crowd. However, it's always a good idea to let the native French speaker initiate your first exchange with **tu**.

The pronoun **on** has several meanings. It may mean *one*, *we*, or *they* depending on how it is used. **On** can replace an indefinite person.

On voudrait tout réussir.	*One would like to succeed in everything.*
On ne peut pas penser à tout.	*One cannot think of everything.*

On means *people* in general. It often refers to habits and customs of a culture.

En France, **on boit** du vin.	*In France, one drinks wine.*
Au Japon, **on boit** du saké.	*In Japan, one drinks sake.*

In informal conversation, **on** takes on the meaning of **nous**.

On va au cinéma cet après-midi?	*Shall we go to the movies this afternoon?*
Julien et moi, **on passe** toujours nos vacances en Corse.	*Julien and I, we always spend our vacation in Corsica.*

Another informal use of **on** replaces the pronoun **tu**.

Ah, **on s'amuse** ici!	*So, we are having fun here!*
Alors, **on se promène** au lieu de faire ses devoirs!	*So, we are taking a walk instead of doing our homework!*

On can also replace a passive voice in English.

Ici, **on parle** anglais.	*English is spoken here.*
On n'a pas encore trouvé de solution.	*A solution has not yet been found.*

VOCABULAIRE

un acteur, une actrice	*an actor, an actress*	**un(e) informaticien(ne)**	*a computer specialist*
		un ingénieur	*an engineer*
un(e) architecte	*an architect*	**un(e) journaliste**	*a journalist*
un(e) artiste	*an artist*	**un mannequin**	*a model*
un(e) avocat(e)	*a lawyer*	**un médecin**	*a doctor, a physician*
un coiffeur, une coiffeuse	*a hairdresser, a barber*	**un metteur en scène**	*a film/theater director*
un(e) commerçant(e)	*a store owner*	**un(e) musicien(ne)**	*a musician*
un(e) comptable	*an accountant*	**un ouvrier, une ouvrière**	*a (factory) worker*
un cuisinier, une cuisinière	*a cook*	**un(e) pharmacien(ne)**	*a pharmacist*
		un(e) photographe	*a photographer*
un(e) dentiste	*a dentist*	**un(e) pilote**	*a pilot*
un directeur, une directrice	*a manager*	**un plombier**	*a plumber*
		un pompier	*a firefighter*
un écrivain	*a writer*	**un professeur**	*a teacher, a professor*
un homme, une femme d'affaires	*a businessman, -woman*	**un rédacteur, une rédactrice**	*an editor*
un(e) fleuriste	*a florist*	**une sage-femme**	*a midwife*
un infirmier, une infirmière	*a (hospital) nurse*	**un serveur, une serveuse**	*a waiter, a waitress*

Direct object pronouns

Another type of pronoun is the *direct object pronoun* (**le pronom objet direct**). In English there are seven direct object pronouns: *me, you, him, her, it, us, them*. Note that in French there are two forms of the direct object pronoun *you*: the informal **te** and the formal or plural **vous**. English distinguishes between a direct object pronoun that replaces a person (*him* or *her*) or a thing (*it*); in French **le, la, les** can replace both people and things. **Les** refers to both masculine and feminine. **Me, te, le,** and **la** become **m', t',** and **l'** before vowels and mute **h**.

SINGULAR		PLURAL	
me (m')	*me*	**nous**	*us*
te (t')	*you* (familiar)	**vous**	*you* (plural or formal)
le (l')	*him* or *it* (masculine)	**les**	*them* (masc. and fem.)
la (l')	*her* or *it* (feminine)		

Pronouns allow speakers to avoid being repetitious, to make communication more efficient, and to link ideas across sentences. An object is called *direct* if it immediately follows the verb without a preposition. The direct object pronoun replaces the direct object noun. In French, the direct object pronoun agrees in gender and number with the noun it replaces. Note that the French direct object pronoun precedes the verb. In a sentence with auxiliary or compound verbs, the direct object pronoun precedes the verb to which it directly refers. The direct object pronoun can replace a noun with a definite article (**le, la, les**), with a possessive adjective (**mon, ton, son,** etc.), or with a demonstrative adjective (**ce, cet, cette, ces**).

L'artiste **chante la chanson.**	*The artist sings the song.*
L'artiste **la chante.**	*The artist sings it.*
Quentin **appelle son ami.**	*Quentin calls his friend.*
Quentin **l'appelle.**	*Quentin calls him.*
Il **prend la décision.**	*He makes the decision.*
Il **la prend.**	*He makes it.*
L'infirmier **soigne ses patients.**	*The nurse takes care of his patients.*
L'infirmier **les soigne.**	*The nurse takes care of them.*
Il **m'appelle.**	*He is calling me.*
Nous **vous remercions.**	*We thank you.*
Elle **t'invite.**	*She invites you.*
Ils **nous accueillent.**	*They greet us.*

In a negative sentence, the direct object pronoun also comes immediately before the conjugated verb.

Nous n'acceptons **pas l'offre.**	*We do not accept the offer.*
Nous **ne l'acceptons pas.**	*We do not accept it.*
Ils **ne** comprennent **pas la question.**	*They do not understand the question.*
Ils **ne la** comprennent **pas.**	*They do not understand it.*
Elle **ne** suit **pas les directives.**	*She does not follow the directions.*
Elle **ne les** suit **pas.**	*She does not follow them.*

In the interrogative form, when using the inversion, the direct object pronoun comes immediately before the verb.

Connaissez-vous **ce dentiste?**	*Do you know this dentist?*
Le connaissez-vous?	*Do you know him?*
Approuvez-vous **sa décision?**	*Do you approve of his decision?*
L'approuvez-vous?	*Do you approve of it?*
Aimez-vous **les chansons de Brel?**	*Do you like Brel's songs?*
Les aimez-vous?	*Do you like them?*
Emmenez-vous **les enfants** au cirque?	*Are you taking the children to the circus?*
Les emmenez-vous au cirque?	*Are you taking them to the circus?*

When an infinitive has a direct object, the direct object pronoun immediately precedes the infinitive.

Pouvez-vous contacter **le journaliste?**	*Can you contact the journalist?*
Pouvez-vous **le** contacter?	*Can you contact him?*

Il doit finir **son article**.	*He must finish his article.*
Il doit **le** finir.	*He must finish it.*
Je vais lire tous **les documents**.	*I am going to read all the documents.*
Je vais tous **les** lire.	*I am going to read all of them.*
Nous venons de voir **son nouveau film**.	*We just saw his new film.*
Nous venons de **le** voir.	*We have just seen it.*

In the **passé composé** and other compound tenses, the direct object pronoun is placed before the auxiliary verb. The past participle agrees in number and gender when the direct object precedes the verb.

Le journaliste a pris **les photos**.	*The journalist took the pictures.*
Le journaliste **les** a prises.	*The journalist took them.*
Le comptable avait trié tous **ces papiers**.	*The accountant had sorted all these papers.*
Le comptable **les** avait tous triés.	*The accountant had sorted them all out.*
Le pompier a éteint **les flammes**.	*The fireman extinguished the flames.*
Le pompier **les** a éteintes.	*The fireman extinguished them.*
Le guitariste a joué **ses morceaux favoris**.	*The guitarist played his favorite pieces.*
Le guitariste **les** a joués.	*The guitarist played them.*

In the affirmative imperative, the direct object pronoun follows the verb. **Me (m')** and **te (t')** change to **moi** and **toi**. Remember to link the verb to the pronoun with a hyphen. In the negative imperative, the direct object pronoun remains before the verb.

Appelez **Jacques**!	*Call Jacques!*
Appelez-**le**!	*Call him!*
Rendez **les clés** à Antoine!	*Give the keys back to Antoine!*
Rendez-**les** à Antoine!	*Give them back to Antoine!*
Achetez **ces fleurs**!	*Buy these flowers!*
Achetez-**les**!	*Buy them!*
N'éteins pas **la lumière**!	*Do not turn off the light!*
Ne **l'**éteins **pas**!	*Do not turn it off!*
N'appelle pas **Caroline** si tard!	*Do not call Caroline so late!*
Ne **l'**appelle **pas** si tard!	*Do not call her so late!*
Invitez-**moi** à la soirée, s'il vous plaît.	*Please invite me to the party.*

EXERCICE
21·1

Remplacer les mots en caractères gras par un pronom objet direct.

1. Elle achète **les fleurs bleues**. _____

2. Il consulte **le médecin**. _____

3. Nous soutenons **votre projet**. _____

4. Ils construisent **la maison de leurs rêves**. _____

5. J'ouvre **la porte**. _____

6. Elle conduit **la voiture de son père**. _____

7. Il accepte **les résultats**. _____

8. Nous comprenons **leur décision**. _____

9. Tu visites **le château de Fontainebleau**. _____

10. Elle étudie **sa leçon**. _____

*Traduire les phrases suivantes en utilisant **vous** et l'inversion si nécessaire.*

1. He thanks me. _____

2. The writer sends them. _____

3. They invite us. _____

4. We accept it. _____

5. She called them. _____

6. Bring them! _____

7. I am going to buy it. _____

8. Do not sell it! _____

9. We must see it. _____

10. Do you know her? _____

Indirect object pronouns

Now that you have mastered the **pronom objet direct**, let's take a look at the **pronom objet indirect** (*indirect object pronoun*).

In English there are five indirect object pronouns *me, you, him, her, us*. As always, French distinguishes between an informal *you* (**te**) and a formal or plural *you* (**vous**). The French indirect object pronoun does not, however, distinguish gender; **lui** and **leur** replace both masculine and feminine nouns. In French, the indirect object pronoun replaces only animate indirect objects (people, animals). Inanimate ideas and things are replaced with the indirect object pronouns **y** and **en**, which will be discussed later in this chapter. Let's look at the indirect object pronouns:

SINGULAR		PLURAL	
me (m')	*me*	**nous**	*us*
te (t')	*you* (familiar)	**vous**	*you* (formal or plural)
lui	*him, her*	**leur**	*them* (masc. and fem.)

The object is called *indirect* when the verb is controlled by a preposition (**parler à, répondre à, écrire à**, etc.). The indirect object pronoun is placed before the conjugated verb and before **avoir** in the compound tenses. Although the past participle agrees in gender and number with the *preceding* direct object, the past participle *never* agrees with an indirect object pronoun. The indirect object pronouns **me** and **te** become **m'** and **t'** before vowels and mute **h**. Make sure to distinguish between **leur**, the indirect object pronoun, and **leur(s)**, the possessive adjective.

Tu parles **au journaliste**.	*You are talking to the journalist.*
Tu **lui** parles.	*You are talking to him.*
Tu réponds **à Andrée**.	*You answer Andrée.*
Tu **lui** réponds.	*You answer her.*
Vous écrivez **à l'agent**.	*You write to the agent.*
Vous **lui** écrivez.	*You write to him.*
Vous expliquez la situation **aux clients**.	*You explain the situation to the customers.*
Vous **leur** expliquez la situation.	*You explain the situation to them.*
Elle **nous** enverra une confirmation.	*She'll send us a confirmation.*
Je **vous** donnerai un jour de congé.	*I'll give you a day off.*
Il **me** rendra le livre demain.	*He'll return the book to me tomorrow.*
Ils **t'**apporteront des fleurs.	*They'll bring you some flowers.*

In the interrogative or negative, the indirect object pronoun is placed immediately before the verb.

Lui as-tu parlé de ce livre?	*Did you talk to him about this book?*
M'avez-vous envoyé un courriel?	*Did you send me an e-mail?*
Vous fournit-il de bons produits?	*Does he provide you with good products?*
Leur avez-vous envoyé les révisions?	*Did you send them the revisions?*
Elle **ne nous** envoie **jamais rien**.	*She never sends us anything.*
Tu **ne m'**apportes **que** des mauvaises nouvelles.	*You only bring me bad news.*
Vous **ne lui** avez **pas** dit la vérité.	*You did not tell him the truth.*
Ils **te** prêteront leur voiture.	*They'll lend you their car.*

Indirect object pronouns in the imperative

In the affirmative imperative, the indirect object pronoun follows the verb. **Me (m')** and **te (t')** become **moi** and **toi**. Remember to link the verb to the following pronoun with a hyphen. In the negative imperative, the indirect object pronoun remains before the verb.

Téléphone-**moi** demain matin!	*Call me tomorrow morning!*
Prêtez-**lui** votre dictionnaire!	*Lend him your dictionary!*
Apportez-**nous** de nouveaux accessoires!	*Bring us new props!*
Envoyez-**leur** le script!	*Send them the script!*
Ne lui donnez **rien**!	*Don't give him anything!*
Ne nous téléphonez **pas** si tard!	*Don't call us so late!*

EXERCICE
21·3

Remplacer les mots en caractères gras par un pronom objet indirect.

1. La grand-mère a raconté une histoire **aux petits-enfants**.

_____

2. Nous avons fait un cadeau **à Marie**.

_____

3. Je ferai parvenir le dossier **à Jean** dès que possible.

_____

4. Nous enverrons des fleurs **à notre collègue**.

_____

5. Ce théâtre appartient **à un ancien comédien**.

_____

6. Est-ce que tu as écrit **au rédacteur en chef**?

_____

7. Téléphonez **à Louise** aussitôt que possible!

_____

8. Ne mentionnez rien **à Odile**!

_____

9. Il annoncera sa décision **à ses employés** demain.

_____

10. Il donnera le scénario **aux acteurs** en fin de journée.

_____

EXERCICE

21·4

Traduire les phrases suivantes en utilisant **tu** et l'inversion si nécessaire.

1. Bring me a book!

_____

2. Do not call them after eight P.M.!

_____

3. Send us your new play!

_____

4. I will write him a letter.

_____

5. She'll give me an answer on Monday.

_____

6. He did not return the books to me.

_____

7. This pen belongs to her.

_____

8. He does not talk to us.

_____

9. They told us a good story.

_____

10. They'll lend you their house for the weekend.

_____

The pronoun y

Y is an indirect object pronoun that precedes the verb. It usually replaces an inanimate object (thing or idea). The object replaced by **y** is considered indirect because it is preceded by a preposition, usually the preposition **à**, but sometimes **sur**.

Elle répond **à l'annonce**.	_She answers the ad._
Elle y répond.	_She answers it._
Ils s'habituent **à cette ville**.	_They are getting used to this city._
Ils s'y habituent.	_They are getting used to it._
Nous pensons **à la situation**.	_We are thinking about the situation._
Nous y pensons.	_We are thinking about it._
Tu t'intéresses **à cette pièce**?	_Are you interested in this play?_
Tu t'y intéresses?	_Are you interested in it?_

In the **passé composé** and other compound tenses the indirect object pronoun **y** is placed before the auxiliary verb. Note that the past participle _does not_ agree in gender or number with the indirect object **y**.

Ils ont réfléchi **à cette question**.	_They thought about this issue._
Ils y ont réfléchi.	_They thought about it._
Nous avons répondu **à vos questions**.	_We answered your questions._
Nous y avons répondu.	_We answered them._
Il a renoncé **à sa carrière**.	_He gave up his career._
Il y a renoncé.	_He gave it up._
Je n'ai pas goûté **à cette sauce**.	_I did not taste this sauce._
Je n'y ai pas goûté.	_I did not taste it._

EXERCICE

21·5

Remplacer les éléments en caractères gras par y.

1. Elle s'habitue **à tout**.

_____

2. Tu devrais prêter attention **à ce qu'il dit**.

_____

3. Nous nous intéressons **à son œuvre**.

_____

4. Je m'abonne **à ce magazine**.

_____

5. Elle tient **à ses bijoux**.

_____

6. Nous ne croyons pas **à cette nouvelle théorie scientifique**.

_____

7. Il ne pense jamais **aux conséquences de ses actes**.

_____

8. Ils n'obéissent pas **à la loi**.

_____

9. Elle réfléchira **au rôle que vous lui proposez**.

_____

10. Pourquoi n'avez-vous jamais répondu **à notre demande**?

_____

The pronoun en

En is an indirect object pronoun that precedes the verb. It usually replaces an inanimate object (thing or idea) preceded by **de**. The pronoun **en** immediately precedes the verb, except in the affirmative imperative where it follows the verb.

Nous nous occuperons **de tous les détails**.	_We'll take care of all the details._
Nous nous **en** occuperons.	_We'll take care of them._
Elle ne se souvient pas **de cette histoire**.	_She does not remember this story._
Elle ne s'**en** souvient pas.	_She does not remember it._
Avez-vous peur **de sa réaction**?	_Are you afraid of his reaction?_
En avez-vous peur?	_Are you afraid of it?_

In the **passé composé** and other compound tenses the indirect object pronoun **en** is placed before the auxiliary verb. Note that the past participle _does not_ agree in gender and number with the indirect object **en**.

Il a parlé **de sa nouvelle idée** à Théo.	_He talked about his new idea to Théo._
Il **en** a parlé à Théo.	_He talked about it to Théo._
Elle s'est chargée **de cette affaire difficile**.	_She took care of this difficult business._
Elle s'**en** est chargée.	_She took care of it._
Je me suis approché **des remparts**.	_I came closer to the ramparts._
Je m'**en** suis approché.	_I came closer to them._
Tu t'es débarrassé **de toutes ces choses inutiles**.	_You got rid of all these useless things._
Tu t'**en** es débarrassé.	_You got rid of them._

*Remplacer les éléments en caractères gras par le pronom **en**.*

1. J'ai parlé **de tous nos problèmes**.

_____

2. Ils ont envie **d'aller en France en mai**.

_____

3. Nous avons besoin **d'un logiciel plus performant**.

_____

4. Il s'est approché **du château** très lentement.

_____

5. Je me chargerai **de tout ce qui facilitera son séjour à Aix**.

_____

6. Tu te sers **de ce dictionnaire**?

_____

7. Il a peur **des changements**.

_____

8. Je ne me souviens pas **de sa conférence**.

_____

9. Elle s'est occupée **des réservations**.

_____

10. Il ne pourra jamais se débarrasser **de ses livres de l'école primaire**.

_____

Faire correspondre les deux colonnes.

_____ 1. Il a peur   a. d'un ordinateur portable

_____ 2. Elle s'intéresse   b. à un magazine hebdomadaire

_____ 3. Je me sers   c. du nom de l'hôtel

_____ 4. Ils ne se souviennent pas   d. à ce nouveau candidat

_____ 5. Tu t'abonnes   e. des insectes

The order of object pronouns

When a direct and indirect pronoun appear in the same sentence, the indirect object pronoun comes first, unless the direct and indirect pronouns are in the third person, in which case the direct object pronoun comes first.

INDIRECT OBJECT	DIRECT OBJECT
me (m') **te (t')** ⎱ **nous** ⎰ **vous**	+ **le, la, l', les**

Elle **te** donne **le rôle.**	*She gives you the part.*
Elle **te le** donne.	*She gives it to you.*
Nous **vous** envoyons **le contrat.**	*We are sending you the contract.*
Nous **vous l'**envoyons.	*We are sending it to you.*
Vous **nous** montrez **les costumes.**	*You show us the costumes.*
Vous **nous les** montrez.	*You show them to us.*
Il **m'**offre **la bague de sa mère.**	*He gives me his mother's ring.*
Il **me l'**offre.	*He gives it to me.*

If the direct and indirect pronouns in the third person are combined, the direct object pronoun comes first.

DIRECT OBJECT	INDIRECT OBJECT
le (l') **la (l')** ⎱ **les** ⎰	+ **lui, leur**

J'envoie **la lettre au rédacteur.**	*I send the letter to the editor.*
Je **la lui** envoie.	*I send it to him.*
Elle tend **le document au médecin.**	*She hands the document to the doctor.*
Elle **le lui** tend.	*She hands it to him.*
Nous offrons **ce livre aux participants.**	*We give this book to the participants.*
Nous **le leur** offrons.	*We give it to them.*
Nous montrons **la route aux touristes.**	*We show the road to the tourists.*
Nous **la leur** montrons.	*We show it to them.*

In the **passé composé** and other compound tenses, the direct object pronoun is placed before the auxiliary verb. The past participle agrees in number and gender with the direct object when the direct object precedes the verb.

Il a écrit **ces articles.**	*He wrote these articles.*
Il **les** a écrits.	*He wrote them.*
Elle a fait **ces tartes délicieuses.**	*She made these delicious pies.*
Elle **les** a faites.	*She made them.*
J'ai envoyé **les lettres.**	*I sent the letters.*
Je **les** ai envoyées.	*I sent them.*
Tu as mis **ta nouvelle chemise.**	*You put on your new shirt.*
Tu **l'**as mise.	*You put it on.*

When **en** is combined with an indirect object pronoun, it is always in second position. The past participle *does not* agree in number and gender with **en** (nor does it agree with any other indirect object pronoun).

Elle **lui** a offert **des fleurs**.	*She gave her some flowers.*
Elle **lui en** a offert.	*She gave her some.*
Il **leur** a donné **des explications**.	*He gave them some explanations.*
Il **leur en** a donné.	*He gave them some.*
Nous **lui** avons prêté **de la farine**.	*We lent him some flour.*
Nous **lui en** avons prêté.	*We lent him some.*
Tu **nous** enverras **des photos**.	*You'll send us some pictures.*
Tu **nous en** enverras.	*You'll send us some.*

EXERCICE
21·8

Remplacer les éléments en caractères gras par les pronoms appropriés.

1. Ne parlez pas **de ce détail à Zoé**!

_____

2. Elle a emprunté **de l'argent à sa sœur**.

_____

3. Je ferai parvenir **ce document à votre avocat**.

_____

4. Patrick a raconté **ses aventures** (*f.pl.*) **à son frère**.

_____

5. Le musicien a envoyé **sa nouvelle composition à son agent**.

_____

6. L'ouvrier a donné **la lettre au patron**.

_____

7. J'ai demandé **la photo au photographe**.

_____

8. Il vendra **sa maison à son cousin**.

_____

9. Le médecin **a prescrit ce médicament au malade**.

_____

10. Je recommande **cet hôtel à tous mes amis**.

_____

*Traduire les phrases suivantes en utilisant **tu** si nécessaire.*

1. I am thinking about it.

_____

2. He is not interested in it.

_____

3. She took care of it.

_____

4. I sent it (*f.*) to you.

_____

5. We gave it (*m.*) to them.

_____

6. I use it every day.

_____

7. He spoke about it.

_____

8. I need it.

_____

9. She borrowed some from me.

_____

10. They gave us some.

_____

Disjunctive pronouns

There are many ways to use *disjunctive pronouns*, also known as stressed or tonic pronouns.

moi	me	nous	us
toi	you	vous	you
lui	him	eux	them
elle	her	elles	them (feminine)

The disjunctive pronouns can be used to add extra *emphasis* to a thought.

Lui, c'est un grand musicien!	*He is a great musician!*
Moi, je déteste les lentilles!	*I hate lentils!*

Lui, il est toujours contre tout!   *He is always against everything!*
Elle, c'est vraiment ma meilleure amie!   *She is really my best friend!*

Disjunctive pronouns are used after **c'est** or **ce sont** in order to stress identification. In this case, they are used where English would use intonation.

C'est moi qui ai trouvé la solution.   *I found the solution.*
C'est lui qui a raison.   *He is right.*
C'est toi qui dois aller les chercher.   *You have to go pick them up.*
Ce ne sont pas eux qui pourront le faire!   *They won't be able to do it!*

You'll find disjunctive pronouns in conjunction with another subject.

Bruno et moi, nous allons à Tokyo.   *Bruno and I are going to Tokyo.*
Lui et sa mère, ils sont toujours d'accord sur tout.   *He and his mother always agree on everything.*
Toi et ta collègue, vous avez gâché la soirée!   *You and your colleague spoiled the party!*
Elle et Michel, ce sont les meilleurs voisins.   *She and Michel are the best neighbors.*

Disjunctive pronouns are also used as one-word questions or answers when there isn't a verb present.

Qui était absent hier? —**Moi!**   *Who was absent yesterday? —I was.*
Qui ne veut pas travailler le dimanche? —**Nous!**   *Who does not want to work on Sundays? —We don't!*
Elle aime le chocolat. **Moi aussi.**   *She likes chocolate. So do I.*
Elle n'aime pas le bruit. **Moi non plus.**   *She does not like noise. Neither do I.*

The disjunctive pronouns can also be used to solicit an opinion or ask for a contrasting piece of information.

Lui, il est pharmacien. **Et elle**, qu'est-ce qu'elle fait?   *He is a pharmacist. And what does she do?*
Moi, je pense que cette décision est absurde. **Et toi**, quelle est ton opinion?   *I think this decision is absurd. And what is your opinion?*
Eux, ils ne dépensent jamais un centime! **Et lui**, est-ce qu'il est moins radin?   *They never spend a cent! Is he less cheap?*
Elle, elle a toujours de la chance. **Et lui**, a-t-il la même veine?   *She is always lucky. Does he have the same luck?*

You'll see disjunctive pronouns used after a preposition.

Qu'est-ce qu'il a **contre eux**?   *What does he have against them?*
Cet employé travaille **pour nous**.   *This employee works for us.*
Vous allez **chez eux** ce soir?   *Are you going to their place tonight?*
Il n'achète rien **sans elle**.   *He never buys anything without her.*

Disjunctive pronouns are also used with **être** to indicate possession.

À qui est cette écharpe? —C'est **à moi**!   *Whose scarf is it? —It's mine!*
À qui sont ces gants? —Ce sont **à lui**!   *Whose gloves are these? —They are mine!*
C'est **à toi**? —Non, ce n'est pas à moi!   *Is it yours? —No, it's not mine!*

You can use disjunctive pronouns to make comparisons.

Caroline est **plus** intelligente **que lui**.	*Caroline is brighter than he is.*
Il court **plus** vite **que toi**.	*He runs faster than you do.*
Ils sont **aussi** riches **qu'elle**.	*They are as rich as she is.*
Elle n'est pas **aussi** douée **que vous**.	*She is not as gifted as you are.*

You can use disjunctive pronouns with -**même** (-*self*) to reinforce the pronoun.

Elle rédige tous ses discours **elle-même**.	*She writes all her speeches herself.*
Écrivez-le **vous-même**!	*Write it yourself!*
C'est **lui-même** qui l'a dit.	*He said it himself.*
On est **soi-même** conscient de ses propres erreurs.	*One is aware of one's own mistakes.*

Disjunctive pronouns are used with certain verbs when the indirect object is a *person*. Compare:

Je parle **de ce film**.	*I am talking about this film.*
J'**en** parle.	*I am talking about it.*

and

Je parle **de ce metteur en scène**.	*I am talking about this film director.*
Je parle **de lui**.	*I am talking about him.*
Je pense **à ce livre**.	*I am thinking about this book.*
J'**y** pense.	*I am thinking about it.*

and

Je pense **à cette photographe**.	*I am thinking about this photographer.*
Je pense **à elle**.	*I am thinking about her.*
Tu as besoin **de cet avocat**.	*You need this lawyer.*
Tu as besoin **de lui**.	*You need him.*
Nous parlons **de nos enfants**.	*We are talking about our children.*
Nous parlons **d'eux**.	*We are talking about them.*
Fais attention **à cet homme**!	*Watch out for this man!*
Fais attention **à lui**!	*Watch out for him!*
Il a peur **de son professeur de chimie**.	*He is afraid of his chemistry teacher.*
Il a peur **de lui**.	*He is afraid of him.*
Nous tenons **à nos amis**.	*We are attached to our friends.*
Nous tenons **à eux**.	*We are attached to them.*
Elle songe **à son fils**.	*She is thinking about her son.*
Elle songe **à lui**.	*She is thinking about him.*

If a reflexive verb is followed by an animate indirect object (person, animal), the disjunctive pronoun is used and placed after the verb.

Nous nous intéressons **à cette candidate**.	*We are interested in this candidate.*
Nous nous intéressons **à elle**.	*We are interested in her.*
Elle s'est débarrassée **de cet employé incompétent**.	*She got rid of this incompetent employee.*
Elle s'est débarrassée **de lui**.	*She got rid of him.*
Il ne veut pas s'occuper **de vos enfants**.	*He does not want to take care of your children.*
Il ne veut pas s'occuper **d'eux**.	*He does not want to take care of them.*
Nous nous méfions **de ce consultant**.	*We do not trust this consultant.*
Nous nous méfions **de lui**.	*We do not trust him.*

Mettre en relief le pronom sujet avec un pronom disjoint en utilisant l'expression
C'est... qui.

1. **Il** a gagné le prix.

_____

2. **Je** prendrai la décision.

_____

3. **Vous** écrirez le discours.

_____

4. **Nous** préparons le dîner.

_____

5. **Tu** as fait cette erreur.

_____

6. **Elle** lui fait toujours de beaux cadeaux.

_____

7. **Je** vous ai invité.

_____

8. **Ils** sont responsables de cette situation désastreuse.

_____

9. **Elles** s'occuperont de tous les détails.

_____

10. **Il** fait les courses.

_____

EXERCICE

21·11

*Traduire les phrases suivantes en utilisant un pronom disjoint et la forme **tu** si nécessaire.*

1. He will go to France with me.

_____

2. I hate coffee!

_____

3. She works for us.

_____

4. Whose book is this?

_____

5. Do it yourself!

_____

6. I can't make this decision without you.

_____

7. He is taller than you are.

_____

8. I am thinking about her.

_____

9. They are afraid of him.

_____

10. She said it herself.

_____

EXERCICE

21·12

*Formuler une question-réponse en reliant les phrases et en utilisant **aussi** ou **non plus**.*

1. Il n'aime pas le froid. Je n'aime pas le froid.

_____

2. Nous allons en France. Ils vont en France.

_____

3. Je prends des vacances. Elle prend des vacances.

_____

4. Nous commandons un dessert. Elles commandent un dessert.

_____

5. Il lit beaucoup. Nous lisons beaucoup.

_____

Adjectives and comparisons

Agreement of adjectives

To describe things and people, we use qualificative adjectives. In French, adjectives agree in gender and number with the noun they modify. The feminine form of an adjective is very often created by adding an -**e** to the masculine form.

Frank est **allemand**.	*Frank is German.*
Heidi est **allemande**.	*Heidi is German.*
Le jardin est **grand**.	*The garden is big.*
La fille de Vincent est **grande**.	*Vincent's daughter is tall.*

Note that the final consonant **d** of **allemand** and **grand** is silent, while the **d** of **allemande** and **grande** is pronounced.

If an adjective ends with an -**e** in the masculine form, the feminine form remains the same.

Cet homme est **coupable**.	*This man is guilty.*
Cette femme est **coupable**.	*This woman is guilty.*
Cet éléphant est **énorme**.	*This elephant is huge.*
Cette baleine est **énorme**.	*This whale is huge.*

Note several irregular feminine forms of adjectives:

Il est **vietnamien**.	*He is Vietnamese.*
Elle est **vietnamienne**.	*She is Vietnamese.*
Marco est **italien**.	*Marco is Italian.*
Stefania est **italienne**.	*Stefania is Italian.*
Charles est **généreux**.	*Charles is generous.*
Caroline est **généreuse**.	*Caroline is generous.*
Ce produit est **dangereux**.	*This product is dangerous.*
Cette route est **dangereuse**.	*This road is dangerous.*
Ce jeu est **interactif**.	*This game is interactive.*
Cette activité est **interactive**.	*This activity is interactive.*
Cet employé est très **passif**.	*This employee is very passive.*
Cette femme est très **passive**.	*This woman is very passive.*
C'est un **faux** témoignage.	*It's perjury.*
C'est une **fausse** alerte.	*It's a false alarm.*

Many adjectives are simply irregular. See the boldfaced adjectives in the following list. Note the special forms of these adjectives when they precede a masculine singular noun that starts with a vowel:

Ce jeu est **fou**.	*This game is crazy.*
Tu as vu le film *Docteur **fol** amour*?	*Have you seen the film Dr. Strangelove?*

Cette idée est **folle**.	*This idea is crazy.*
Ce château est **vieux**.	*This castle is old.*
Ce **vieil édifice** appartenait à un prince.	*This old building belonged to a prince.*
Cette maison est **vieille**.	*This house is old.*
Son **nouveau** patron est suédois.	*His new boss is Swedish.*
Son **nouvel emploi** est ennuyeux.	*Her new job is boring.*
Ma **nouvelle** voiture est grise.	*My new car is gray.*
Ce village est très **beau**.	*This village is very beautiful.*
Ce **bel homme** est son cousin.	*This handsome man is her cousin.*
Quelle **belle** histoire!	*What a beautiful story!*
Le pelage de ce chien est **roux**.	*This dog's coat is red.*
Est-elle **rousse**?	*Is she a redhead?*

VOCABULAIRE

beige	*beige*	**orange**	*orange*
blanc, blanche	*white*	**rose**	*pink*
bleu(e)	*blue*	**rouge**	*red*
bleu ciel	*sky blue*	**vert(e)**	*green*
bleu clair	*light blue*	**vert olive**	*olive green*
bleu foncé	*dark blue*	**violet(te)**	*purple*
bleu marine	*navy blue*	**à carreaux**	*checked*
bordeaux	*burgundy*	**à rayures**	*striped*
gris(e)	*gray*	**à fleurs**	*flowered*
jaune	*yellow*	**à pois**	*polka-dotted*
marron	*brown*	**à volants**	*flounced*
noir(e)	*black*	**à plis**	*pleated*
ocre	*ochre*		

The placement of adjectives

As you continue studying French, you'll become familiar with the irregular feminine forms of certain adjectives. What is often more difficult is knowing where to place adjectives. In French, most qualificative adjectives follow the noun.

Carole aime les **plats italiens**.	*Carole loves Italian dishes.*
Danielle préfère la **cuisine chinoise**.	*Danielle prefers Chinese cooking.*
Il porte des **chaussures noires**.	*He is wearing black shoes.*
C'est un **remède efficace**.	*This is an efficient remedy.*

Some adjectives precede the noun. You just need to memorize them.

C'est un **long trajet**.	*It's a long commute.*
C'est une **longue distance**.	*It's a long distance.*
C'est un **beau compliment**.	*It's a beautiful compliment.*
J'adore cette **belle chanson**.	*I love this beautiful song.*
Son **nouveau livre** est un polar.	*His new book is a detective novel.*
Sa **nouvelle armoire** est magnifique.	*His new armoire is magnificent.*
C'est un **bon prix**.	*It's a good price.*
C'est une **bonne affaire**.	*It's a good deal.*
C'est un **mauvais signe**.	*It's a bad sign.*
C'est une **mauvaise critique**.	*It's a bad review.*

Je déteste mon **vieux canapé**.	*I hate my old couch.*
Cette **vieille maison** est à vendre.	*This old house is for sale.*
Ce **jeune chef** est vraiment doué.	*This young chef is really talented.*
Cette **jeune femme** est écrivain.	*This young woman is a writer.*

Beware: Some adjectives have different meanings, depending on whether they precede or follow the noun.

son ancien mari	*her former husband*	**une statue ancienne**	*an antique statue*
ma chère Carole	*my dear Carole*	**un cadeau cher**	*an expensive gift*
Notre pauvre chien!	*Our poor dog!*	**des pays pauvres**	*poor countries*
sa propre idée	*his own idea*	**une nappe propre**	*a clean tablecloth*
une sale affaire	*a nasty business*	**une fenêtre sale**	*a dirty window*
un grand homme	*an important man*	**une femme grande**	*a tall woman*
le dernier métro	*the last subway train*	**l'an dernier**	*last year*

Adjectives of color

Adjectives describing colors usually agree in gender and number with the noun they modify.

Elle a les **yeux verts**.	*She has green eyes.*
Il a acheté des **chemises blanches**.	*He bought some white shirts.*
Les **fleurs** sur la table sont **rouges**.	*The flowers on the table are red.*
En hiver, cette **pièce** est **froide**.	*In the winter, this room is cold.*
Ses trois **chats** sont **noirs**.	*His three cats are black.*
Tes **lunettes** sont **nouvelles**?	*Are your glasses new?*

Adjectives of color that are also nouns of fruit or plants generally remain in the masculine singular form.

Ces **chaussures orange** sont moches.	*These orange shoes are ugly.*
Mon frère a les **yeux marron**.	*My brother has brown (chestnut-colored) eyes.*
Ces **échantillons safran** sont parfaits!	*These saffron-colored samples are perfect!*

Another exception: **les adjectifs composés**. When two adjectives are combined to provide more specificity, both adjectives generally remain in the masculine singular form.

Cette peinture **vert clair** ne me plaît pas.	*I don't like this light-green paint.*
Sa veste **gris foncé** lui va très bien.	*Her dark gray jacket suits her well.*
Ces robes **rose bonbon** sont trop voyantes.	*These candy pink dresses are too flashy.*
Achète ces coussins **bleu azur**!	*Buy these azur blue cushions!*
Sa fille a les cheveux **châtain clair**.	*Her daughter has light-brown hair.*

EXERCICE
22·1

Traduire les adjectifs entre parenthèses.

1. Ta grand-mère est (*French*)? —Non, elle est (*Italian*).

_____

2. Ces fenêtres sont (*clean*)? —Non, ces fenêtres sont (*dirty*).

_____

3. Sa femme est (*blond*)? —Non, elle est (*redhead*).

_____

4. Il porte ses chaussures (*black*)? —Non, il porte des chaussures (*navy blue*).

_____

5. C'est une situation (*serious*)? —Oui, c'est une situation très (*serious*).

_____

6. C'est une histoire (*tragic*)? —Non, c'est une histoire (*funny*).

_____

7. C'est un (*long*) voyage? —Non, c'est assez (*short*).

_____

8. Votre projet est (*ambitious*). —Non, c'est la directrice qui est (*ambitious*).

_____

9. Ses idées sont (*good*)? —Oui, ses idées sont (*better*) que les nôtres.

_____

10. Ton travail est (*boring*)? —Non, mon travail est très (*interesting*).

_____

EXERCICE
22·2

Choisir l'adjectif logique.

1. Les antiquités sont _____ méchantes/vieilles/courtes.

2. Mon chat est _____ adorable/bavard/immense.

3. Le musée du Louvre est _____ brave/dernier/fascinant.

4. Le professeur d'italien est _____ silencieux/intéressant/final.

5. Sa nouvelle histoire est _____ première/folle/violette.

EXERCICE
22·3

Mettre les adjectifs au féminin en remplaçant Patrick *par* Sonia.

1. Patrick est français. Sonia est _____.

2. Patrick est charmant. Sonia est _____.

3. Patrick est amoureux. Sonia est _____.

4. Patrick est beau. Sonia est _____.

5. Patrick est agressif. Sonia est _____.

6. Patrick est actif. Sonia est _____.

7. Patrick est fou. Sonia est _____.

8. Patrick est généreux. Sonia est _____.

9. Patrick est roux. Sonia est _____.

10. Patrick est doué. Sonia est _____.

Comparatives and superlatives

Comparison of adjectives and adverbs

In French, comparisons of adjectives and adverbs can take three forms, **plus... que** (*more . . . than*), **moins... que** (*less . . . than*), **aussi... que** (*as . . . as*). For example:

Ce modèle est **plus** récent **que** le mien.	*This model is more recent than mine.*
New York est **plus** grand **que** San Francisco.	*New York is bigger than San Francisco.*
Marc est **moins** riche que **Paul**.	*Mark is less rich than Paul.*
Luc est **aussi** célèbre **que** Bertrand.	*Luc is as famous as Bertrand.*

Comparison of nouns

To compare quantities, use the following expressions. Note the use of **de (d')** with expressions of quantity:

Elle a **plus de** temps **que** Valérie.	*She has more time than Valérie.*
Il a **moins de** chance **que** toi.	*He is less lucky than you are.*
Elle a **autant de** jouets **que** toi.	*She has as many toys as you do.*

Irregular comparatives

Some comparatives have irregular forms.

Ce livre est **bon**.	*This book is good.*
Ce livre-ci est **meilleur que** ce livre-là.	*This book is better than that book.*
Il se porte **bien**.	*He's feeling well.*
Il se porte **mieux qu'**avant.	*He is feeling better than before.*
La situation économique est **mauvaise**.	*The economic situation is bad.*
La situation économique est **pire qu'**avant.	*The economic situation is worse than before.*
Cela n'a pas **le moindre** intérêt.	*That does not have the slightest interest.*

Superlatives

To express the ideas of *the most, the least, the best, the worst*, etc., one uses the *superlative*. To form the superlative in French, simply precede the comparative form by the definite article. Note that before naming a group or entity, the superlative is followed by **de** + the definite article.

C'est **le plus grand** spectacle **du monde**.   It's the greatest show on earth.
C'est **la plus belle** histoire que j'aie jamais lue.   It's the most beautiful story I ever read.
C'est l'endroit **le moins ennuyeux de toute**   It's the least boring place in the whole city.
la ville.

The irregular adjectives you learned with the comparatives are also used in the superlative.

Ce roman est **bon**.   This novel is good.
C'est son **meilleur** roman.   It's his best novel.
C'est un **mauvais** cauchemar.   It's a bad nightmare.
C'est son **pire** cauchemar.   It's his worst nightmare.

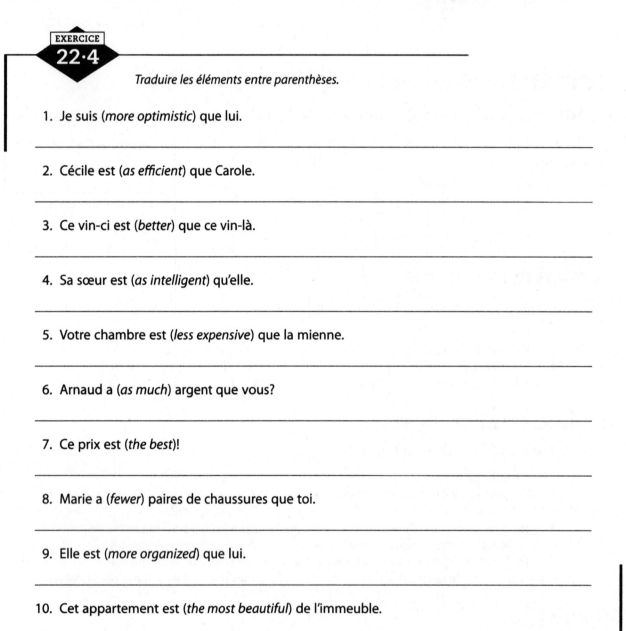

EXERCICE 22·4

Traduire les éléments entre parenthèses.

1. Je suis (*more optimistic*) que lui.

_____

2. Cécile est (*as efficient*) que Carole.

_____

3. Ce vin-ci est (*better*) que ce vin-là.

_____

4. Sa sœur est (*as intelligent*) qu'elle.

_____

5. Votre chambre est (*less expensive*) que la mienne.

_____

6. Arnaud a (*as much*) argent que vous?

_____

7. Ce prix est (*the best*)!

_____

8. Marie a (*fewer*) paires de chaussures que toi.

_____

9. Elle est (*more organized*) que lui.

_____

10. Cet appartement est (*the most beautiful*) de l'immeuble.

_____

EXERCICE
22·5

Formuler une phrase avec les éléments ci-dessous.

1. Charlotte/Lucie/grande/+

_____

2. Charles/Xavier/drôle/=

_____

3. Véronique/Sébastien/optimiste/−

_____

4. Lucien/sa sœur/intelligent/+

_____

5. Élodie/Thérèse/bronzée/=

_____

EXERCICE
22·6

Traduire les phrases suivantes.

1. It's a good idea.

_____

2. They bought an old house in Normandy.

_____

3. This young man is ambitious.

_____

4. This white shirt is mine.

_____

5. Her aunt loves old French songs.

_____

6. I do not have your new address.

_____

7. England is smaller than France.

_____

8. She does not like this yellow jacket.

_____

9. She is as ambitious as he is.

_____

10. This story is boring.

_____

EXERCICE
22·7

Faire correspondre les deux colonnes.

_____ 1. Il travaillait ici dans le passé.   a. Elles sont toutes sales.

_____ 2. Ils n'ont pas d'argent.   b. Elle mesure 1,80 m.

_____ 3. Il n'a pas de chemise à porter.   c. Son pauvre genou!

_____ 4. C'est une femme grande.   d. Ils sont pauvres.

_____ 5. Elle est tombée.   e. C'est l'ancien directeur.

Demonstrative adjectives and pronouns

Demonstrative adjectives

Sometimes you need to be very specific when identifying things. To do so, you use demonstrative adjectives (*this, that, these, those*). In French, demonstratives, like all adjectives, agree in gender and number with the noun they modify.

Masculine singular

ce livre	*this book*
cet auteur	*this author*
cet homme	*this man*

Note that the demonstrative adjective **ce** adds a -**t** before a masculine singular noun that starts with a vowel or a mute **h** (**cet appartement, cet arbre**).

Feminine singular

cette lampe	*this lamp*
cette télévision	*this television*
cette histoire	*this story*

Masculine and feminine plural

ces cahiers (*m.pl.*)	*these notebooks*
ces arbres (*m.pl.*)	*these trees*
ces chemises (*f.pl.*)	*these shirts*
ces homards (*m.pl.*)	*these lobsters*

To make a distinction between two elements, -**ci** and -**là** are added to the noun following the demonstrative adjective.

Préférez-vous **cette** chemise-**ci** ou **cette** chemise-**là**?	*Do you prefer this shirt or that shirt?*
Combien coûtent **ce** livre-**ci** et **ce** livre-**là**?	*How much do this book and that book cost?*
Préférez-vous **ces** lunettes-**ci** ou **ces** lunettes-**là**?	*Do you prefer these glasses or those glasses?*
Vous recommandez **cet** hôtel-**ci** ou **cet** hôtel-**là**?	*Do you recommend this hotel or that hotel?*

une famille	a family	un oncle	an uncle
un(e) adulte	an adult	une tante	an aunt
un mari	a husband	un(e) cousin(e)	a cousin
une femme	a wife, a woman	un beau-père	a father-in-law,
un père	a father		a stepfather
une mère	a mother	une belle-mère	a mother-in-law
un fils	a son		a stepmother
une fille	a daughter, a girl	un beau-frère	a brother-in-law
un enfant	a child	une belle-sœur	a sister-in-law
un bébé	a baby	un neveu	a nephew
un frère	a brother	une nièce	a niece
une sœur	a sister	un grand-père	a grandfather
ainé(e)	older, eldest	une grand-mère	a grandmother
cadet(te)	younger, youngest	un petit-fils	a grandson
un(e) benjamin(e)	a youngest son,	une petite-fille	a granddaughter
	daughter	les petits-enfants	grandchildren
un(e) parent(e)	a relative	(m.pl.)	

EXERCICE
23·1

Compléter avec ce, cet, cette ou ces.

1. Ma sœur n'aime pas (*this*) _____ robe rouge.

2. Mon petit frère préfère (*this*) _____ dessin animé.

3. Nos parents arrivent (*this*) _____ semaine.

4. Tu vas voir ton cousin (*this*) _____ soir.

5. J'achète (*these*) _____ cadeaux pour mes enfants.

6. (*This*) _____ maison est trop petite pour notre famille.

7. Son neveu trouve (*this*) _____ jeu difficile.

8. Ma cousine fait toujours (*these*) _____ plats pour sa belle-mère.

9. (*This*) _____ famille habite ici depuis longtemps et les enfants aiment (*this*) _____ quartier.

10. (*This*) _____ bébé est adorable.

*Faire la distinction entre les deux éléments en ajoutant **-ci** et **-là** aux noms qui suivent les adjectifs démonstratifs.*

1. Ma mère achète les biscuits dans (*this*) _____ pâtisserie et les gâteaux dans (*that*) _____ pâtisserie.

2. Leur enfant joue avec (*this*) _____ jouet mais il ne joue pas avec (*that*) _____ jouet.

3. Mes parents habitent loin d'ici. (*This*) _____ cousin habite à San Francisco, (*that*) _____ cousin est à New York.

4. (*This*) _____ maison appartient à Tante Marthe, (*that*) _____ maison appartient à son fils.

5. (*This*) _____ neveu et (*that*) _____ neveu sont nés le même jour.

6. Mon mari aime (*this*) _____ belle-sœur, mais il n'aime pas (*that*) _____ belle-sœur.

7. Son frère a écrit (*this*) _____ roman, mais il n'a pas écrit (*that*) _____ roman.

8. Leurs enfants aiment (*this*) _____ jeu mais ils n'aiment pas (*that*) _____ jeu.

9. (*This*) _____ poupée et (*that*) _____ poupée sont des cadeaux de Tante Agathe.

10. Notre tante a envoyé (*this*) _____ carte à son fils et (*that*) _____ carte à sa mère, notre grand-mère.

Possessive adjectives

Possessive adjectives modify nouns and are used to express relationship and ownership. They agree in gender and number with the noun they modify.

Masculine singular

mon ordinateur	*my computer*	**notre ordinateur**	*our computer*
ton ordinateur	*your computer*	**votre ordinateur**	*your computer*
son ordinateur	*his/her computer*	**leur ordinateur**	*their computer*

Feminine singular

ma vie	*my life*	**notre vie**	*our life*
ta vie	*your life*	**votre vie**	*your life*
sa vie	*his/her life*	**leur vie**	*their life*

Masculine and feminine plural

mes cousin(e)s	*my cousins*	**nos cousin(e)s**	*our cousins*
tes cousin(e)s	*your cousins*	**vos cousin(e)s**	*your cousins*
ses cousin(e)s	*his/her cousins*	**leurs cousin(e)s**	*their cousins*

Note that the masculine singular form of the possessive adjective (**mon, ton, son**) is used before *singular feminine* nouns beginning with a vowel or a mute **h**.

Mon amie Suzanne travaille à Rennes.	*My friend Suzanne works in Rennes.*
Ton amitié est importante.	*Your friendship is important.*
Son honnêteté est suspecte.	*His honesty is suspect.*

Son, sa, ses can mean either *his* or *hers*, since they modify the noun (not the owner). The context will usually prevent any ambiguity about the identity of the owner. If there is ambiguity, the sentence needs to be rephrased for clarity.

son roman	*his/her novel*
sa pièce	*his/her play*
ses contes de fée	*his/her fairy tales*

Another way of expressing possession is to use **à** + a noun or a disjunctive pronoun.

C'est **à qui?**	*Whose is it?*
C'est **à Pierre?**	*Is it Pierre's?*
Non, ce n'est pas **à Pierre**.	*No, it's not Pierre's.*
C'est **à moi**.	*It's mine.*

EXERCICE
23·3

*Compléter avec l'adjectif possessif approprié en utilisant **vous** si nécessaire.*

1. Aimez-vous (*his*) _____ nouvelle pièce?

2. Non, mais j'aime (*his*) _____ nouveau conte de fée.

3. Que penses-tu de (*her*) _____ dernier roman?

4. (*Her*) _____ dernière pièce est plus intéressante.

5. As-tu besoin de (*our*) _____ voiture?

6. Oui, j'ai besoin de (*your*) _____ voiture.

7. (*Your*) _____ sœur est actrice?

8. Non, (*my*) _____ sœur est architecte.

9. Quel âge a (*their*) _____ fille?

10. (*Their*) _____ filles sont jumelles. Elles ont quatre ans.

Faire correspondre les deux colonnes.

_____ 1. frère   a. ma

_____ 2. amies   b. mon

_____ 3. oncle   c. ma

_____ 4. maison   d. mon

_____ 5. belle-sœur   e. mes

Possessive pronouns

Possessive pronouns replace nouns used with possessive adjectives. They agree in gender and number with the noun they replace, not with the possessor.

MASCULINE SINGULAR		FEMININE SINGULAR	
le mien	*mine*	**la mienne**	*mine*
le tien	*yours*	**la tienne**	*yours*
le sien	*his/hers*	**la sienne**	*his/hers*
le nôtre	*ours*	**la nôtre**	*ours*
le vôtre	*yours*	**la vôtre**	*yours*
le leur	*theirs*	**la leur**	*theirs*

MASCULINE PLURAL		FEMININE PLURAL	
les miens	*mine*	**les miennes**	*mine*
les tiens	*yours*	**les tiennes**	*yours*
les siens	*his/hers*	**les siennes**	*his/hers*
les nôtres	*ours*	**les nôtres**	*ours*
les vôtres	*yours*	**les vôtres**	*yours*
les leurs	*theirs*	**les leurs**	*theirs*

J'apporte mes notes et tu apportes **les tiennes**.	*I bring my notes and you bring yours.*
Tu fais tes devoirs et elle fait **les siens**.	*You do your homework and she does hers.*
Nous aimons votre chien et vous aimez **le nôtre**.	*We like your dog and you like ours.*
Les leurs sont de grande valeur.	*Theirs are quite valuable.*
Vous prenez vos billets et nous prenons **les nôtres**.	*You take your tickets and we take ours.*

When the possessive pronoun is preceded by **à** or **de**, the article is contracted as shown below.

Il a téléphoné à son avocat et elle a téléphoné **au sien**.	*He called his lawyer and she called hers.*
Elle a besoin de mon aide et tu as besoin **de la sienne**.	*She needs your help and you need hers.*

Expressing possession with être + à

Remember that the most common way of expressing possession is by using **être** + **à** + the disjunctive pronoun.

Cette valise **est à moi**.	*This suitcase is mine.*
Ce blouson en cuir **est à lui**.	*This leather jacket is his.*
Ces vélos **sont à eux**.	*These bikes are theirs.*
Ces journaux **sont à elles**.	*These newspapers are theirs.*

When one wants to stress the ownership or identify different items of a similar nature, the possessive pronoun is used.

C'est **le sien**? —Non, c'est **le mien**!	*Is it his? —No, it's mine!*
C'est ton avis et c'est aussi **le sien**.	*It's your opinion and it's also his.*

Contrary to English, sometimes a possessive adjective rather than a possessive pronoun is required in French.

C'est **un de vos associés**?	*Is he a business partner of yours?*
C'est **un de mes collègues**.	*He is a colleague of mine.*

Possessive pronouns are also used in idiomatic expressions.

À la tienne!	*Cheers!* (informal singular)
À la vôtre!	*Cheers!* (formal or plural)
Après des mois de cauchemar, elle est de nouveau **parmi les siens**.	*After some nightmarish months, she is back with her family again.*
Leur benjamin **a** encore **fait des siennes**!	*Their youngest son has been acting up again!*
Il faut **y mettre du tien**!	*You have to make an effort!*
Si elle n'**y met** pas **du sien**, elle ne réussira jamais.	*If she does not make an effort, she'll never succeed.*

EXERCICE
23·5

Traduire les pronoms possessifs entre parenthèses.

1. Mes documents sont en anglais. (*His*) _____ sont en français.

2. Ses parents viennent d'Écosse. (*Mine*) _____ viennent d'Irlande.

3. Il n'a pas trouvé son acte de naissance. Voici (*mine*) _____.

4. Nous avons choisi notre itinéraire. Avez-vous choisi (*yours*) _____?

5. Elle a fini son roman. As-tu fini (*yours*) _____?

6. Ses idées sont étranges. Et (*theirs*) _____ aussi.

7. Je suis vos conseils et je vous demande de suivre (*ours*) _____.

8. Mon blouson est en cuir marron et (*hers*) _____ est en cuir noir.

9. Ton plat est trop épicé et (*mine*) _____ est trop salé.

10. Mon neveu est trop âgé et (*his*) _____ est trop jeune pour ce spectacle.

Traduire les phrases suivantes en utilisant **vous** *si nécessaire.*

1. My family is larger than yours.

_____

2. Our situation is more difficult than his.

_____

3. Her brothers are younger than she is.

_____

4. Their city is cleaner than ours.

_____

5. My exercise is more advanced than theirs.

_____

6. Your dog is more handsome than his.

_____

7. Our neighbors are nicer than yours.

_____

8. Your winters are colder than ours.

_____

9. Their products are more expensive than yours.

_____

10. Your children are more active than mine.

_____

Possessive pronouns with aussi and non plus

The possessive pronoun is also often used with **aussi** and **non plus** to confirm an affirmative or negative statement.

Son appartement coûtait cher.
   —Le mien aussi.
	His apartment was expensive.
	   —So was mine.

Nos meubles sont très modernes.
   —Les miens aussi.
	Our furniture is very modern.
	   —So is mine.

Vos réponses ne sont pas correctes.
   —Les siennes non plus.
	Your answers are not right.
	   —His either. (Nor are his.)

Son appartement n'est pas bruyant.
   —Le tien non plus.
	His apartment is not noisy.
	   —Yours either. (Nor is yours.)

Demonstrative pronouns

Earlier, you studied the demonstrative adjectives **ce, cet, cette, ces** (*this, that, these, those*) used to point out things and people.

ce restaurant	*this restaurant*	**cette galerie**	*this gallery*
ces chaises	*these chairs*	**ces bagues**	*these rings*

A demonstrative pronoun replaces a demonstrative adjective + a noun. It agrees in gender and number with the noun it replaces. It can refer to people or things. In a sentence, it can be the subject or object of the verb and be followed by **que, qui, de**, or another prepositional phrase.

Singular

celui	*the one* (masculine)	**celle**	*the one* (feminine)

Plural

ceux	*the ones* (masc.; masc. and fem.)	**celles**	*the ones* (feminine)

Cette dame est **celle qui habitait** autrefois à côté.	*That woman is the one who used to live next door.*
Il a adopté la méthode de Gérard. —Non, c'est **celle de Francine**.	*He adopted Gérard's method. —No, it's Francine's.*
À qui est ce téléphone? —C'est **celui de Juliette**?	*Whose phone is it? —Is it Juliette's?*

Compound demonstrative pronouns

Compound demonstrative pronouns are used to compare elements of the same nature or to indicate a choice between two objects or two people. The particles **-ci** and **-là** are added to demonstrative pronouns to indicate *this one, that one*, etc.

Singular

celui-ci	*this one* (masculine)	**celui-là**	*that one* (masculine)
celle-ci	*this one* (feminine)	**celle-là**	*that one* (feminine)

Plural

ceux-ci	*these* (*ones*) (masc.; masc. and fem.)	**ceux-là**	*those* (*ones*) (masc.; masc. and fem.)
celles-ci	*these* (*ones*) (fem.)	**celles-là**	*those* (*ones*) (feminine)

Celui-ci est en argent. **Celui-là** est en or.	*This one is silver. That one is gold.*
Celle-ci coûte cher. **Celle-là** est bon marché.	*This one is expensive. That one is cheap.*
Ceux-ci sont vrais. **Ceux-là** sont faux.	*These are real. Those are fake.*
Celles-ci sont belles. **Celles-là** sont laides.	*These are beautiful. Those are ugly.*

Note that **celui-ci** (**celle-ci**) and **celui-là** (**celle-là**) may carry a condescending or derogatory meaning when used to talk about a person who is not present. Therefore, be careful if you decide to use it to refer to a person.

Tu connais son frère? —Ah, **celui-là**! Il est odieux!	*Do you know his brother? —Ah, that one! He is obnoxious!*
Tu as posé la question à ta voisine? —Ah, **celle-là**, je ne lui adresse jamais la parole!	*Did you ask your neighbor? —Ah! That one! I don't talk to her!*

The demonstrative pronoun ce

The demonstrative pronoun **ce** (**c'**) is invariable and is often the subject of the verb **être**. It refers to an idea previously introduced. The adjective following **ce** (**c'**) is always in the masculine even if it refers to a feminine antecedent. See the example sentences below:

Les erreurs qu'elle a faites! **C'est idiot!**   *The mistakes she made! It's so stupid!*
Cette ville en hiver! **C'est si beau!**   *This city in the winter! It's so beautiful!*

Ceci, cela, and ça

The indefinite demonstrative pronouns **ceci** (*this*), **cela** (*that*), and **ça** (*this/that*, familiar) refer to indefinite things or ideas. **Ceci** may initiate a statement and also announce a following sentence. **Cela** may reflect on something already mentioned.

Mangez **ceci!**   *Eat this!*
Enlevez **cela!**   *Remove that!*
Ceci n'est pas une pipe.   *This is not a pipe.*
Ça, c'est de l'art!   *That's (really) art!*
Ça ne fait rien.   *It does not matter.*
Ça m'est égal.   *I don't mind.*

EXERCICE
23·7

*Traduire les phrases suivantes en utilisant **tu** et l'inversion si nécessaire.*

1. What dress are you going to wear? —The one (that) I bought in Paris.

_____

2. What do you think of his new novel? —It's awful!

_____

3. What are these rings made of? —This one is gold and that one is silver.

_____

4. What do you think of my new house? —It's beautiful!

_____

5. What dishes can we prepare? —We can prepare the ones you prefer.

_____

6. Are these films available? —This one is available but that one is not.

_____

7. Are they subtitled? —This one is subtitled in French and that one is in German.

_____

8. Their children like games but not the ones that are difficult.

_____

9. Look at these two books. Do you think my mother would like this one or that one?

_____

10. Here are two bracelets. This one is Indian. That one is Egyptian.

_____

EXERCICE
23·8

Remplacer l'adjectif démonstratif par le pronom démonstratif.

1. Cette robe est rose. Cette robe est blanche.

_____

2. Ces écrivains sont inconnus. Ces écrivains sont célèbres.

_____

3. Cet oncle est jeune. Cet oncle est plus âgé.

_____

4. Ce rendez-vous est trop tôt. Ce rendez-vous est trop tard.

_____

5. Ce roman est un best-seller. Ce roman est épuisé.

_____

6. Cet ordinateur est vieux. Cet ordinateur est le dernier modèle.

_____

7. Cette peinture est trop claire. Cette peinture est trop foncée.

_____

8. Ces articles sont bien écrits. Ces articles sont mal écrits.

_____

9. Cette valise est légère. Cette valise est lourde.

_____

10. Ces arguments sont bons. Ces arguments sont nuls.

_____

*Traduire les phrases suivantes en utilisant des expressions idiomatiques contenant un pronom possessif et la forme **tu** si nécessaire.*

1. After ten difficult years, she went back to her family.

_____

2. My friend René is not at ease among his peers.

_____

3. His young dog has been acting up again!

_____

4. Their granddaughter has been acting up again in school!

_____

5. Cheers! It's your birthday.

_____

6. You are going to lose everything if you don't make an effort!

_____

7. If he does not contribute his share, the presentation will be a disaster!

_____

Relative pronouns

It is essential to know how to connect several elements in the same sentence. One way to link ideas back to persons and things already mentioned is by using **pronoms relatifs** (*relative pronouns*). Relative pronouns link two sentences, making one dependent on the other. The dependent phrase is also called the subordinate clause; it contains a verb, but usually cannot stand alone. Choosing the correct relative pronoun depends on its function in the sentence (subject, direct object, or object of a preposition).

Qui

Let's start with the relative pronoun **qui** used as a subject. **Qui** may refer to people or things and may mean *who, whom, which, what,* or *that*.

J'écoute la personne **qui parle**.	*I am listening to the person who is speaking.*
Il aime les histoires **qui finissent** bien.	*He likes stories that end well.*
Elle remercie la cousine **qui l'a invitée**.	*She thanks the cousin who invited her.*
Nous félicitons l'artiste **qui a pris** cette photo.	*We congratulate the artist who took this picture.*

Note that the -**i** of **qui** is *never* dropped in front of a vowel sound (see above: **qui a pris**). **Qui** as a *subject* precedes the verb in the dependent clause.

When **qui** is the *subject* of the dependent clause, the verb following **qui** agrees with the noun or pronoun that **qui** replaces.

C'est **moi qui lui ai vendu** cette lampe.	*I am the one who sold him this lamp.*
C'est **toi qui es** responsable.	*You are the one who is responsible.*
C'est **vous qui avez restauré** cette chaise?	*Did you restore (Was it you who restored) this chair?*
C'est **vous qui êtes** le propriétaire?	*Are you the owner?*

VOCABULAIRE			
un(e) antiquaire	*an antiques dealer*	**une vente aux enchères**	*an auction*
		faire une offre	*to bid*
un marché aux puces	*a flea market*	**baisser le prix**	*to lower the price*

202

marchander	*to bargain*	une lampe	*a lamp*
un meuble	*a piece of furniture*	une lampe de chevet	*a bedside lamp*
les meubles (*m.pl.*)	*furniture*	un miroir	*a mirror*
une chaise	*a chair*	une coiffeuse	*a dressing table*
un tabouret	*a stool*	un vase	*a vase*
une table	*a table*	un secrétaire	*a writing desk*
une table basse	*a coffee table*	une commode	*a chest of drawers*
un fauteuil	*an armchair*	un coffre	*a chest*
un canapé	*a sofa*	une bibliothèque	*a bookcase, a library*
un buffet	*a sideboard*	une étagère	*a shelf*
un lit	*a bed*	un tapis	*a rug*
un placard	*a closet, a cupboard*	une horloge	*a clock*
une penderie	*a wardrobe, a closet*	un rideau	*a curtain*
une armoire	*a wardrobe, a cupboard*	cher, chère	*expensive*
une armoire à pharmacie	*a medicine cabinet*	bon marché	*cheap, inexpensive*

EXERCICE
24·1

Conjuguer les verbes entre parenthèses au présent.

1. C'est moi qui (être) _____ en charge de l'exposition.

2. C'est lui qui (suivre) _____ l'affaire.

3. C'est nous qui (avoir) _____ les documents d'authenticité.

4. Ce sont eux qui (pouvoir) _____ prendre cette décision.

5. C'est elle qui (savoir) _____ la vérité.

6. C'est moi qui (avoir) _____ l'armoire de grand-mère.

7. C'est vous qui (devoir) _____ nous aider à choisir.

8. C'est lui qui (faire) _____ la restauration.

9. C'est toi qui (écrire) _____ l'article?

10. C'est eux qui (vouloir) _____ acheter ce buffet.

Que

When the dependent clause introduced by a relative pronoun already has a subject noun or pronoun, the relative pronoun **que** (*whom, which, that*) is used. Like **qui**, the relative pronoun **que** refers to both people and things.

Elle n'aime pas le cadre **que vous lui montrez**.	*She does not like the frame you are showing her.*
Voici le lustre **que Daniel a acheté**.	*Here's the chandelier Daniel bought.*

J'ai contacté l'ébéniste **que tu as recommandé**.	*I contacted the cabinetmaker you recommended.*
Rends-moi le livre **que je t'ai prêté**.	*Give me back the book I lent you.*

In the following sentences, note that the **-e** of **que** is dropped before a vowel (**qu'**).

Les articles **qu'il vend** sont chers.	*The items he sells are expensive.*
Les statues **qu'il a chez lui** viennent d'Afrique.	*The statues that he has at home come from Africa.*
L'article **qu'elle écrit** sera publié en mai.	*The article she is writing will be published in May.*
Les objets **qu'ils fabriquent** sont de grande valeur.	*The objects they make are of great value.*

In the compound tenses, if the direct object is placed before the verb, the past participle agrees in gender and number with that direct object. This includes sentences where **que** (**qu'**) refers back to a direct object noun. See the following examples:

C'est **la table en marbre que** nous avons trouvée au marché aux puces.	*Here's the marble table we found at the flea market.*
La pièce qu'il a écrite n'a jamais été jouée.	*The play he wrote was never performed.*
Montrez-moi **la photo que** vous avez prise.	*Show me the picture you took.*
Les chaises qu'ils ont restaurées sont comme neuves.	*The chairs they restored look new.*

Note the following sentences where **qui** is the *object* of the verb in the dependent clause. In this case, a subject noun or pronoun comes between **qui** and the verb form. Remember that the **-i** of **qui** is never dropped.

Je ne sais pas **qui il est**.	*I don't know who he is.*
Le président n'a pas dit **qui il nommerait** à ce poste.	*The president did not say who(m) he would appoint to this position.*
Nous ignorons **qui elle renverra**.	*We don't know who(m) she'll fire.*
Le policier a révélé **qui il avait attrapé**.	*The police officer revealed who(m) he had caught.*

EXERCICE
24·2

Qui ou que?

1. Le magasin _____ se trouve place d'Italie a beaucoup de choix.

2. L'antiquaire _____ elle a conseillé est fermé le dimanche.

3. Tu veux me vendre le coffre _____ est dans le salon?

4. Les manteaux sont dans le placard _____ est à gauche de la porte.

5. Le livre _____ je lis en ce moment est passionnant.

6. Les clients _____ sont dans le magasin sont indécis.

7. Il choisit toujours des gravures _____ je déteste.

8. Achète quelque chose _____ fera plaisir aux enfants.

9. Le dessert _____ tu as acheté est délicieux.

10. Il n'est pas satisfait du tableau _____ il peint.

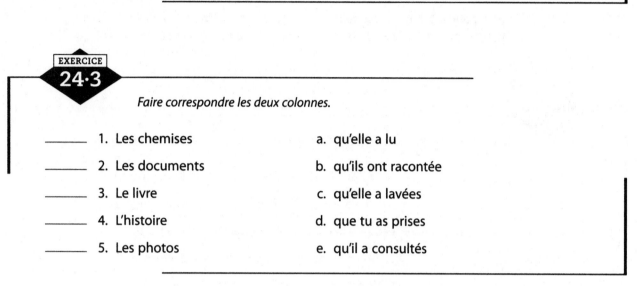

EXERCICE
24·3

Faire correspondre les deux colonnes.

_____ 1. Les chemises	a. qu'elle a lu
_____ 2. Les documents	b. qu'ils ont racontée
_____ 3. Le livre	c. qu'elle a lavées
_____ 4. L'histoire	d. que tu as prises
_____ 5. Les photos	e. qu'il a consultés

The relative clause is often inserted into the main clause. Note again that **qui** and **que** can refer to either people or things.

La commode **qui est dans la vitrine**, a appartenu à Talleyrand.	*The chest of drawers that is in the window belonged to Talleyrand.*
L'homme **que vous voyez au fond de l'atelier** est un des meilleurs artisans du pays.	*The man you see in the back of the shop is one of the best craftsmen in the country.*

Lequel

When verbs are followed by prepositions, the relative pronouns **qui** (*whom*), **quoi** (*what*), **lequel**, **laquelle**, **lesquels**, **lesquelles** (*that, which, whom*) are used. The preposition precedes these pronouns. **Qui** refers only to people; **quoi** is an indefinite thing or object; and **lequel**, **laquelle**, **lesquels**, **lesquelles** refer to specific things. (**Lequel**, **laquelle**, **lesquels**, **lesquelles** may also be used for people; but this use is less common.)

C'est l'antiquaire **à qui** je pensais. (Less common: C'est l'antiquaire auquel je pensais.)	*He's the antiques dealer I was thinking about.*
C'est le tableau **auquel** je pensais.	*It is the painting (that) I was thinking about.*
Tu sais **à quoi** il pense?	*Do you know what he is thinking about?*
C'est **le client pour lequel** je travaille.	*It's the client for whom I am working.*
C'est **la société pour laquelle** je travaille.	*It's the company for which I am working.*
Voici **le collègue avec qui** j'écris le rapport.	*Here is the colleague with whom I am writing the report.*
Les outils avec lesquels il travaille appartenaient à son père.	*The tools with which he is working belonged to his father.*
Je vous présente **la personne sans qui** je n'aurai pas pu réussir.	*Let me introduce you to the person without whom I would not have been able to succeed.*

Merci pour **ces documents sans lesquels** je n'aurais pas pu authentifier ces œuvres.

Thank you for these documents without which I would not have been able to authenticate these works.

Note that **qui** cannot be used with the preposition **parmi** (*among*).

Plusieurs peintres, parmi lesquels celui-ci, étaient nés en Angleterre.

Several painters, among whom this one, were born in England.

EXERCICE 24·4

Compléter avec un pronom relatif en utilisant la préposition entre parenthèses.

1. La femme, _____ je restaure ces meubles, est australienne. (pour)

2. La route _____ nous devons passer, est dangereuse. (par)

3. Le tissu _____ il recouvre le canapé, est de la soie sauvage. (avec)

4. L'époque _____ ils s'intéressent, est le dix-neuvième siècle. (à)

5. Les livres _____ je fais mes recherches, sont à Sylvie. (avec)

6. Le fauteuil _____ il est assis, appartenait à sa tante. (dans)

7. Le poste _____ elle aspire, sera vacant d'ici la fin de l'année. (à)

8. Les amis, _____ nous avons déjeuné dimanche, ont une belle collection de gravures. (chez)

9. Il pense à ses vacances? À ses projets? Je ne sais pas _____ il pense. (à)

10. Merci à Julie _____ ce projet n'aurait jamais vu le jour. (sans)

Où

The relative pronoun **où**, referring to a place, often replaces **dans lequel, sur lequel, par lequel**, etc. **Où** is more common in modern language.

C'est **le magasin dans lequel** je fais mes courses.

It's the store where I do my shopping.

C'est **le magasin où** je fais mes courses.

It's the store where I do my shopping.

La région dans laquelle ils habitent est très calme.

The area where they live is very quiet.

La région où ils habitent est très calme.

The area where they live is very quiet.

The relative pronoun **où** is also used when the antecedent expresses time.

Tu te souviens de **l'année où** il est arrivé dans la région?

Do you remember the year (when) he arrived in the region?

Le jour où il a été élu, tout le monde était content.

The day (when) he was elected, everyone was happy.

L'instant où nous sommes partis, il a commencé à pleuvoir.	*The moment (when) we left, it started to rain.*
Le dix-neuvième siècle fut **un siècle où** il y eut de nombreuses inventions.	*The nineteenth century was a century (when) there were many inventions.*

Dont

The relative pronoun **dont** acts as an object of the main clause and can refer to both people and things. It is used to refer to objects of verbs or verbal expressions that include the preposition **de**. (You may wish to review the verbs and their prepositions in Chapter 14.)

Il **a besoin de** ces documents.	*He needs these documents.*
Voici les documents **dont il a besoin**.	*Here are the documents he needs.*
Elle **se sert d'**un pinceau.	*She uses a paintbrush.*
Montrez-moi le pinceau **dont elle se sert**.	*Show me the paintbrush she uses.*
Tu **as parlé d'**un souffleur de verre.	*You talked about a glassblower.*
Où habite le souffleur de verre **dont tu nous as parlé**?	*Where does the glassblower you told us about live?*
Elle **est fière de** son fils.	*She is proud of her son.*
Denis est le fils **dont elle est fière**.	*Denis is the son she is proud of.*

In modern French, **dont** usually replaces **duquel**, **de laquelle**, **desquels**, and **desquelles**.

Le marchand **dont (duquel) je me souviens** est à Saint-Ouen.	*The merchant I remember is in Saint-Ouen.*
Les forgerons, **dont (desquels) je parle** dans mon roman, vivent dans ce quartier.	*The blacksmiths I talk about in my book live in this neighborhood.*

Dont is also used to express possession (*whose, of whom, of which*). After this construction, the word order is subject + verb + object.

Un artisan, **dont j'ai aussi rencontré le père**, m'a encouragé à devenir verrier.	*A craftsman, whose father I also met, encouraged me to become a glassworker.*
Ils ont des voisins **dont les amis sont bergers**.	*They have neighbors whose friends are shepherds.*

EXERCICE
24·5

*Compléter avec **qui**, **que** ou **dont**.*

1. L'artisan _____ tu parles est à la retraite.

2. Le film _____ nous regardons est sous-titré.

3. Le dictionnaire _____ ils se servent est bilingue.

4. Le cadre _____ vous plaît n'est pas à vendre.

5. Les pinceaux _____ elle a besoin sont dans l'autre atelier.

6. Le livre d'art _____ est sur la table appartient à un client.

7. Le seul incident _____ je me souviens c'est celui-ci.

8. Le coussin _____ tu regardes est en soie.

9. La maison _____ ils veulent acheter est en Camargue.

10. Les ouvriers _____ il est content recevront une augmentation de salaire.

EXERCICE
24·6

*Traduire les phrases suivantes en utilisant **vous** si nécessaire.*

1. I can remember the year he opened his shop.

_____

2. The chandelier he bought is for the living room.

_____

3. The tool with which she is working is very old.

_____

4. Are you the owner?

_____

5. The armchair you are sitting on belonged to my grandfather.

_____

6. The city where they live is quite beautiful.

_____

7. I know the person he is talking about.

_____

8. It's the only detail I remember.

_____

9. The documents you need are at Valérie's.

_____

10. I don't know what he is thinking about.

_____

Ce que, ce qui, ce dont, ce à quoi

When there is no specific word or antecedent for the relative pronoun to refer to, the antecedent **ce** is combined with the pronoun. **Ce qui**, **ce que**, **ce dont**, and **ce à quoi**, all meaning *what*, refer to ideas, not to persons, and do not have gender or number. Choosing the correct indefinite relative pronoun again depends on the pronoun's function in the sentence (subject, direct object, or object of a preposition). Here again, it will be useful to review the verbs and their prepositions in Chapter 14.

Ce qui is used as the subject of the dependent clause.

J'aime **ce qui est fabriqué** dans cet atelier.	*I like what is made (what they make) in this workshop.*
Il ne sait pas **ce qui a provoqué** leur réaction.	*He does not know what triggered their reaction.*
Qui sait **ce qui est arrivé**?	*Who knows what happened?*
J'aimerais savoir **ce qui lui plairait**.	*I'd like to know what she would like.*

Ce que is used as the direct object of the dependent clause.

Savez-vous **ce qu'il fait** ces jours-ci?	*Do you know what he is doing these days?*
Tu comprends **ce que ce journaliste écrit** (**ce qu'écrit ce journaliste**)?	*Do you understand what this journalist writes?*
Ils ont fait **ce qu'il ne fallait pas faire**.	*They did what shouldn't have been done.*
Elle écrit **ce qu'elle vit**.	*She writes what she lives.*

Ce dont is used when verbs take the preposition **de**.

Elle ne comprend pas **ce dont il a peur**. (avoir peur de)	*She does not understand what he's afraid of.*
Fais-moi voir **ce dont tu te sers**. (se servir de)	*Show me what you use.*
La police veut savoir **ce dont elle se souvient**. (se souvenir de)	*The police want to know what she remembers.*
Je m'intéresse à **ce dont vous avez parlé** ce matin. (parler de)	*I am interested in what you talked about this morning.*

Ce à quoi is used with verbs that take the preposition **à**.

J'ignore **ce à quoi il s'abonne**. (s'abonner à)	*I don't know what he subscribes to.*
C'est exactement **ce à quoi je m'attendais** de sa part. (s'attendre à)	*It's exactly what I expected from him.*
Ils ne savent pas **ce à quoi tu t'opposes**. (s'opposer à)	*They don't know what you are opposed to.*
Je voudrais savoir **ce à quoi elle aspire**. (aspirer à)	*I'd like to know what she is aspiring to.*

The indefinite relative pronouns **ce qui**, **ce que**, **ce à quoi**, and **ce dont** are frequently placed at the beginning of a sentence to stress a point. This construction compensates for the English intonation that is much more marked. When a verb requires a preposition, it is repeated in the second clause.

Ce qui est amusant, c'est les marchés aux puces.	*Flea markets are fun!*
Ce qu'elle adore, c'est acheter des vieilles chaises.	*She loves buying old chairs!*

Ce **dont** il a envie, c'est **de** cet automate.   *What he'd like is this automaton!*
Ce **à quoi** il s'intéresse, c'est **à**   *He is interested in aromatherapy!*
l'aromathérapie.

EXERCICE
24·7

*Compléter par **ce qui**, **ce que**, **ce à quoi** ou **ce dont**.*

1. _____ ils s'intéressent, c'est à l'opéra.

2. _____ elle se souvient, c'est de son enfance en Indochine.

3. _____ ils aiment, c'est l'art déco.

4. _____ tu as envie est beaucoup trop cher.

5. _____ j'ai besoin, c'est de votre aide.

6. _____ est arrivé hier risque d'avoir des conséquences graves.

7. _____ je ne comprends pas, c'est son indifférence.

8. _____ est fascinant, c'est sa collection.

9. _____ il parle n'a aucun intérêt.

10. _____ je décris dans mon roman, c'est le paysage savoyard.

EXERCICE
24·8

*Traduire les phrases suivantes en commençant par **ce qui**, **ce que**, **ce à quoi** ou **ce dont**.*

1. What he wants is more free time.

_____

2. What the glassblower uses is in the other workshop.

_____

3. What I can't remember is this incident in Camargue.

_____

4. What I expected was different.

_____

5. What he needs is this book.

_____

6. What they are talking about is interesting.

_____

7. What he does is difficult.

_____

8. What she is interested in is this art collection.

_____

9. What they love is chocolate.

_____

10. What happened last night is very sad.

_____

The relative pronouns **qui** and **que** can sometimes be followed by the subjunctive. If there is a doubt about the existence of someone or the possible realization of anything, the subjunctive may be used after the relative pronoun.

Il cherche un artisan **qui puisse restaurer** ce fauteuil Louis XV.
He is looking for an artisan who might be able to restore this Louis XV armchair.

Connaîtriez-vous un antiquaire **qui vende des pièces rares?**
Would you know of an antiques dealer who sells rare coins?

When the antecedent of the relative pronoun **qui** or **que** is a superlative such as **le plus** (*the most*), **le moins** (*the least*), **le seul** (*the only*), **l'unique** (*the unique*), **le premier** (*the first*), **le dernier** (*the last*), etc., the subjunctive may be used.

Paolo est **le meilleur artisan qui vende** des objets à Burano.
Paolo is the best artisan who sells pieces in Burano.

C'est **le seul marché aux puces que je connaisse** dans cette ville.
It's the only flea market I know in this city.

EXERCICE
24·9

Compléter avec le pronom relatif qui convient.

1. Pourquoi la bibliothèque, _____ est dans le coin à gauche, est-elle si chère?

2. L'artiste _____ tu parles vit actuellement à Paris.

3. La chaise sur _____ elle est assise a besoin d'être repeinte.

4. _____ j'ai envie, c'est de faire le tour du monde.

5. Le chinois est une langue étrangère _____ est très utile de nos jours.

6. Je ne comprends pas _____ vous demandez.

7. C'est un lustre _____ vient d'Espagne.

8. Les objets _____ il s'intéresse sont du dix-huitième siècle.

9. L'ottoman _____ je veux faire recouvrir appartenait à un des mes ancêtres.

10. _____ est fait, est fait.

Adverbs and expressions of time, frequency, and location

Adverbs and expressions of time

The following expressions are useful when talking about time:

aujourd'hui	*today*
demain	*tomorrow*
hier	*yesterday*
après-demain	*the day after tomorrow*
avant-hier	*the day before yesterday*
dans trois jours	*in three days (from today)*
dans une quinzaine	*in two weeks*
dans un mois	*in a month*
dans un an	*in a year*
la semaine prochaine	*next week*
la semaine dernière	*last week*

Il ira en France **dans un an**.	*He'll go to France in a year.*
Je t'appellerai **après-demain**.	*I'll call you the day after tomorrow.*

The adverbs listed above are ordinarily used when you are speaking directly to people, in what is known as direct style or direct speech. If you are discussing past and future events, or telling a story, you are more likely to use an indirect style, the **discours indirect** (*indirect speech*), which you studied in Chapter 18. Here are a few time expressions typically used in indirect speech:

la veille	*the day before*
le jour même	*the very day*
le lendemain	*the day after*
l'avant-veille	*two days before*
le surlendemain	*two days later*
la semaine suivante	*the following week*
la dernière semaine	*the last week (of a sequence)*

Elle est arrivée **la veille** de mon anniversaire.	*She arrived the day before my birthday.*
Nous sommes partis **le lendemain**.	*We left the day after.*

Here are some additional adverbs or expressions of time:

chaque jour	*every day*	tous les jours	*every day*
maintenant	*now*	en ce moment	*at this present time*
actuellement	*presently*	à l'heure actuelle	*at this very moment*
d'habitude	*usually*	d'ordinaire	*ordinarily*
toujours	*always, still*	souvent	*often*
ne... jamais	*never*	longtemps	*for a long time*
autrefois	*formerly*	rarement	*seldom*
tôt	*early*	tard	*late*
parfois	*sometimes*	quelquefois	*sometimes*
de temps en temps	*from time to time*	de temps à autre	*from time to time*

Il assiste **rarement** aux réunions.   *He rarely attends meetings.*
Que fait-elle **actuellement**?   *What is she presently doing?*

EXERCICE 25·1

Compléter les phrases avec l'adverbe approprié.

1. Virginie arrive (*tomorrow*) _____? —Oui, elle arrive (*tomorrow evening*) _____.

2. Vous êtes libres (*next week*) _____? —Non, nous ne sommes pas libres (*next week*) _____.

3. Où vas-tu (*today*) _____? —Je vais à Nantes (*today*) _____.

4. Vous mangez des fruits (*every day*) _____? —Non, je mange des fruits (*every other day*) _____.

5. Tu rentres (*late*) _____ ce soir? —Non, je rentre vers sept heures.

6. Est-ce qu'ils arrivent (*often*) _____ en avance? —Non, ils arrivent (*rarely*) _____ en avance.

7. Est-ce qu'elles vont (*sometimes*) _____ à la plage? —Non, elles ne vont (*never*) _____ à la plage.

8. Vous avez beaucoup de travail (*right now*) _____? —Non, (*right now*) _____, c'est très calme.

9. Ton anniversaire est (*next week*) _____? —Non, mon anniversaire est (*the day after tomorrow*) _____.

10. Il est parti (*yesterday*) _____? —Non, il est parti (*the day before yesterday*) _____.

*Traduire les phrases suivantes en utilisant **tu** et la forme **est-ce que** si nécessaire.*

1. Today is the first day of winter.

   _____

2. She often travels.

   _____

3. I am never on time. I am always late.

   _____

4. He arrives the day after tomorrow.

   _____

5. Her appointment is in two weeks.

   _____

6. We are working tomorrow, but we are not working the day after tomorrow.

   _____

7. They sold their house last week.

   _____

8. Are you going to the opera tonight?

   _____

9. You are early. I am not ready.

   _____

10. The bakery will be closed next week.

   _____

VOCABULAIRE

une agence de voyages	*a travel agency*	**un épicier, une épicière**	*a grocer*
un(e) antiquaire	*an antiques dealer*	**un(e) fleuriste**	*a florist*
une banque	*a bank*	**un horloger**	*a watchmaker*
une bijouterie	*a jewelry store*	**un kiosque à journaux**	*a newsstand*
un boucher, une bouchère	*a butcher*	**un magasin**	*a store*
un boulanger, une boulangère	*a baker*	**un magasin d'appareils photo**	*a camera store*
un bureau de tabac	*a tobacco shop*	**un magasin de chaussures**	*a shoe shop*
un coiffeur, une coiffeuse	*a hairdresser*	**un magasin de disques**	*a record store*
une confiserie	*a candy store*	**un magasin de jouets**	*a toy store*
un cordonnier	*a shoemaker*		

un(e) marchand(e) au détail	a retailer	une papeterie	a stationery store
un(e) marchand(e) de gros	a wholesaler	une pharmacie	a pharmacy
un(e) marchand(e) de journaux	a newspaper dealer	un(e) pharmacien(ne)	a pharmacist
un(e) marchand(e) de légumes	a produce dealer	un pâtissier,	a pastry cook
un(e) marchand(e) de poisson	a fishmonger	une pâtissière	
un(e) marchand(e) de tableaux	an art dealer	une poissonnerie	a fish market
un(e) marchand(e) de vin	a wine merchant	une quincaillerie	a hardware store
un(e) libraire	a bookseller	un salon de coiffure	a hairdressing salon
une librairie	a bookstore	un supermarché	a supermarket
un(e) opticien(ne)	an optician	un pressing,	a dry cleaner
		une teinturerie	

Expressing duration

Remember: If you are asking a question about the duration of an action that began in the past and still continues in the present, you have several options: **depuis**, **il y a... que**, or **cela (ça) fait... que**, used along with the duration. Note that French uses a present tense verb whereas English uses the past.

Let's review **depuis**. To ask a question about the duration of an action, use **Depuis quand?** (*Since when?*) or **Depuis combien de temps?** (*How long?*)

Depuis quand (Depuis combien de temps) Julie est-elle pharmacienne?	*Since when has Julie been a pharmacist?*
—Julie est pharmacienne **depuis dix ans**.	*—Julie has been a pharmacist for ten years.*
J'achète mes livres chez ce libraire **depuis des années**.	*I have been buying my books at this bookseller's for years.*

EXERCICE
25·3

Traduire les éléments entre parenthèses.

1. (*Since when*) _____ habites-tu à New York? —J'habite à New York depuis 1998.

2. (*How long*) _____ est-ce que ce boulanger est installé ici? —Depuis cinq ans.

3. (*Since when*) _____ est-elle malade? —Elle est malade depuis jeudi.

4. (*How long*) _____ est-il fleuriste? —Depuis six mois.

5. (*Since when*) _____ cette bijouterie est-elle ouverte? —Elle est ouverte depuis le premier septembre.

6. (*How long*) _____ est-ce que vous attendez? —Nous attendons (*for*) _____ quinze minutes.

7. (*Since when*) _____ voyages-tu en France régulièrement? —Depuis plusieurs années.

8. (*Since when*) _____ êtes-vous amis? —Nous sommes amis depuis notre enfance.

9. (*How long*) _____ le marchand de journaux a-t-il pris sa retraite? Depuis

   trois mois.

10. Cette laverie se trouve ici (*for*) _____ plusieurs années.

There is an important exception to the construction with **depuis**: In negative sentences, the **passé composé** is used instead of the present. For example:

Il n'a pas revu sa sœur depuis dix ans.	*He has not seen his sister for ten years.*
Nous ne sommes pas allées à Madrid **depuis** dix ans.	*We have not been to Madrid for ten years.*

EXERCICE

25·4

Répondre aux questions à l'aide des éléments entre parenthèses.

1. Depuis combien de temps travailles-tu pour cette agence de voyages? (5 ans)

   _____

2. Depuis combien de temps cherches-tu un nouvel appartement? (le mois de janvier)

   _____

3. Depuis quand allez-vous chez cet opticien? (des années)

   _____

4. Cela fait longtemps que vous êtes mariés? (14 ans)

   _____

5. Cela fait combien de temps que nous nous connaissons? (9 ans)

   _____

6. Cela fait longtemps que tu m'attends sous la pluie? (45 minutes)

   _____

7. Vous prenez cette ligne de métro depuis combien de temps? (5 ans)

   _____

8. Cela fait longtemps que le coiffeur est situé par ici? (6 mois)

   _____

9. Depuis quand ne fumes-tu plus? (la semaine dernière)

   _____

10. Depuis combien de temps est-il en vacances? (3 semaines)

    _____

*Changer **depuis** ou **cela fait... que** en **il y a... que**.*

1. J'attends depuis une demi-heure.

_____

2. Cela fait quatre mois que Valérie a sa voiture.

_____

3. Cela fait dix jours que nous essayons de joindre le banquier.

_____

4. Il est en voyage d'affaires depuis deux jours.

_____

5. Sophie étudie le chinois depuis un an.

_____

6. Elle veut adopter un enfant depuis cinq ans.

_____

7. Cela fait des semaines que nous cherchons un appartement.

_____

8. Cela fait trois mois que j'attends votre réponse.

_____

9. Ses idées sont dénuées d'intérêt depuis longtemps.

_____

10. Le chien de nos voisins est perdu depuis une semaine.

_____

Using adverbs with the **passé composé**

In the **passé composé**, shorter adverbs of quantity, quality, and frequency are placed between **avoir** or **être** and the past participle. See the following example sentences:

Elle étudie **beaucoup**.	*She studies a lot.*
Elle a **beaucoup** étudié.	*She studied a lot.*
Ils dépensent **trop**.	*They spend too much.*
Ils ont **trop** dépensé.	*They spent too much.*
Nous travaillons **assez**.	*We work enough.*
Nous avons **assez** travaillé.	*We worked enough.*
Il écrit **très bien** la musique.	*He writes music very well.*
Il a **très bien** écrit la musique.	*He wrote music very well.*
Tu t'exprimes **mal**.	*You express yourself badly.*
Tu t'es **mal** exprimé(e).	*You expressed yourself badly.*

Je voyage **souvent** en Italie.   *I often travel in Italy.*
J'ai **souvent** voyagé en Italie.   *I often traveled in Italy.*
Vous mentez **rarement**.   *You rarely lie.*
Vous avez **rarement** menti.   *You have rarely lied.*

To express time with the **passé composé**, **pendant** (*for, during*) is commonly used (although it can actually be omitted). However, **pour** (*for*) is *never* used to talk about duration in the past.

Il a habité **pendant cinq ans** à Londres.   *He lived for five years in London.*
Il a habité **cinq ans** à Londres.   *He lived five years in London.*
Nous avons voyagé **pendant un mois**   *We traveled for a month in Italy.*
    en Italie.
Nous avons voyagé **un mois** en Italie.   *We traveled one month in Italy.*

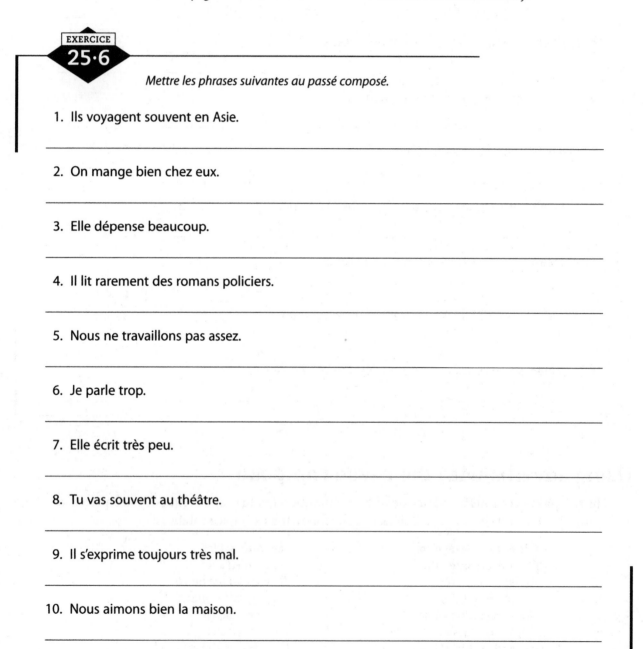

EXERCICE 25·6

Mettre les phrases suivantes au passé composé.

1. Ils voyagent souvent en Asie.

_____

2. On mange bien chez eux.

_____

3. Elle dépense beaucoup.

_____

4. Il lit rarement des romans policiers.

_____

5. Nous ne travaillons pas assez.

_____

6. Je parle trop.

_____

7. Elle écrit très peu.

_____

8. Tu vas souvent au théâtre.

_____

9. Il s'exprime toujours très mal.

_____

10. Nous aimons bien la maison.

_____

Interrogative forms; question words

When you want to formulate questions, interrogative words come in handy. Here are some important ones:

pourquoi	*why*
où	*where*
quand	*when*
comment	*how*
combien	*how much*
que	*what*
qui	*who, whom*
dans quelle mesure	*to what extent*

EXERCICE 25·7

Traduire les mots entre parenthèses.

1. (*How many*) _____ livres lisez-vous? —Je lis deux livres.

2. (*How*) _____ allons-nous à la plage? —Nous allons à la plage en voiture.

3. (*Who*) _____ loue la maison bleue? —Suzanne loue la maison bleue.

4. (*What*) _____ pensez-vous de ce roman? —C'est un mauvais roman.

5. (*How much*) _____ coûte l'appartement de Stéphane? —L'appartement de

   Stéphane coûte cher.

6. (*Where*) _____ travaille votre mari? —Il travaille à Berlin.

7. (*When*) _____ vont-ils au théâtre? —Ils vont au théâtre samedi soir.

8. (*Why*) _____ étudiez-vous le français? —J'étudie le français pour mon travail.

9. (*When*) _____ arrive-t-il? —Il arrive la semaine prochaine.

10. (*Who*) _____ chante? —C'est Laurent qui chante.

Adverbs and expressions of location

Here are some words that are helpful when talking about location:

ici	*here*	**là**	*there*
là-bas	*over there*	**ailleurs**	*elsewhere*
ça et là	*here and there*	**à cet endroit**	*in this place*
là-haut	*up there*	**partout**	*everywhere*
près	*near, close*	**loin**	*far*
à côté	*next to, beside*	**auprès**	*next to, close to*
dehors	*outside*	**dedans**	*inside*
devant	*in front of*	**derrière**	*behind*
dessus	*on top*	**dessous**	*under*

Ici, tout est possible.	*Here, everything is possible.*
Les femmes **d'ici** sont très belles.	*Local women are very beautiful.*
Fitzgerald est mort **ici** même.	*Fitzgerald died in this very place.*
Je le vois **là**, sur l'étagère.	*I see it over there, on the shelf.*
Mets ton sac **dessous**.	*Put your bag underneath.*
C'est écrit **dessus**.	*It's written on it.*
Nous désirons voyager **ailleurs**.	*We want to travel elsewhere.*
Tu es juste **devant**.	*You are right in front of it.*
Vous êtes juste **derrière**.	*You are right behind it.*
C'est beaucoup trop **loin**.	*It is much too far.*
Je vois des erreurs **ça et là**.	*I see mistakes here and there.*

EXERCICE

25·8

*Traduire les phrases suivantes en utilisant **vous** et l'inversion si nécessaire.*

1. He planted flowers everywhere.

_____

2. Do you want to live here?

_____

3. My car is parked just behind yours.

_____

4. We'll go somewhere else.

_____

5. He is outside.

_____

6. I live near the river.

_____

7. You live too far.

_____

8. I see strange things here and there.

_____

9. He is in front of you.

_____

10. Come sit next to me.

_____

Numbers

The numbers 0 to 50

Let's start with numbers from 0 to 50. Although consonants are generally silent in French, they are pronounced in the following numbers: **cinq, six, sept, huit, neuf, dix**. With **sept**, the -**p**- is silent, but the final -**t** is pronounced. The final -**x** in **six** and **dix** is pronounced like an **s**.

When the numbers **cinq, six, huit**, and **dix** are followed by a word beginning with a consonant, their final consonant is mute (silent).

zéro	*zero*	**vingt**	*twenty*
un	*one*	**vingt et un**	*twenty-one*
deux	*two*	**vingt-deux**	*twenty-two*
trois	*three*	**vingt-trois**	*twenty-three*
quatre	*four*	**vingt-quatre**	*twenty-four*
cinq	*five*	**vingt-cinq**	*twenty-five*
six	*six*	**vingt-six**	*twenty-six*
sept	*seven*	**vingt-sept**	*twenty-seven*
huit	*eight*	**vingt-huit**	*twenty-eight*
neuf	*nine*	**vingt-neuf**	*twenty-nine*
dix	*ten*	**trente**	*thirty*
onze	*eleven*	**trente et un**	*thirty-one*
douze	*twelve*	**trente-deux**	*thirty-two*
treize	*thirteen*	**trente-trois**	*thirty-three*
quatorze	*fourteen*	**quarante**	*forty*
quinze	*fifteen*	**quarante et un**	*forty-one*
seize	*sixteen*	**quarante-deux**	*forty-two*
dix-sept	*seventeen*	**quarante-trois**	*forty-three*
dix-huit	*eighteen*	**cinquante**	*fifty*
dix-neuf	*nineteen*		

EXERCICE

26·1

Écrire les nombres suivants en toutes lettres.

1. 6 _____

2. 14 _____

3. 23 _____

4. 28 _____

5. 35 _____

6. 39 _____

7. 41 _____

8. 46 _____

9. 49 _____

10. 52 _____

Ordinal numbers

Ordinal numbers, for the most part, follow a regular pattern, ending with **-ième**. **Premier/première** (*first*) and **dernier/dernière** (*last*) are the exceptions.

premier, première	*first*
deuxième	*second*
troisième	*third*
quatrième	*fourth*
cinquième	*fifth*
sixième	*sixth*
septième	*seventh*
huitième	*eighth*
neuvième	*ninth*
dixième	*tenth*
vingtième	*twentieth*
vingt et unième	*twenty-first*
vingt-deuxième	*twenty-second*
vingt-troisième	*twenty-third*
trentième	*thirtieth*
quarantième	*fortieth*
cinquantième	*fiftieth*

In France, **le premier étage** corresponds to the American second floor. The American first or ground floor is called **le rez-de-chaussée** in France. Note the following examples:

La première fois que j'ai pris l'avion, j'avais cinq ans.	*The first time I took the plane, I was five years old.*
L'appartement d'Olivier est **au dixième étage.**	*Olivier's apartment is on the eleventh floor.*

VOCABULAIRE

l'accès haut-débit (*m.*)	*high-speed Internet access*	**une adresse IP**	*an Internet protocol address*
un administrateur, une administratrice de site	*a webmaster*	**les autoroutes de l'information** (*m.pl.*)	*information highways*
une adresse URL	*a URL*	**une bibliothèque numérique**	*a digital library*

---

un blog	a blog	naviguer	to browse
un domaine	a domain	une page d'accueil	a home page
une fenêtre	a window	une page Web	a Web page
un fil RSS	an RSS feed	un pirate	a hacker
une foire aux questions (FAQ)	frequently asked questions (FAQ)	rechercher	to search
		un site Web	a website
un fournisseur d'accès	an access provider	un serveur	a server (Internet)
glisser-déposer	to drag and drop	un signet	a bookmark
un(e) internaute	a cybernaut, a Web user	surfer	to surf
		la Toile	the World Wide Web
un moteur de recherche	a search engine	le Web 2.0 (Web deux point zéro)	Web 2.0

EXERCICE 26·2

Traduire en anglais les phrases suivantes.

1. Il a perdu pour la troisième fois.

_____

2. J'habite au trente et unième étage.

_____

3. Elle a vendu sa deuxième voiture.

_____

4. C'est son cinquante-huitième anniversaire.

_____

5. Nous avons fait du ski pour la première fois.

_____

6. C'est la quatrième fois que nous nous croisons dans la rue.

_____

7. Il a obtenu la quarante-huitième place.

_____

8. J'adore la neuvième symphonie de Beethoven.

_____

9. Il habite au coin de la vingt-troisième rue et de la septième avenue.

_____

10. C'est sa deuxième année?

_____

The numbers 50 to 99

Last time we stopped counting at fifty, right? OK, let's keep going.

cinquante	*fifty*
cinquante et un	*fifty-one*
cinquante-deux	*fifty-two*
cinquante-trois	*fifty-three*
cinquante-quatre	*fifty-four*
cinquante-cinq	*fifty-five*
cinquante-six	*fifty-six*
cinquante-sept	*fifty-seven*
cinquante-huit	*fifty-eight*
cinquante-neuf	*fifty-nine*
soixante	*sixty*
soixante et un	*sixty-one*
soixante-deux	*sixty-two*
soixante-trois	*sixty-three*
soixante-quatre	*sixty-four*
soixante-cinq	*sixty-five*
soixante-six	*sixty-six*
soixante-sept	*sixty-seven*
soixante-huit	*sixty-eight*
soixante-neuf	*sixty-nine*
soixante-dix	*seventy*

From seventy-one to seventy-nine, you add the teen numbers.

soixante et onze	*seventy-one*
soixante-douze	*seventy-two*
soixante-treize	*seventy-three*
soixante-quatorze	*seventy-four*
soixante-quinze	*seventy-five*
soixante-seize	*seventy-six*
soixante-dix-sept	*seventy-seven*
soixante-dix-huit	*seventy-eight*
soixante-dix-neuf	*seventy-nine*

Eighty is really four times twenty. Therefore from eighty to ninety-nine, you'll keep adding to **quatre-vingts**. Note that **quatre-vingts** has an **-s**. But once you attach another number to **quatre-vingts**, the **-s** will drop.

quatre-vingts	*eighty*
quatre-vingt-un	*eighty-one*
quatre-vingt-deux	*eighty-two*
quatre-vingt-trois	*eighty-three*
quatre-vingt-quatre	*eighty-four*
quatre-vingt-cinq	*eighty-five*
quatre-vingt-six	*eighty-six*
quatre-vingt-sept	*eighty-seven*
quatre-vingt-huit	*eighty-eight*
quatre-vingt-neuf	*eighty-nine*
quatre-vingt-dix	*ninety*
quatre-vingt-onze	*ninety-one*
quatre-vingt-douze	*ninety-two*
quatre-vingt-treize	*ninety-three*
quatre-vingt-quatorze	*ninety-four*

quatre-vingt-quinze	*ninety-five*
quatre-vingt-seize	*ninety-six*
quatre-vingt-dix-sept	*ninety-seven*
quatre-vingt-dix-huit	*ninety-eight*
quatre-vingt-dix-neuf	*ninety-nine*

Transcrire en chiffres les nombres suivants.

1. cinquante-trois _____

2. cinquante-neuf _____

3. soixante-deux _____

4. soixante-dix _____

5. soixante et onze _____

6. soixante-dix-huit _____

7. quatre-vingt-trois _____

8. quatre-vingt-sept _____

9. quatre-vingt-dix _____

10. quatre-vingt-treize _____

The numbers 100 to 999

Now we have reached one hundred! Let's keep going.

cent	*one hundred*
cent un	*one hundred one*
cent deux	*one hundred two*
cent trois	*one hundred three*
cent quatre	*one hundred four*
cent cinq	*one hundred five*
cent six	*one hundred six*
cent sept	*one hundred seven*
cent huit	*one hundred eight*
cent neuf	*one hundred nine*
cent dix	*one hundred ten*
cent onze	*one hundred eleven*
cent douze	*one hundred twelve*
cent treize	*one hundred thirteen*
cent quatorze	*one hundred fourteen*
cent quinze	*one hundred fifteen*
cent vingt	*one hundred twenty*
cent vingt et un	*one hundred twenty-one*
cent vingt-deux	*one hundred twenty-two*
cent trente	*one hundred thirty*

cent trente et un	*one hundred thirty-one*
cent trente-deux	*one hundred thirty-two*
cent quarante	*one hundred forty*
cent quarante et un	*one hundred forty-one*
cent quarante-deux	*one hundred forty-two*
cent cinquante	*one hundred fifty*
cent soixante	*one hundred sixty*
cent soixante-dix	*one hundred seventy*
cent soixante et onze	*one hundred seventy-one*
cent soixante-douze	*one hundred seventy-two*
cent quatre-vingts	*one hundred eighty*
cent quatre-vingt-un	*one hundred eighty-one*
cent quatre-vingt-dix	*one hundred ninety*
cent quatre-vingt-onze	*one hundred ninety-one*
cent quatre-vingt-douze	*one hundred ninety-two*

EXERCICE
26·4

Écrire les nombres suivants en toutes lettres.

1. 101 _____

2. 114 _____

3. 126 _____

4. 139 _____

5. 145 _____

6. 156 _____

7. 160 _____

8. 178 _____

9. 181 _____

10. 199 _____

Add an -s to **cent** greater than one hundred (**deux cents, trois cents**), except when **cent** is followed by another number.

deux cents	*two hundred*
trois cents	*three hundred*
quatre cents	*four hundred*
cinq cents	*five hundred*
six cents	*six hundred*
sept cents	*seven hundred*
huit cents	*eight hundred*
neuf cents	*nine hundred*

Note the following examples:

huit cent vingt-quatre	*eight hundred twenty-four*
deux cent quatre-vingt-trois	*two hundred eighty-three*

Traduire (en toutes lettres) les nombres suivants.

1. two hundred twelve _____

2. three hundred fifteen _____

3. four hundred twenty _____

4. five hundred thirty-one _____

5. six hundred twenty-three _____

6. seven hundred ninety _____

7. eight hundred forty-eight _____

8. nine hundred four _____

9. six hundred forty-five _____

10. one hundred one _____

Écrire les nombres suivants en toutes lettres.

1. 205 _____

2. 389 _____

3. 456 _____

4. 504 _____

5. 678 _____

6. 745 _____

7. 800 _____

8. 815 _____

9. 901 _____

10. 940 _____

The numbers 1,000 and greater

Never add an -s to **mille** (*one thousand*).

mille	*one thousand*
mille un	*one thousand one*
mille deux	*one thousand two*

mille dix	*one thousand ten*
mille vingt	*one thousand twenty*
mille trente	*one thousand thirty*
mille onze	*one thousand eleven*
mille vingt-trois	*one thousand twenty-three*
mille deux cents	*one thousand two hundred*
mille deux cent cinquante-trois	*one thousand two hundred fifty-three*
mille quatre cents	*one thousand four hundred*
deux mille	*two thousand*
deux mille cinq cents	*two thousand five hundred*
deux mille sept cent soixante-treize	*two thousand seven hundred seventy-three*
dix mille	*ten thousand*

In French, an **-s** is added to **million** and **milliard** greater than **un** (*one*).

un million	*a million*
un milliard	*a billion*

quatre millions trois cent mille quatre cent vingt-cinq	*four million three hundred thousand four hundred twenty-five*
deux milliards quatre cent millions cinq cent mille	*two billion four hundred million five hundred thousand*

Years are written out as follows in French:

1978   **mille neuf cent soixante-dix-huit**
          or
        dix-neuf cent soixante-dix-huit
2008   **deux mille huit**

EXERCICE
26·7

Écrire les nombres suivants en toutes lettres.

1. 1 005 _____

2. 2 456 _____

3. 3 021 _____

4. 4 789 _____

5. 10 450 _____

6. 24 008 _____

7. 170 890 _____

8. 1 230 000 _____

9. 30 030 000 _____

10. 1 600 000 000 _____

Dans les phrases suivantes, transcrire les nombres.

1. Leur bibliothèque numérique sera prête en 2015.

_____

2. Cet appartement coûte 150 000 euros.

_____

3. Hier, j'ai bu du Saint-Émilion 1978.

_____

4. Le soixantième Festival de Cannes a lieu en mai 2007.

_____

5. Il y a plus d'1 000 000 000 d'étoiles dans le ciel.

_____

6. Il a remporté la médaille d'or du 1 500 mètres.

_____

7. D'après une étude en 2006, plus d'1 000 000 de personnes écrivent un blog en France.

_____

8. Victor Hugo est mort en 1885.

_____

9. Cet administrateur de site gagne 5 000 euros par mois.

_____

10. Nous sommes plus de 6 000 000 000 sur cette planète.

_____

Pot pourri

VOCABULAIRE

un aspirateur	*a vacuum cleaner*	**une fourchette**	*a fork*
une assiette	*a plate, a (soup) bowl*	**un grille-pain**	*a toaster*
		un lave-vaisselle	*a dishwasher*
un bol	*a bowl, wide cup (for morning coffee)*	**une louche**	*a ladle*
		une nappe	*a tablecloth*
		un ouvre-boîtes	*a can opener*
une cafetière	*a coffee pot*	**un plateau**	*a tray*
une casserole	*a pan, a pot*	**une poêle**	*a frying pan*
un congélateur	*a freezer*	**un réfrigérateur**	*a refrigerator*
un couteau	*a knife*	**une serviette**	*a napkin*
une cuillère	*a spoon*	**une soucoupe**	*a saucer*
une cuisinière	*a stove*	**une tasse**	*a cup*
un four	*an oven*	**une théière**	*a teapot*
un four à micro-ondes	*a microwave oven*	**un tire-bouchon**	*a corkscrew*
		un verre	*a glass*

In previous chapters we have seen how complicated verbs and their conjugations can be. Some verbs can be very capricious as they change preposition and meaning. Here are a few more examples, just for the fun of it!

Verbs that use different prepositions

It is important to remember that the same verb can be used with no preposition, simply followed by a direct object noun, or followed by different prepositions. The meaning of the verb changes. Such verbs have to be memorized with their meanings. For example:

finir *to finish, to end*	
As-tu fini ton café?	*Have you finished your coffee?*
Elle **a fini** le tournage du film.	*She completed the shooting of the film.*
Elle **n'a pas fini d'**écrire son article.	*She hasn't finished writing her article.*
J'ai fini de manger.	*I am done eating.*
Il **a fini par** lui dire la vérité.	*He finally told her the truth.*
Elle **a fini par** accepter.	*She finally accepted.*

commencer to begin, to start

J'ai **commencé** un nouveau livre.	*I started a new book.*
Tu **as** bien **commencé** l'année?	*Did you start the year on the right foot?*
Il **commence à** pleuvoir.	*It's starting to rain.*
Tout à coup, il **a commencé à** pleurer.	*Suddenly, he started crying.*
Elle **a commencé par** se présenter.	*She started by introducing herself.*
On **va commencer par** des escargots.	*We'll start with snails.*

décider to decide

C'est **décidé**.	*It's (has been) decided.*
J'ai **décidé d'**aller au cinéma.	*I decided to go to the movies.*
Nous **avons décidé d'**aller au Japon.	*We decided to go to Japan.*
Ils **se sont** enfin **décidés à** se marier.	*They finally decided to get (got around to getting) married.*
Décide-toi!	*Make up your mind!*

demander to ask

Il lui **demande** une explication.	*He is asking her for an explanation.*
Demande-moi tout ce que tu veux.	*Ask me anything you want.*
Elle nous **a demandé de** ne rien dire.	*She asked us not to say anything.*
Je vous **demande d'**attendre.	*I am asking you to wait.*
Je **demande à** voir les preuves.	*I'm asking to see the evidence.*
Le patient **demande à** quitter l'hôpital.	*The patient is asking (permission) to leave the hospital.*

donner to give

Je te le **donnerai** demain.	*I'll give it to you tomorrow.*
Elle m'**a donné** sa réponse.	*She gave me her answer.*
L'hôtel **donne sur** la mer?	*The hotel faces the sea?*
Mon appartement **donne sur** la Place de la Bastille.	*My apartment looks out onto Place de la Bastille.*

jouer to play

Il faut **jouer le jeu**.	*You've got to play the game.*
Marie et Émile **jouent aux échecs**.	*Marie and Émile play chess.*
Marc **joue au poker** tous les jeudis.	*Marc plays poker every Thursday.*
Ils **jouent au chat et à la souris**.	*They are playing cat and mouse.*
Thierry **joue de la guitare**.	*Thierry plays the guitar.*
Pierre **joue de l'accordéon**.	*Pierre plays the accordion.*
Valérie aime **jouer des castagnettes**.	*Valérie likes to play castanets.*

parler to speak

Laisse-moi **parler à** ta sœur.	*Let me talk to your sister.*
Puis-je **lui parler**?	*May I talk to her/him?*
Il **a parlé de toi** à la radio.	*He talked about you on the radio.*
De quoi voulez-vous **parler** aujourd'hui?	*What do you want to talk about today?*

croire to believe

La police **le croit**.	*The police believe him.*
Je **crois sa version** de l'histoire.	*I believe his version of the story.*
Il ne **croit** pas **à la magie**.	*He doesn't believe in magic.*
Je **crois au progrès**.	*I believe in progress.*
Crois-tu **en Dieu**?	*Do you believe in God?*
Je **crois en toi**, mon fils.	*I have confidence in you, my son.*

Je **crois en l'humanité.**	*I have faith in mankind.*
Je **crois pouvoir** vous **dire** ce qui s'est réellement passé.	*I think I can tell you what really happened.*
Il **croit avoir garé** sa voiture dans cette rue.	*He thinks he parked his car in that street.*

tenir to hold

Je **tiens à mes amis.**	*I am attached to my friends.*
Je **tiens à voir** ce film.	*I am eager to see that movie.*
Tu **tiens de ton père.**	*You look like your father.*
Elle **tient de sa mère.**	*She takes after her mother.*

rêver to dream

La nuit dernière, j'**ai rêvé de lui.**	*Last night I dreamt about him.*
Patrice **rêve à une autre vie.**	*Patrice is dreaming of a different life.*
Ils **rêvent à un avenir meilleur.**	*They are hoping for better days (a better future).*

EXERCICE
27·1

Compléter avec la préposition appropriée.

1. Elle aime jouer _____ la clarinette.

2. Paul a décidé _____ partir tôt.

3. La chambre donne _____ une cour très calme.

4. Je crois _____ la vertu médicinale des plantes.

5. J'ai rêvé _____ toi.

6. Émilie tient _____ ses livres.

7. Hier, nous avons parlé _____ toi.

8. Est-ce qu'il croit _____ Dieu?

9. Nous nous sommes décidés _____ prendre de très longues vacances.

10. Elle m'a demandé _____ fermer la porte.

The verb **manquer**

Note how the preposition (or lack of preposition) changes the meaning of the verb **manquer** (*to miss*) in these examples:

J'**ai manqué le cours** la semaine dernière.	*I missed the class last week.*
Elle **a manqué le début** de la pièce.	*She missed the beginning of the play.*
Cette pièce **manque d'air.**	*This room lacks air.*
Tu **manques de générosité.**	*You lack generosity.*
Je **ne manque de rien.**	*I lack nothing.*
Frédérique **a manqué à sa promesse.**	*Frédérique failed to keep her word.*
Laura **a manqué à tous ses devoirs.**	*Laura neglected all of her duties.*
Tu **me manques.**	*I miss you (i.e., you are lacking to me)*
Paris **me manque.**	*I miss Paris.*

Traduire en anglais les phrases suivantes.

1. Paul me manque.

_____

2. Mon frère a manqué à sa parole.

_____

3. Cet écrivain manque de talent.

_____

4. J'ai manqué le début du cours.

_____

5. Le patron a manqué à ses devoirs.

_____

Whatever, whenever, wherever, whoever

The present subjunctive is used with the indefinite expressions that are the French equivalents of *whatever, whenever, wherever,* and *whoever.*

When the English *whatever* is followed by subject + verb, use the neuter **quoi que** + present subjunctive.

Quoi que tu fasses, je t'aimerai toujours.	*Whatever you do, I will always love you.*
Quoi qu'elle dise, je ne changerai pas d'avis.	*Whatever she says, I will not change my mind.*

When the English *whatever* is followed by a noun, use **quel que** (**quelle que, quels que, quelles que**) + the subjunctive of **être** + noun. **Quel que** agrees in gender and number with the noun that follows it.

Quel que soit votre conseil, je prendrai rendez-vous avec le patron.	*Whatever your advice, I will make an appointment with the boss.*
Quelle que soit leur décision, elle démissionnera.	*Whatever their decision, she will resign.*

Look at the following examples that express *wherever* (**où que**) in French:

Où que tu sois, appelle-moi.	*Wherever you are, call me.*
Où qu'elle aille, il ira aussi.	*Wherever she goes, he will go, too.*

The subjunctive is also used following the expression of *whoever* (**qui que**). For example:

Qui que tu sois, tu peux lui parler.	*Whoever you are, you can talk to him.*
Qui que vous soyez, ouvrez votre cœur.	*Whoever you are, open up your heart.*

*Traduire les phrases entre parenthèses en utilisant **tu** si nécessaire.*

1. (*Whatever you say*), je reste sur ma position.

_____

2. (*Whatever her decision*), la mienne est prise.

_____

3. (*Whoever you are*), je ne t'autorise pas à me parler sur ce ton.

_____

4. (*Wherever you go*), j'irai avec toi.

_____

5. (*Whoever she is*), elle n'est pas autorisée à venir!

_____

6. (*Whatever you think*), je m'en moque.

_____

7. (*Wherever they live*), je les retrouverai.

_____

8. (*Whatever their suggestion*), je trouve mon idée très bonne.

_____

9. (*Whoever you are*), aide-moi.

_____

10. (*Whatever your mother may think*), c'est ta décision.

_____

Avoir beau and quitte à

The expression **avoir beau** + infinitive can usually be translated by *although* or *however*.

Il a beau être aisé, il n'est pas heureux.	*Although he has a lot of money, he is not happy.*
Il a beau dormir, il est toujours fatigué.	*However much he sleeps, he is always tired.*
Il avait beau habiter au bord de la mer, il n'a jamais appris à nager.	*Although he lived by the sea, he never learned how to swim.*
Elle aura beau essayer, ce sera inutile.	*However much she tries, it will be useless.*

The expression **quitte à** + infinitive can usually be translated by *even if it means*.

Je vais lui dire ce que je pense, **quitte à me fâcher** avec elle.	*Even if it means arguing with her, I am going to tell her what I think.*

Quitte à payer plus, je préfère voyager en première classe.	*Even if it means paying more, I prefer traveling first class.*
Je n'accepterai pas leur offre, **quitte à être renvoyé**.	*I won't accept their offer even if it means being fired.*
Quitte à s'ennuyer, ils préfèrent rester chez eux.	*They prefer to stay home even if it means being bored.*

*Traduire les phrases suivantes en utilisant **tu** si nécessaire.*

1. Even if it means not sleeping, I am going with you to that party.

_____

2. He will resign even if it means having financial problems.

_____

3. However intelligent he is, he is very lonely.

_____

4. Although they are friends, they cannot talk politics together.

_____

5. I'll take two years off even if it means losing my position.

_____

6. However hard they tried, they failed.

_____

7. However magnificent this teapot is, it is not worth 200 euros.

_____

8. Although you are swearing to tell the truth, I still have doubts.

_____

9. Even if it means bothering you, I need to ask you a few questions.

_____

10. He will not leave the room even if it means bothering everyone.

_____

Verb tables

Note that in these tables, verb forms are shown without subject pronouns. In context, subject pronouns are always used in French (except with the imperative, infinitive, and present participle).

Regular verbs

There are three categories of regular verbs: those ending in **-er**, those ending in **-re**, and those ending in **-ir**.

Simple tenses

Indicative mood

PRESENT INDICATIVE

regarder	regarde	regardes	regarde	regardons	regardez	regardent
vendre	vends	vends	vend	vendons	vendez	vendent
partir	pars	pars	part	partons	partez	partent

IMPERFECT INDICATIVE

regarder	regardais	regardais	regardait	regardions	regardiez	regardaient
vendre	vendais	vendais	vendait	vendions	vendiez	vendaient
partir	partais	partais	partait	partions	partiez	partaient

HISTORICAL PAST

regarder	regardai	regardas	regarda	regardâmes	regardâtes	regardèrent
vendre	vendis	vendis	vendit	vendîmes	vendîtes	vendirent
partir	partis	partis	partit	partîmes	partîtes	partirent

SIMPLE FUTURE

regarder	regarderai	regarderas	regardera	regarderons	regarderez	regarderont
vendre	vendrai	vendras	vendra	vendrons	vendrez	vendront
partir	partirai	partiras	partira	partirons	partirez	partiront

CONDITIONAL MOOD

regarder	regarderais	regarderais	regarderait	regarderions	regarderiez	regarderaient
vendre	vendrais	vendrais	vendrait	vendrions	vendriez	vendraient
partir	partirais	partirais	partirait	partirions	partiriez	partiraient

regarder	regarde	regard**ons**	regard**ez**
vendre	vends	vend**ons**	vend**ez**
partir	pars	part**ons**	part**ez**

Subjunctive mood

PRESENT SUBJUNCTIVE

regarder	regarde	regardes	regarde	regard**ions**	regard**iez**	regard**ent**
vendre	vende	vend**es**	vende	vend**ions**	vend**iez**	vend**ent**
partir	parte	part**es**	parte	part**ions**	part**iez**	part**ent**

IMPERFECT SUBJUNCTIVE

regarder	regard**asse**	regard**asses**	regard**ât**	regard**assions**	regard**assiez**	regard**assent**
vendre	vend**isse**	vend**isses**	vend**ît**	vend**issions**	vend**issiez**	vend**issent**
partir	part**isse**	part**isses**	part**ît**	part**issions**	part**issiez**	part**issent**

Compound tenses

Compound tenses are formed with the appropriate tense of the auxiliary verb, either **avoir** or **être**, followed by the past participle of the verb.

Indicative mood

CONVERSATIONAL PAST OR PRESENT PERFECT

regarder	ai regardé	as regardé	a regardé	avons regardé	avez regardé	ont regardé
vendre	ai vendu	as vendu	a vendu	avons vendu	avez vendu	ont vendu
partir	suis parti(e)	es parti(e)	est parti(e)	sommes parti(e)s	êtes parti(e)(s)	sont parti(e)s

PLUPERFECT INDICATIVE

regarder	avais regardé	avais regardé	avait regardé	avions regardé	aviez regardé	avaient regardé
vendre	avais vendu	avais vendu	avait vendu	avions vendu	aviez vendu	avaient vendu
partir	étais parti(e)	étais parti(e)	était parti(e)	étions parti(e)s	étiez parti(e)(s)	étaient parti(e)s

PAST PERFECT

regarder	eus regardé	eus regardé	eut regardé	eûmes regardé	eûtes regardé	eurent regardé
vendre	eus vendu	eus vendu	eut vendu	eûmes vendu	eûtes vendu	eurent vendu
partir	fus parti(e)	fus parti(e)	fut parti(e)	fûmes parti(e)s	fûtes parti(e)(s)	furent parti(e)s

FUTURE PERFECT

regarder	aurai regardé	auras regardé	aura regardé	aurons regardé	aurez regardé	auront regardé
vendre	aurai vendu	auras vendu	aura vendu	aurons vendu	aurez vendu	auront vendu
partir	serai parti(e)	seras parti(e)	sera parti(e)	serons parti(e)s	serez parti(e)(s)	seront parti(e)s

PAST CONDITIONAL

regarder	aurais regardé	aurais regardé	aurait regardé	aurions regardé	auriez regardé	auraient regardé
vendre	aurais vendu	aurais vendu	aurait vendu	aurions vendu	auriez vendu	auraient vendu
partir	serais parti(e)	serais parti(e)	serait parti(e)	serions parti(e)s	seriez parti(e)(s)	seraient parti(e)s

Subjunctive mood

regarder	aie regardé	aies regardé	ait regardé	ayons regardé	ayez regardé	aient regardé
vendre	aie vendu	aies vendu	ait vendu	ayons vendu	ayez vendu	aient vendu
partir	sois parti(e)	sois parti(e)	soit parti(e)	soyons parti(e)s	soyez parti(e)(s)	soient parti(e)s

PLUPERFECT SUBJUNCTIVE

regarder	eusse regardé	eusses regardé	eût regardé	eussions regardé	eussiez regardé	eussent regardé
vendre	eusse vendu	eusses vendu	eût vendu	eussions vendu	eussiez vendu	eussent vendu
partir	fusse parti(e)	fusses parti(e)	fût parti(e)	fussions parti(e)s	fussiez parti(e)(s)	fussent parti(e)s

Verbs with spelling changes

Verbs ending in **-ger** include the -**e**- as part of the stem with endings that begin with the letter **a** or **o**. Examples: **manger (nous mangeons)**, **plonger (il plongeait)**, **ronger (il rongea)**, **arranger (nous arrangeâmes)**.

Verbs ending in **-er** change the **c** to **ç** when endings begin with the letter **a** or **o**. Examples: **commencer (nous commençons)**, **lancer (elle lança)**.

PRESENT INDICATIVE

manger	mange	manges	mange	mangeons	mangez	mangent
commencer	commence	commences	commence	commençons	commencez	commencent

IMPERFECT INDICATIVE

manger	mangeais	mangeais	mangeait	mangions	mangiez	mangeaient
commencer	commençais	commençais	commençait	commencions	commenciez	commençaient

Verbs with stem changes

A number of verbs ending in **-er** change their stem depending on the verb tense. These changes may involve changes in spelling or additions/changes of accent. Here are some of the more common ones:

PRESENT INDICATIVE

acheter	achète	achètes	achète	achetons	achetez	achètent
appeler	appelle	appelles	appelle	appelons	appelez	appellent
payer	paie/paye	paies/payes	paie/paye	payons	payez	paient/payent
préférer	préfère	préfères	préfère	préférons	préférez	préfèrent

IMPERFECT INDICATIVE

acheter	achetais	achetais	achetait	achetions	achetiez	achetaient
appeler	appelais	appelais	appelait	appelions	appeliez	appelaient
payer	payais	payais	payait	payions	payiez	payaient
préférer	préférais	préférais	préférait	préférions	préfériez	préféraient

Other verbs that follow the same patterns:

Verbs like **acheter: mener, amener, emmener, se promener, lever, se lever, élever**
Verbs like **appeler: se rappeler, jeter**
Verbs like **payer: essayer, employer, ennuyer, essuyer, nettoyer**
Verbs like **préférer: espérer, répéter, célébrer, considérer, suggérer, protéger**

Irregular verbs

Here is a list of some of the more commonly used irregular verbs. The infinitive and past participle are given for each verb, along with a full conjugation of the present indicative tense.

Indicative mood

INFINITIVE	PAST PARTICIPLE			PRESENT INDICATIVE			
acquérir	acquis	acquiers	acquiers	acquiert	acquérons	acquérez	acquièrent
aller	allé	vais	vas	va	allons	allez	vont
apprendre	appris	apprends	apprends	apprend	apprenons	apprenez	apprennent
(s')asseoir	assis	assieds	assieds	assied	asseyons	asseyez	asseyent
avoir	eu	ai	as	a	avons	avez	ont
battre	battu	bats	bats	bat	battons	battez	battent
boire	bu	bois	bois	boit	buvons	buvez	boivent
comprendre	compris	comprends	comprends	comprend	comprenons	comprenez	comprennent
conclure	conclus	conclus	conclus	conclut	concluons	concluez	concluent
conduire	conduit	conduis	conduis	conduit	conduisons	conduisez	conduisent
connaître	connu	connais	connais	connaît	connaissons	connaissez	connaissent
courir	couru	cours	cours	court	courons	courez	courent
craindre	craint	crains	crains	craint	craignons	craignez	craignent
croire	cru	crois	crois	croit	croyons	croyez	croient
cueillir	cueilli	cueille	cueilles	cueille	cueillons	cueillez	cueillent
devoir	dû	dois	dois	doit	devons	devez	doivent
dire	dit	dis	dis	dit	disons	dites	disent
dormir	dormi	dors	dors	dort	dormons	dormez	dorment
écrire	écrit	écris	écris	écrit	écrivons	écrivez	écrivent
envoyer	envoyé	envoie	envoies	envoie	envoyons	envoyez	envoient
être	été	suis	es	est	sommes	êtes	sont
faire	fait	fais	fais	fait	faisons	faites	font
falloir	fallu			faut			
fuir	fui	fuis	fuis	fuit	fuyons	fuyez	fuient
haïr	haï	hais	hais	hait	haïssons	haïssez	haïssent
lire	lu	lis	lis	lit	lisons	lisez	lisent
mettre	mis	mets	mets	met	mettons	mettez	mettent
mourir	mort	meurs	meurs	meurt	mourons	mourez	meurent
naître	né	nais	nais	naît	naissons	naissez	naissent
offrir	offert	offre	offres	offre	offrons	offrez	offrent
ouvrir	ouvert	ouvre	ouvres	ouvre	ouvrons	ouvrez	ouvrent
peindre	peint	peins	peins	peint	peignons	peignez	peignent
plaire	plu	plais	plais	plaît	plaisons	plaisez	plaisent
pleuvoir	plu			pleut			
pouvoir	pu	peux/puis	peux	peut	pouvons	pouvez	peuvent
prendre	pris	prends	prends	prend	prenons	prenez	prennent
recevoir	reçu	reçois	reçois	reçoit	recevons	recevez	reçoivent
résoudre	résolu	résous	résous	résout	résolvons	résolvez	résolvent
rire	ri	ris	ris	rit	rions	riez	rient
savoir	su	sais	sais	sait	savons	savez	savent
suivre	suivi	suis	suis	suit	suivons	suivez	suivent
tenir	tenu	tiens	tiens	tient	tenons	tenez	tiennent
vaincre	vaincu	vaincs	vaincs	vainc	vainquons	vainquez	vainquent
venir	venu	viens	viens	vient	venons	venez	viennent
vivre	vécu	vis	vis	vit	vivons	vivez	vivent
voir	vu	vois	vois	voit	voyons	voyez	voient
vouloir	voulu	veux	veux	veut	voulons	voulez	veulent

French-English glossary

Regular adjectives in French are listed in their masculine singular form.

A

à carreaux checked
à fleurs flowered
à la campagne in the country
à la mer by the sea
à la montagne in the mountains
à la plage at the beach
à midi at noon
à minuit at midnight
à peine hardly
à plis pleated
à pois polka-dotted
à rayures striped
à volants flounced
abonner à (s') to subscribe to
accepter to accept
accès haut-débit (*m.*) high-speed access
accessoire (*m.*) accessory, stage prop
accompagner to accompany
accomplir to accomplish
accorder to grant
accroupir (s') to squat, to crouch
accueillir to welcome
accusé(e) (*m./f.*) accused (person)
acheter to buy
achever to complete
acquérir to acquire
acteur, actrice (*m./f.*) actor, actress
actuel(le) present, present day
actuellement currently
addition (*f.*) bill
administrateur, administratrice de site (*m./f.*) webmaster
ADN (*m.*) DNA
adoucir to soften, to mellow
adresse IP (*f.*) Internet protocol address
adresse URL (*f.*) URL
affaires (*f.pl.*) business
affiche (*f.*) poster
affirmer to say, to claim
agence de voyages (*f.*) travel agency
agrandir to enlarge

agréable pleasant
agression (*f.*) mugging, assault
aimer to like, to love
ainsi thus
ajouter to add
allemand (*m.*) German
aller to go
allumer to turn on
alors que while, whereas
améliorer to improve
amende (*f.*) fine
amer, amère bitter
amusant funny
analyser to analyze
ancêtre (*m./f.*) ancestor
anglais (*m.*) English
anniversaire (*m.*) birthday
annoncer to announce
annuler to cancel
antiquaire (*m./f.*) antiques dealer
apercevoir to see, to perceive
apercevoir (s') to realize
appareil (*m.*) (still) camera, device
appeler to call
applaudir to applaud
apprécier to value
apprendre to learn
après que after
aquarelle (*f.*) watercolor
arabe (*m.*) Arabic
argent (*m.*) money
armoire (*f.*) wardrobe, cupboard
armoire à pharmacie (*f.*) medicine cabinet
arracher to pull out
arrêter to arrest
arriver to arrive
arriver sur les lieux du crime to arrive at the crime scene
artisan(e) (*m./f.*) craftsman, craftswoman
ascenseur (*m.*) elevator
assaisonner to season
assister to attend

assurer to ensure, to maintain
attendre to wait
attentat (*m.*) terrorist attack
atterrir to land
attraper to catch
aube (*f.*) dawn
augmentation de salaire (*f.*) salary increase
augmenter to increase
aujourd'hui today
aussitôt que as soon as
autobus (*m.*) bus
autoroutes de l'information (*f.pl.*) information highways
autrefois formerly
avancer to advance
avenir (*m.*) future
aventure (*f.*) adventure
avion (*m.*) plane
avoir to have
avoir (trente-cinq) ans to be (thirty-five) years old
avoir besoin to need
avoir chaud to be hot
avoir de la chance to be lucky
avoir envie to feel like
avoir faim to be hungry
avoir froid to be cold
avoir honte to be ashamed
avoir l'air to seem, to look
avoir la grippe to have the flu
avoir mal to hurt, to have pain
avoir mal à la tête to have a headache
avoir mal au dos to have a backache
avoir mal au ventre to have a stomachache
avoir peur to be afraid
avoir raison to be right
avoir soif to be thirsty
avoir tort to be wrong
avoir un rhume to have a cold
avouer to confess

B

bague (*f.*) ring
bail (*m.*) lease
baisser to lower
baisser le prix to lower the price
balancer to swing, to finger (betray)
balcon (*m.*) balcony
banque (*f.*) bank
banque de données (*f.*) data bank
base de données (*f.*) database
bateau (*m.*) boat
bâtir to build
battre to beat
bavarder to chat
beau (bel, belle) beautiful
beige beige
belle-sœur (*f.*) sister-in-law

bénir to bless
bibliothèque (*f.*) bookcase, library
bibliothèque numérique (*f.*) digital library
bijou (*m.*) jewel
bijouterie (*f.*) jewelry store
blanc(he) white
blanchiment d'argent (*m.*) money laundering
bleu blue
bleu ciel sky blue
bleu clair light blue
bleu foncé dark blue
bleu marine navy blue
blog (*m.*) blog
boire to drink
bois (*m.*) wood
boîte (*f.*) box
boîte vocale (*f.*) voice mail
bon(ne) good
bon marché cheap, inexpensive
bondé crowded
bordeaux burgundy (*color*)
bouche (*f.*) mouth
boucher, bouchère (*m./f.*) butcher
boucherie (*f.*) butcher shop
bouger to move
bouillir to boil
boulanger, boulangère (*m./f.*) baker
bouteille (*f.*) bottle
braiser to braise
brancher to plug in
bras (*m.*) arm
brosser to brush
brouillon (*m.*) first draft
broyer to grind, to crush
bruiner to drizzle
bruit (*m.*) noise
brûler to burn
buffet (*m.*) sideboard
bureau (*m.*) office, desk
bureau de tabac (*m.*) tobacco shop

C

cadeau (*m.*) gift
cambriolage (*m.*) burglary
cambrioler to burglarize
canapé (*m.*) sofa
caraméliser to caramelize
casser to break
céder to yield
célébrer to celebrate
célibataire single
cesser de to stop, to cease
chaise (*f.*) chair
chaleur (*f.*) heat, warmth
champignon (*m.*) mushroom
changer to change

chanson (*f.*) song
chantage (*m.*) blackmail
chanter to sing
chapeau (*m.*) hat
chaque année every year
chaque jour every day
chaque mois every month
chaque semaine every week
charmant charming
chat (*m.*) cat
château (*m.*) castle
chaud hot
chaussure (*f.*) shoe
chef-d'œuvre (*m.*) masterpiece
chemin (*m.*) path
cheminée (*f.*) chimney, fireplace
chemise (*f.*) shirt
cher, chère expensive
chercher to look for
cheveux (*m.pl.*) hair
cheville (*f.*) ankle
chien (*m.*) dog
chinois (*m.*) Chinese
chirurgien(ne) (*m./f.*) surgeon
choisir to choose
chorale (*f.*) chorus
ciel (*m.*) sky
cinéma (*m.*) cinema
au cinéma at the movies
circonstances (*f.pl.*) circumstances
circulation (*f.*) traffic
clavier (*m.*) keyboard
climatisé air-conditioned
cliquer to click
clôture (*f.*) closing
cocher to check off
coffre (*m.*) chest
coiffeur, coiffeuse (*m./f.*) hairdresser
coiffeuse (*f.*) dressing table
collectionneur, collectionneuse (*m./f.*) collector
combien how much
commander to order
comme as, since
comme à l'accoutumée as usual
commencer to begin
commode (*f.*) chest of drawers
comporter to consist of
comprendre to understand
compter to intend, to plan
concurrent(e) (*m./f.*) competitor
conduire to drive
confier to confide
confiserie (*f.*) candy store
confiture (*f.*) jam
conjugaison (*f.*) conjugation
connaître to know

connecter (se) to log on
conseiller to advise
conservateur, conservatrice (*m./f.*) curator
considérer to consider
constater to note, to notice
consulter to consult
convaincre to convince
cordonnier (*m.*) shoemaker
correspondre to correspond
corriger to correct
coude (*m.*) elbow
coulisses (*f.pl.*) backstage, wings
couper to cut
courir to run
cours (*m.*) course
cousin(e) (*m./f.*) cousin
couvrir to cover
craindre to fear
créatif (créative) creative
créole Creole
crier to shout
croire to believe
cueillir to pick (produce)
cuire to cook
cuisine (*f.*) kitchen, cooking

D

d'accord OK, all right
d'habitude usually
d'ordinaire ordinarily
danser to dance
de temps en temps from time to time
débâcle (*f.*) disaster
débarquer to get off
décevoir to disappoint
déchirer to tear up
déclarer to state
décoller to take off (plane)
décontracté casual
décortiquer to shell (shrimp), to husk
défendre to defend, to forbid
défoncer to smash in
dégager to release, to free
déjeuner to have lunch
déléguer to delegate
demain tomorrow
demander to ask
déménager to move
démissionner to resign
déplacer to move
depuis since
déranger to disturb
derrière behind
dès que as soon as
descendre to go down
désirer to desire, to wish

dessiner to draw
détendre to release, to relax
détester to hate
détournement d'avion (*m.*) hijacking
dette (*f.*) debt
devancer to get ahead of
devenir to become
devoir to have to
diamant (*m.*) diamond
dictionnaire (*m.*) dictionary
dinde (*f.*) turkey
dire to say
discuter to discuss
disponible available
disque dur (*m.*) hard drive
divertissement (*m.*) entertainment
divorcé divorced
documentaire (*m.*) documentary
doigt (*m.*) finger
domaine (*m.*) area
donner to give
dormir to sleep
dos (*m.*) back
doublé dubbed
douleur (*f.*) pain
droite (*f.*) right

E

écailler to scale (fish)
échouer à un examen to fail an exam
éclairage (*m.*) lighting
éclaircir to lighten, to clear
écosser to shell (peas)
écouter to listen
écran (*m.*) screen
écraser to crush, to squash
écrire to write
écumer to skim (soup)
effacer to erase
efficace efficient
élève (*m./f.*) student, pupil
élire to elect
embarquer to board
embouteillage (*m.*) traffic jam
émincer to slice thinly
émission (*f.*) broadcast
emmener to take along, to escort
émouvoir to move, to stir (emotion)
emporter to take away
empreinte (*f.*) imprint, print
empreintes digitales (*f.pl.*) fingerprints
emprunter to borrow
encourager to encourage
enfuir (s') to flee
engagement (*m.*) commitment
engager to commit, to hire

enlever to remove
enseigner to teach
ensemble (*m.*) group
ensorceler to bewitch
entendre to hear
entraîner (s') to train
entreprendre to undertake
entrer to enter
envahir to invade
envisager to contemplate
envoyer to send
épanouir (s') to bloom
épeler to sell
épicer to spice
épicier, épicière (*m./f.*) grocer
éplucher to peel (vegetables)
équipe (*f.*) team
escalader to climb
escalier (*m.*) staircase, stairs
escroc (*m.*) crook
escroquerie (*f.*) swindle, fraud
espagnol (*m.*) Spanish
espérer to hope
essuyer to wipe
étage (*m.*) floor
étagère (*f.*) shelf
étant donné que given, in view of
étape (*f.*) stopover (car travel)
étendre to spread out, to extend
étinceler to sparkle, to glitter
étiquette (*f.*) label
étoile (*f.*) star
étranger, étrangère (*m./f.*) stranger, foreigner
être to be
être condamné(e) à to be sentenced to
être rouillé(e) to be rusty
étudiant(e) (*m./f.*) student (college)
étudier to study
Europe (*f.*) Europe
évanouir (s') to faint
éveillé alert, awake
exagérer to exaggerate
examen (*m.*) exam
exiger to demand
expédition (*f.*) expedition
expliquer to explain
explorer to explore
exposition (*f.*) exhibition
exprimer to express
extranet (*m.*) extranet

F

façonner to craft, to manufacture
faire to do, to make
faire des grimaces to make faces
faire l'école buissonnière to play hooky

faire la cuisine to cook
faire la queue to stand in line
faire la sieste to take a nap
faire le ménage to do the housework
faire le plein to fill up (gas)
faire revenir to brown (foods)
faire sauter to sauté (cooking)
faire une offre to bid
falloir to be necessary
famille (*f.*) family
farcir to stuff
fauteuil (*m.*) armchair
favori (*m.*) bookmark
feindre to feign, to pretend
féliciter to congratulate
fenêtre (*f.*) window
fermer to close
fête (*f.*) celebration
feu (*m.*) fire
ficeler to tie
fichier (*m.*) file
fil RSS (*m.*) RSS feed
filière (*f.*) channel(s)
film (*m.*) film, movie
financer to finance
finir to finish
flamber to flambé (cooking)
flâner to stroll
fleur (*f.*) flower
fleuriste (*m./f.*) florist
foire aux questions (FAQ) (*f.*) FAQ
formulaire (*m.*) form (to fill out)
foulard (*m.*) scarf
fournisseur d'accès (*m.*) access provider
frais (fraîche) fresh
français (*m.*) French
frapper to hit
fredonner to hum
fréquemment frequently
frire to fry
fuir to flee
fusillade (*f.*) shoot-out, gun battle

G

gaffe (*f.*) blunder
gagner to win, to earn
garder to keep
garnir to garnish
gaspiller to waste
gauche (*f.*) left (side)
genou (*m.*) knee
gentil(le) kind, nice
gérer to manage
glacer to glaze (cooking)
glisser-déposer drag and drop
gouvernement (*m.*) government

gouverner to govern
grand tall
grandir to grow up
gratiner to brown, to cook au gratin
gravure (*f.*) etching
griller to grill, to toast
grimacer to make faces
gris gray
grossir to put on weight
guerre (*f.*) war
guillotiner to guillotine

H

habiter to live
habitude (*f.*) habit
habituellement usually
hacher to chop, to mince
hanche (*f.*) hip
harcèlement (*m.*) harassment
haricot (*m.*) bean
héberger to host
heureux (heureuse) happy, content, glad
hier yesterday
hindi (*m.*) Hindi
histoire (*f.*) story
horloge (*f.*) clock
horloger (*m.*) watchmaker
huile (*f.*) oil
humeur (*f.*) mood

I

idée (*f.*) idea
ignorer to be unaware
île (*f.*) island
immobilier (*m.*) real estate
impliqué implicated
imprimante (*f.*) printer (device)
imprimer to print
influencer to influence
informatique (*f.*) computer science
inquiet (inquiète) worried
inquiétant disturbing
interdire to forbid
internaute (*m./f.*) cybernaut, Web user
Internet (*m.*) Internet
intranet (*m.*) intranet
intrigue (*f.*) plot
investir to invest
inviter to invite
italien (*m.*) Italian

J

jadis in times past
jambe (*f.*) leg
japonais (*m.*) Japanese
jardin (*m.*) garden

jaune yellow
jeter to throw
jeune young
jouer (à, de) to play
joueur, joueuse (*m./f*) player
journée (*f.*) day
jurer to swear

K

kiosque à journaux (*m.*) newsstand

L

laisser to let
lampe (*f.*) lamp
lampe de chevet (*f.*) bedside lamp
lancer to throw
laver to wash
le mardi on Tuesdays
le vendredi on Fridays
lécher to lick
légume (*m.*) vegetable
lever to raise
lèvres (*f.pl.*) lips
libraire (*m./f.*) bookseller
librairie (*f.*) bookstore
libre free
lire to read
lit (*m.*) bed
livres (*f.pl.*) pounds (English currency, weight)
logiciel (*m.*) software
loi (*f.*) law
loin far
loisirs (*m.pl.*) leisure time
lorsque when
louer to rent
loyer (*m.*) rent
lumière (*f.*) light
lunettes (*f.pl.*) (eye)glasses

M

macérer to macerate, to soak (cooking)
machine à laver (*f.*) washing machine
magasin (*m.*) store
magasin d'appareils photo (*m.*) camera store
magasin de chaussures (*m.*) shoe store
magasin de disques (*m.*) record store
magasin de jouets (*m.*) toy store
maigrir to lose weight
main (*f.*) hand
maintenant now
malade sick
malheureusement unfortunately
malle (*f.*) trunk
manger to eat
manifester to demonstrate
manoir (*m.*) manor, estate

manquer le train to miss the train
marchand(e) (*m./f.*) merchant, storekeeper
marchand(e) au détail retailer
marchand(e) de journaux news dealer
marchand(e) de légumes greengrocer, produce seller
marchand(e) de poisson fishmonger
marchand(e) de tableaux art dealer
marchand(e) de vin wine merchant
marchand(e) en gros wholesaler
marchander to bargain
marchandise (*f.*) merchandise
marché (*m.*) market
marché aux puces (*m.*) flea market
marguerite (*f.*) daisy
marié married
mariner to marinate (cooking)
marron brown
médicament (*m.*) medicine
mélanger to mix
même same
menacer to threaten
mener to lead
mentir to lie, to tell a lie
mériter to deserve
méthode (*f.*) method
métier (*m.*) job
metteur en scène (*m.*) director (film, theater)
mettre to put
mettre au four to put in the oven
meuble (*m.*) piece of furniture
meubles (*m.pl.*) furniture
meurtre (*m.*) murder
meurtrier, meurtrière (*m./f.*) murderer
mijoter to simmer (cooking)
mincir to slim down
miroir (*m.*) mirror
mode (*f.*) fashion
monter to go up
montre (*f.*) (wrist)watch
montrer to show
mordre to bite
moteur de recherche (*m.*) search engine
mourir to die
mouton (*m.*) sheep
musée (*m.*) museum
musicien(ne) (*m./f.*) musician

N

nager to swim
naissance (*f.*) birth
naître to be born
nappe (*f.*) tablecloth
nature morte (*f.*) still life
navette (*f.*) shuttle
navigateur Web (*m.*) Web browser
naviguer to browse

nécessaire necessary
négliger to neglect
neiger to snow
nettoyer to clean
nez (*m.*) nose
nièce (*f.*) niece
n'importe où anywhere
n'importe quoi anything
niveler to level
noir black
nom (*m.*) name
non no
note (*f.*) grade
notre our
nouveau (nouvel, nouvelle) new
numérique digital
numériser to digitize

O

obéir to obey
objet (*m.*) object
observer to notice, to observe
obtenir to get
occupé occupied
ocre ochre
odeur (*f.*) odor
œuvre (*f.*) work (of art)
offrir to offer
omelette (*f.*) omelet(te)
ongle (*m.*) fingernail, toenail
opéra (*m.*) opera
opticien(ne) (*m./f.*) optician
orange orange
ordinateur (*m.*) computer
ordonnance (*f.*) prescription
oreille (*f.*) ear
oser to dare
oublier to forget
oui yes
ouvrir to open

P

pagaille (*f.*) mess
page d'accueil (*f.*) home page
page Web (*f.*) Web page
pâlir to turn pale
paner to coat with bread crumbs
papeterie (*f.*) stationery store
par hasard by chance
paraître to appear
parapluie (*m.*) umbrella
parc (*m.*) park
parce que because
parenté (*f.*) kinship
paresse (*f.*) laziness
parfois sometimes

parfum (*m.*) perfume
parler to speak
parler l'anglais couramment to speak English fluently
partager to share
parti (*m.*) political party
partir to leave
passer les menottes à quelqu'un to handcuff someone
passer un examen to take an exam
pâtissier, pâtissière (*m./f.*) pastry cook
patron(ne) (*m./f.*) boss, employer
pause-café (*f.*) coffee break
pauvre poor
paysage (*m.*) landscape
peau (*f.*) skin
peindre to paint
peine (*f.*) sentence
peintre (*m.*) painter
peinture (*f.*) painting
pèlerinage (*m.*) pilgrimage
pelouse (*f.*) lawn
pencher to lean
pendant que while
penderie (*f.*) wardrobe, closet
penser to think
percer to pierce
perdre to lose
permis de conduire (*m.*) driver's license
peser to weigh
petit small
pétrir to knead
pharmacie (*f.*) pharmacy
pharmacien(ne) (*m./f.*) pharmacist
photographe (*m./f.*) photographer
photographie (*f.*) photograph
pied (*m.*) foot
piler to crush
piquer to sting
pirate (*m.*) hacker (software)
piscine (*f.*) swimming pool
placard (*m.*) closet, cupboard
placer to place
plage (*f.*) beach
plagier to plagiarize
plaindre to pity
se plaindre de to complain
plaire à to please
plaisanter to joke
plaisir (*m.*) pleasure
plat (*m.*) dish
pleuvoir to rain
plonger to dive
pluie (*f.*) rain
poche (*f.*) pocket
pocher to poach (cooking)
poisson (*m.*) fish
poissonnerie (*f.*) fish market

polar (*m.*) detective novel
police (*f.*) police
policier (*m.*) police officer
politique (*f.*) politics
polonais (*m.*) Polish
poncer to sand, to smooth
porte (*f.*) door
porter to carry
portugais (*m.*) Portuguese
posséder to own
poste (*f.*) post office
poubelle (*f.*) garbage can
pourquoi why
pourri rotten
poursuivre to chase
pouvoir can, may, to be able to
préférer to prefer
prendre to take
prendre la fuite to flee
prendre un verre to have a glass of wine
prénom (*m.*) first name
préparer to prepare
présenter to present
pressing (*m.*) dry cleaner's
prétendre to claim
prêter to lend
prévenir la police to call the police
prévoir to foresee
professeur (*m.*) teacher, professor
projet (*m.*) plan
promesse (*f.*) promise
promettre to promise
promouvoir to promote
prononcer to pronounce
propriété (*f.*) property
protéger to protect
prudent careful
public (publique) public
puisque since

Q

quand when
quelque chose something
quincaillerie (*f.*) hardware store
quotidien(ne) daily

R

raconter to tell
rafraîchir to refresh
raisonnable reasonable
ralentir to slow down
randonner to go hiking
ranger to put away
râper to grate (cooking)
rapidement quickly
rappeler to remind, to call back

rarement rarely
raser (se) to shave
recevoir to receive
recevoir son diplôme to get one's degree
rechercher to search
recouvrir to recover
réduire to reduce (by boiling)
réfléchir to think, to reflect
refuser to refuse
regarder to watch
régulièrement regularly
remarquer to notice, to observe
remède (*m.*) remedy
remercier to thank
remplacer to replace
remplir to fill
rencontrer to meet
rendre compte de (se) to realize
rendre visite à to visit someone
renoncer to give up
renouveler to renew
renseignement(s) (*m.pl.*) information
rentrer to return
renverser to spill
répandre to spread
répéter to repeat
répondre to answer
résoudre to solve
restaurant (*m.*) restaurant
rester to stay
retard (*m.*) lateness
réunion (*f.*) meeting
réussir to succeed
réussir à un examen to pass an exam
révéler to reveal
revenir to return
rideau (*m.*) curtain
rien nothing
rire to laugh
roi (*m.*) king
rôle (*m.*) part, role
roman (*m.*) novel
romancier, romancière (*m./f.*) novelist
rose pink
rôtir to roast
rouge red
rougir to blush
rumeur (*f.*) rumor
russe (*m.*) Russian

S

saisir to seize
salaire (*m.*) salary
salon de coiffure (*m.*) hairdressing salon
sauter to jump
sauvegarder to save

savoir to know
sec (sèche) dry
secrétaire (*m.*) writing desk
selon according to
sembler to seem
semer to sow
sentir to feel, to smell
séparé separated
serveur (*m.*) server
servir to serve
seul alone, lonely
si if
siècle (*m.*) century
signet (*m.*) bookmark
sirop (*m.*) syrup
site (*m.*) site
site Web (*m.*) website
sœur (*f.*) sister
soie (*f.*) silk
soir (*m.*) evening
soleil (*m.*) sun
sorcier, sorcière (*m./f.*) witch
sortir to go out
souffrir to suffer
souhaiter to wish
souris (*f.*) mouse
sous prétexte que under the pretext of
sous-titré subtitled
souvent often
stage (*m.*) internship, training
succès (*m.*) success
suivre to follow
supermarché (*m.*) supermarket
surfer to surf
surfer sur Internet to surf the Internet
surnom (*m.*) nickname
surprendre to surprise, to discover
survenir to occur
swahili (*m.*) Swahili
sympathique nice, friendly

T

table (*f.*) table
table basse (*f.*) coffee table
tableau (*m.*) painting
tabouret (*m.*) stool
taille (*f.*) waist
tailleur (*m.*) tailor, suit (women's)
tant que as long as
tapis (*m.*) rug
tasse (*f.*) cup
taxi (*m.*) taxi
teindre to dye
teinturerie (*f.*) dry cleaner's
télécharger to download
téléphoner to telephone, to call

témoignage (*m.*) testimony, evidence
témoigner to testify
témoin (*m.*) witness
tendre to stretch, to hold out
tenir à to insist, to be eager
tenir compte de to take into account
terrasse (*f.*) terrace
tête (*f.*) head
thé (*m.*) tea
théâtre (*m.*) theater
théorie (*f.*) theory
timbre (*m.*) stamp
tissu (*m.*) fabric
Toile (*f.*) World Wide Web
toit (*m.*) roof
tomber to fall
tomber en panne to break down (car)
tordre to twist
touche (*f.*) key (keyboard)
toujours always
tour (*f.*) tower
tournage (*m.*) shooting (film)
tourner un film to shoot a film
tous les jours every day
tousser to cough
tout (tous, toute, toutes) all
traduire to translate
train (*m.*) train
traité (*m.*) treaty
traitement (*m.*) treatment
travailler to work
traverser to cross
tremper to soak
tricoter to knit
triste sad
tristesse (*f.*) sadness
trône (*m.*) throne
trouver to find

V

vacances (*f.pl.*) vacation
vague (*f.*) wave (ocean)
valise (*f.*) suitcase
valoir to be worth
valse (*f.*) waltz
vase (*m.*) vase
vedette (*f.*) (movie) star
vendre to sell
venger to avenge
venir to go
vente aux enchères (*f.*) auction
vernissage (*m.*) opening (art show)
verre (*m.*) glass
vers toward
verser to pour
vert green

vert olive olive green
veuf, veuve (*m./f.*) widower, widow
viande (*f.*) meat
vieillir to grow old
vieux (vieil, vieille) old
violet(te) purple
visage (*m.*) face
viser à to aim at
visiter to visit
vitesse (*f.*) speed
vivre to live
voir to see
voiture (*f.*) car
vol (*m.*) theft
vol à l'étalage (*m.*) shoplifting

voler to steal
volontiers willingly
vouloir to want
voyage d'affaires (*m.*) business trip
voyage d'agrément (*m.*) pleasure trip
voyager to travel
vu que given, in view of

W
Web 2.0 (Web deux point zéro) (*m.*) Web 2.0
wolof (*m.*) Wolof

Y
yeux (*m.pl.*) eyes

English-French glossary

Regular adjectives in French are listed in their masculine singular form.

A

accept, to accepter
access, high-speed accès haut-débit (*m.*)
access provider fournisseur d'accès (*m.*)
accessory accessoire (*m.*)
accompany, to accompagner
accomplish, to accomplir
according to selon
acquire, to acquérir
actor, actress acteur, actrice (*m./f.*)
add, to ajouter
advance, to avancer
adventure aventure (*f.*)
advise, to conseiller
afraid, to be avoir peur
after après que
aim at, to viser
air-conditioned climatisé
alert éveillé
all tout, tous, toute, toutes
all right d'accord
alone seul
along le long de
always toujours
analyze, to analyser
ancestor ancêtre (*m./f.*)
ankle cheville (*f.*)
announce, to annoncer
answer, to répondre
antiques dealer antiquaire (*m./f.*)
anything n'importe quoi
appear, to paraître
applaud, to applaudir
Arabic arabe
area domaine (*m.*)
arm bras (*m.*)
armchair fauteuil (*m.*)
arrest, to arrêter
arrive, to arriver
art dealer marchand(e) de tableaux (*m./f.*)
as comme
as long as tant que
as soon as aussitôt que, dès que

as usual comme d'habitude
ashamed, to be avoir honte
ask, to demander
assault agression (*f.*)
at midnight à minuit
at noon à midi
at the beach à la plage
at the movies au cinéma
attack, terrorist attentat (*m.*)
attend, to assister
auction vente aux enchères (*f.*)
available disponible
avenge, to venger
awake éveillé

B

back dos (*m.*)
backache, to have a avoir mal au dos
backstage coulisses (*f.pl.*)
baker boulanger, boulangère (*m./f.*)
bakery boulangerie (*f.*)
bank banque (*f.*)
bargain, to marchander
be, to être
beach plage (*f.*)
bean haricot (*m.*)
beat, to battre
beautiful beau, bel, belle
because parce que
become, to devenir
bed lit (*m.*)
begin, to commencer
believe, to croire
bewitch, to ensorceler
bid, to faire une offre
birth naissance (*f.*)
birthday anniversaire (*f.*)
bite, to mordre
bitter amer, amère
black noir
blackmail chantage (*m.*)
blog blog (*m.*)
bloom, to (s')épanouir

blue bleu
blue, dark bleu foncé
blue, light bleu clair
blue, navy bleu marine
blue, sky bleu ciel
blunder gaffe (*f.*)
blush, to rougir
board, to embarquer
boat bateau (*m.*)
boil, to bouillir
bookcase bibliothèque (*f.*)
bookmark signet (*m.*)
bookseller libraire (*m./f.*)
bookstore librairie (*f.*)
born, to be naître
borrow, to emprunter
boss patron (*m.*)
bother, to déranger
bottle bouteille (*f.*)
box boîte (*f.*)
break, to casser
break down, to tomber en panne
broadcast émission (*f.*)
brown marron
brown, to (cooking) faire revenir
browse, to naviguer
build, to construire, bâtir
burglarize, to cambrioler
burglary cambriolage (*m.*)
burn, to brûler
bus autobus (*m.*)
business affaires (*f.pl.*)
butcher boucher, bouchère (*m./f.*)
butcher shop boucherie (*f.*)
buy, to acheter
by chance par hasard
by heart par cœur
by the sea à la mer

C

call, to appeler
to call back rappeler
to call the police prévenir la police
camera appareil (*m.*)
camera store magasin d'appareils photo (*m.*)
can (may) pouvoir
cancel, to annuler
candy store confiserie (*f.*)
car voiture (*f.*)
careful prudent
carry, to porter
casual décontracté
cat chat (*m.*)
catch, to attraper
cease, to cesser
celebrate, to célébrer
celebration fête (*f.*)

century siècle (*m.*)
chair chaise (*f.*)
change, to changer
channel(s) filière (*f.*)
charming charmant
chase, to poursuivre
chat, to bavarder
cheap bon marché
check off, to cocher
checked à carreaux
cheese fromage (*m.*)
chest coffre (*m.*)
chest of drawers commode (*f.*)
chimney cheminée (*f.*)
Chinese chinois
choose, to choisir
chop, to hacher
chorus chorale (*f.*)
cinema cinéma (*m.*)
circumstances circonstances (*f.pl.*)
claim, to affirmer, prétendre
clean, to nettoyer
clear, to éclaircir
click, to cliquer
climb, to escalader
clock horloge (*f.*)
close, to fermer
closet placard (*m.*)
closing clôture (*f.*)
coat with bread crumbs, to paner
coffee break pause-café (*f.*)
coffee table table basse (*f.*)
cold, to be avoir froid; to have a cold avoir un rhume
collector collectionneur, collectionneuse (*m./f.*)
commit, to engager
commitment engagement (*m.*)
competitor concurrent(e) (*m./f.*)
complain, to se plaindre
complete, to achever
computer ordinateur (*m.*)
computer science informatique (*f.*)
confess, to avouer
confide, to confier
congratulate, to féliciter
conjugation conjugaison (*f.*)
consider, to considérer
consist of, to comporter
consult, to consulter
contemplate, to envisager
content heureux, heureuse
convince, to convaincre
cook, to faire la cuisine, cuire, faire cuire
to cook au gratin gratiner
cooking cuisine (*f.*)
correct, to corriger
correspond, to correspondre
cough, to tousser

course cours (*m.*)
cousin cousin(e) (*m./f.*)
cover, to couvrir
craft, to façonner
craftsman (-woman) artisan(e) (*m./f.*)
creative créatif, créative
Creole créole
crook escroc (*m.*)
cross, to traverser
crouch, to s'accroupir
crowded bondé
crush, to broyer, écraser, piler
cup tasse (*f.*)
curator conservateur, conservatrice (*m./f.*)
curtain rideau (*m.*)
cut, to couper
cybernaut internaute (*m./f.*)

D

daisy marguerite (*f.*)
dance, to danser
dare, to oser
data bank banque de données (*f.*)
database base de données (*f.*)
day jour (*m.*), journée (*f.*)
debt dette (*f.*)
defend, to défendre
degree, to get one's recevoir son diplôme
delegate, to déléguer
demand, to exiger
deserve, to mériter
desire, to désirer
detective novel polar (*m.*)
device appareil (*m.*)
diamond diamant (*m.*)
dictionary dictionnaire (*m.*)
die, to mourir
digital numérique
digital library bibliothèque numérique (*f.*)
digitize, to numériser
director (theater, film) metteur en scène (*m.*)
disappoint, to décevoir
discover, to surprendre
discuss, to discuter
dish plat (*m.*)
disturb, to déranger, ennuyer
disturbing inquiétant
dive, to plonger
divorced divorcé
DNA ADN (*m.*)
do, to faire
to do the housework faire le ménage
documentary documentaire (*m.*)
dog chien (*m.*)
door porte (*f.*)
download, to télécharger
draft, first brouillon (*m.*)

drag and drop glisser-déposer
draw, to dessiner
dressing table coiffeuse (*f*)
drink, to boire
drive, to conduire
driver's license permis de conduire (*m.*)
drizzle, to bruiner
dry sec, sèche
dry cleaner's pressing (*m.*)
dubbed doublé
dye, to teindre

E

eager, to be tenir à
ear oreille (*f.*)
earn, to gagner
eat, to manger
efficient efficace
elbow coude (*m.*)
elect, to élire (*m.*)
elevator ascenseur (*m.*)
encourage, to encourager
end fin (*f.*)
English anglais (*m.*)
enlarge, to agrandir
ensure, to assurer
enter, to entrer
entertainment divertissement (*m.*)
erase, to effacer
escort, to emmener
etching gravure (*f.*)
Europe Europe (*f.*)
evening soir (*m.*)
every day chaque jour, tous les jours
every month chaque mois
every week chaque semaine
every year chaque année
exaggerate, to exagérer
exam examen (*m.*)
exhibition exposition (*f.*)
expedition expédition (*f.*)
expensive cher, chère
explain, to expliquer
explore, to explorer
express, to exprimer
extend, to étendre
extranet extranet (*m.*)
eye(s) œil (*m.*), yeux (*m.pl.*)

F

face visage (*m.*)
fail an exam, to échouer à un examen
failure échec (*m.*)
faint, to s'évanouir
fall, to tomber
family famille (*f.*)
FAQ foire aux questions (FAQ) (*f.*)

fashion mode (*f.*)
fear, to craindre
feel, to sentir
feel like, to avoir envie de
feign, to feindre
fill, to remplir
fill up, to faire le plein
film film (*m.*)
finance, to financer
find, to trouver
fine (penalty) amende (*f.*)
finger doigt (*m.*)
finger, to (betray) balancer
fingerprints empreintes digitales (*f.pl.*)
finish, to finir
fire feu (*m.*)
fireplace cheminée (*f.*)
first name prénom (*m.*)
fish poisson (*m.*)
fish market poissonnerie (*f.*)
fishmonger marchand(e) de poisson (*m./f.*)
flambé, to (cooking) flamber
flea market marché aux puces (*m.*)
flee, to fuir, s'enfuir, prendre la fuite
floor étage (*m.*)
florist fleuriste (*m./f.*)
flounced à volants
flower fleur (*f.*)
flowered à fleurs
flu, to have the avoir la grippe
follow, to suivre
foot pied (*m.*)
forbid, to défendre
foreigner étranger, étrangère (*m./f.*)
foresee, to prévoir
forget, to oublier
form formulaire (*m.*)
formerly autrefois
fraud escroquerie (*f.*)
free libre
free, to dégager
French français (*m.*)
frequently fréquemment
fresh frais, fraîche
Fridays, on le vendredi
friendly sympathique
from time to time de temps en temps
fry, to frire, faire frire
funny amusant
furniture meubles (*m.pl.*)
furniture, piece of meuble (*m.*)

G

garden jardin (*m.*)
garnish, to garnir
German allemand (*m.*)
get, to obtenir

get ahead of, to devancer
get off, to débarquer
gift cadeau (*m.*)
give, to donner
give up, to renoncer
given étant donné que, vu que
glad heureux, heureuse
glass verre (*m.*)
glasses (eye) lunettes (*f.pl.*)
glitter, to étinceler
go, to aller
go down, to descendre
go out, to sortir
go up, to monter
good bon(ne)
govern, to gouverner
government gouvernement (*m.*)
grade (in school) note (*f.*)
grant, to accorder
grate, to (cooking) râper
gray gris
green vert
green, olive vert olive
greengrocer marchand(e) de légumes (*m./f.*)
grill, to griller
grind, to broyer
grocer épicier, épicière (*m./f.*)
group ensemble (*m.*)
grow up, to grandir
guillotine, to guillotiner
guilty coupable

H

habit habitude (*f.*)
hacker (computer) pirate (*m.*)
hair cheveux (*m.pl.*)
hairdresser coiffeur, coiffeuse (*m./f.*)
hairdressing salon salon de coiffure (*m.*)
hand main (*f.*)
handcuff (someone), to passer les menottes (à quelqu'un)
happy heureux, heureuse
harassment harcèlement (*m.*)
hard drive disque dur (*m.*)
hardly à peine
hardware store quincaillerie (*f.*)
hate, to détester
have, to avoir
have to, to devoir
have a glass of wine, to prendre un verre du vin
have lunch, to déjeuner
have pain, to avoir mal
hazelnut noisette (*f.*)
head tête (*f.*)
headache, to have a avoir mal à la tête
hear, to entendre
hijacking détournement d'avion (*m.*)
hiking, to go randonner

hill colline (*f.*)
Hindi hindi (*m.*)
hip hanche (*f.*)
hire, to engager
hit, to frapper
hold out, to tendre
home page page d'accueil (*f.*)
hope, to espérer
host, to héberger
hot, to be avoir chaud
how much combien
hum, to fredonner
hungry, to be avoir faim
hurt, to avoir mal
husk, to décortiquer

I

idea idée (*f.*)
if si
implicated impliqué
imprint empreinte (*f.*)
in the country à la campagne
in the mountains à la montagne
in times past autrefois
in view of étant donné que, vu que
increase, to augmenter
influence, to influencer
information renseignement(s) (*m.pl.*)
information highways autoroutes de l'information (*f.pl.*)
insist on, to tenir à
intend, to compter
Internet Internet (*m.*)
Internet protocol address adresse IP (*f.*)
internship stage (*m.*)
intranet intranet (*m.*)
invade, to envahir
invest, to investir
invite, to inviter
island île (*f.*)
Italian italien (*m.*)

J

jacket veste (*f.*)
jam confiture (*f.*)
Japanese japonais (*m.*)
jewel bijou (*m.*)
jewelry store bijouterie (*f.*)
job métier (*m.*)
joke, to plaisanter
jump, to sauter

K

keep, to garder
key (keyboard) touche (*f.*)
keyboard clavier (*m.*)
kind gentil(le)
king roi (*m.*)

kinship parenté (*f.*)
kiss, to embrasser
kitchen cuisine (*f.*)
knead, to pétrir
knee genou (*m.*)
know, to connaître, savoir
knowledge connaissance (*f.*)

L

label étiquette (*f.*)
lake lac (*m.*)
lamp lampe (*f.*), **bedside lamp** lampe de chevet (*f.*)
land, to atterrir
landscape paysage (*m.*)
language langue (*f.*)
lateness retard (*m.*)
laugh, to rire
lead, to mener
lean, to pencher
learn, to apprendre
leather cuir (*m.*)
leave, to partir
left gauche (*f.*)
leg jambe (*f.*)
leisure time loisirs (*m.pl.*)
lend, to prêter
let, to (allow) laisser
level, to niveler
library bibliothèque (*f.*)
lick, to lécher
lie, to mentir
light, to allumer
lighten, to éclaircir
lighting éclairage (*m.*)
like, to aimer
lips lèvres (*f.pl.*)
listen, to écouter
live, to habiter, vivre
log on, to se connecter
look, to (see) regarder
look, to (seem) avoir l'air
look for, to chercher
lose, to perdre
lose weight, to maigrir
love, to aimer
lower, to baisser
lower the price, to baisser le prix
luck chance (*f.*)
lucky, to be avoir de la chance

M

macerate, to (cooking) macérer
magic magie (*f.*)
maintain, to assurer
make, to faire
make faces, to faire des grimaces, grimacer
manage, to gérer

manufacture, to façonner
marinate, to (cooking) mariner
market marché (*m.*)
married marié
masterpiece chef-d'œuvre (*m.*)
meat viande (*f.*)
medicine médicament (*m.*)
medicine cabinet armoire à pharmacie (*f.*)
meet, to rencontrer
meeting réunion (*f.*)
mellow, to adoucir
merchandise marchandise (*f.*)
mess pagaille (*f.*)
method méthode (*f.*)
mince, to (cooking) hacher
mirror miroir (*m.*)
miss the train, to manquer le train
mix, to mélanger
money argent (*m.*)
money laundering blanchiment d'argent (*m.*)
mood humeur (*f.*)
mouse souris (*f.*)
mouth bouche (*f.*)
move, to (emotionally) émouvoir
move, to (house) déménager
mugging agression (*f.*)
murder meurtre (*m.*)
murderer meurtrier, meurtrière (*m./f.*), assassin (*m.*)
museum musée (*m.*)
mushroom champignon (*m.*)
musician musicien(ne) (*m./f.*)

N

nail (finger, toe) ongle (*m.*)
name nom (*m.*)
necessary nécessaire
necessary, to be falloir
need, to avoir besoin de
neglect, to négliger
new nouveau, nouvel, nouvelle
news dealer marchand(e) de journaux (*m./f.*)
newsstand kiosque à journaux (*m.*)
nice gentil(le), sympathique
nickname surnom (*m.*)
niece nièce (*f.*)
night nuit (*f.*)
no non
nose nez (*m.*)
note, to constater
nothing rien
notice, to constater, observer, remarquer
novel roman (*m.*)
now that maintenant que

O

obey, to obéir
objects objets (*m.pl.*)

observe, to observer, remarquer
occupied occupé
occur, to survenir
ochre ocre
odor odeur (*f.*)
offer, to offrir
often souvent
oil huile (*f.*)
OK d'accord
old vieux, vieil, vieille
old, to grow vieillir
omelet(te) omelette (*f.*)
open, to ouvrir
opening (art) vernissage (*m.*)
opera opéra (*m.*)
optician opticien(ne) (*m./f.*)
orange orange
order, to commander
ordinarily d'ordinaire
our notre, nos
own, to posséder

P

pain douleur (*f*)
paint, to peindre
painter peintre (*m.*)
painting peinture (*f.*), tableau (*m.*)
park parc (*m.*)
part rôle (*m.*)
party (political) parti (*m.*)
pass an exam, to réussir à un examen
pastry cook pâtissier, pâtissière (*m./f.*)
path chemin (*m.*)
peel, to (vegetables) éplucher
pen (writing) stylo (*m.*)
pepper poivre (*m.*)
perceive, to apercevoir
perfume parfum (*m.*)
pharmacist pharmacien(ne) (*m./f.*)
pharmacy pharmacie (*f.*)
photograph photographie, photo (*f.*)
photographer photographe (*m./f.*)
pick, to (produce) cueillir
piece morceau (*m.*)
pierce, to percer
pilgrimage pèlerinage (*m.*)
pink rose
pity, to plaindre
place, to placer
plagiarize, to plagier
plan projet (*m.*)
plan, to compter
plane avion (*m.*)
play pièce (*f.*)
play, to jouer (à, de)
play hooky, to faire l'école buissonnière
player joueur, joueuse (*m./f.*)

pleasant plaisant, agréable
please, to plaire (à)
pleasure plaisir (*m.*)
pleated à plis
plot intrigue (*f.*)
plug in, to brancher
poach, to (cooking) pocher
pocket poche (*f.*)
police police (*f.*)
police officer policier (*m.*)
politics politique (*f.*)
polka-dotted à pois
poor pauvre
Portuguese portugais (*m.*)
post office poste (*f.*)
pounds (English currency, weight) livres (*f.pl.*)
pour, to verser
prefer, to préférer
prepare, to préparer
prescription ordonnance (*f.*)
present, to présenter
pretend, to feindre
print, to imprimer
printer (device) imprimante (*f.*)
promise promesse (*f.*)
promise, to promettre
promote, to promouvoir
pronounce, to prononcer
property propriété (*f.*)
protect, to protéger
public public, publique
pull out, to arracher
purple violet(te)
put, to mettre
put away, to ranger
put in the oven, to mettre au four
put on weight, to grossir

Q

quickly rapidement

R

rain pluie (*f.*)
rain, to pleuvoir
raise, to lever
rarely rarement
read, to lire
real estate immobilier (*m.*)
realize, to s'apercevoir, se rendre compte
reasonable raisonnable
receive, to recevoir
record store magasin de disques (*m.*)
recover, to recouvrir
red rouge
reduce, to réduire
reflect, to réfléchir
refresh, to rafraîchir

refuse, to refuser
regularly régulièrement
relax, to détendre
release, to dégager
remedy remède (*m.*)
remind, to rappeler
remove, to enlever
renew, to renouveler
rent loyer (*m.*)
rent, to louer
repeat, to répéter
replace, to remplacer
resign, to démissionner
resolve, to résoudre
rest, to se reposer
restaurant restaurant (*m.*)
retailer marchand(e) au détail (*m./f.*)
return, to revenir
return home, to rentrer
reveal, to révéler
right droite (*f.*)
right, to be avoir raison
ring bague (*f.*)
roast, to (cooking) rôtir
role rôle (*m.*)
rotten pourri
RSS feed fil RSS (*m.*)
rug tapis (*m.*)
rumor rumeur (*f.*)
run, to courir
Russian russe (*m.*)
rusty rouillé

S

sad triste
sadness tristesse (*f.*)
sail voile (*f.*)
salary salaire (*m.*)
salary increase augmentation de salaire (*f.*)
same même
sand, to poncer
sauté, to (cooking) faire sauter
save, to sauvegarder
say, to dire, affirmer
scale, to (fish) écailler
scarf foulard (*m.*)
school école (*f.*)
screen écran (*m.*)
sea mer (*f.*)
search, to rechercher
search engine moteur de recherche (*m.*)
season, to assaisonner
seduce, to séduire
see, to voir, apercevoir
seem, to sembler, avoir l'air
seize, to saisir
sell, to vendre

send, to envoyer
sentence (criminal) peine (f.)
sentenced, to be être condamné(e) à
separated séparé
serve, to servir
server serveur (m.)
share, to partager
shave, to se raser
sheep mouton (m.)
shelf étagère (f.)
shell, to (peas) écosser
shell, to (shrimp) décortiquer
shelter abri (m.)
shirt chemise (f.)
shoe chaussure (f.)
shoe store magasin de chaussures (m.)
shoemaker cordonnier (m.)
shoot a film, to tourner un film
shooting (film) tournage (m.)
shoot-out fusillade (f.)
shoplifting vol à l'étalage (m.)
shout, to crier
show, to montrer
shuttle navette (f.)
sick malade
sideboard buffet (m.)
simmer, to (cooking) mijoter
since depuis, puisque
sing, to chanter
single célibataire
sister sœur (f.)
sister-in-law belle-sœur (f.)
site site (m.)
skim, to (soup) écumer
skin peau (f.)
sky ciel (m.)
sleep, to dormir
slice thinly, to émincer
slim down, to mincir
slow down, to ralentir
small petit
smash in, to défoncer
smell, to sentir
snow, to neiger
soak, to tremper
soak, to (cooking) macérer
sofa canapé (m.)
soften, to adoucir
software logiciel (m.)
solve, to résoudre
something quelque chose
sometimes parfois
song chanson (f.)
sow, to semer
Spanish espagnol (m.)
sparkle, to étinceler
speak, to parler

speak English fluently, to parler l'anglais couramment
speed vitesse (f.)
spell, to épeler
spice, to épicer
spill, to renverser
spread, to répandre
squash, to écraser
squat, to s'accroupir
staircase escalier (m.)
stand in line, to faire la queue
star étoile (f.)
star (film) vedette (f.)
state, to déclarer
stationery store papeterie (f.)
stay, to rester
steal, to voler
still life nature morte (f.)
sting, to piquer
stir, to émouvoir
stomachache, to have a avoir mal au ventre
stool tabouret (m.)
stop, to cesser de, arrêter (de), s'arrêter (de)
stopover (car travel) étape (f.)
store magasin (m.)
story histoire (f.)
stranger étranger, étrangère (m./f.)
stretch, to tendre
striped à rayures
student (college) étudiant(e) (m./f.)
student (grade school) élève (m./f.)
study, to étudier
stuff, to (cooking) farcir
subscribe, to s'abonner
subtitled sous-titré
succeed, to réussir
success succès (m.)
suffer, to souffrir
suitcase valise (f.)
sun soleil (m.)
supermarket supermarché (m.)
surf, to surfer
surf the Internet, to surfer sur Internet
surgeon chirurgien(ne) (m./f.)
surprise, to surprendre
Swahili swahili (m.)
swim, to nager
swindle escroquerie (f.)
swing, to balancer
syrup sirop (m.)

T

table table (f.)
tablecloth nappe (f.)
tailor tailleur (m.)
take, to prendre
take a nap, to faire la sieste
take along, to emmener

take an exam, to passer un examen
take away, to emporter
take into account, to tenir compte de
take off (plane), to décoller
take off (shoes), to enlever
tall grand
taste, to goûter
taxi taxi (*m.*)
tea thé (*m.*)
teach, to enseigner
teacher professeur (*m.*)
team équipe (*f.*)
tear up, to déchirer
telephone, to téléphoner
tell, to raconter
terrace terrasse (*f.*)
terrorist attack attentat (*m.*)
testify, to témoigner
testimony témoignage (*m.*)
thank, to remercier
thank you merci
theater théâtre (*m.*)
theft vol (*m.*)
theory théorie (*f.*)
think, to penser, réfléchir
thirsty, to be avoir soif
thirty-five years old, to be avoir trente-cinq ans
threaten, to menacer
throne trône (*m.*)
throw, to lancer, jeter
thus ainsi
tie, to ficeler
time fois (*f.*)
toast, to griller
tobacco shop bureau de tabac (*m.*)
today aujourd'hui
tomorrow demain
tongue (language) langue (*f.*)
toward(s) vers
tower tour (*f.*)
toy store magasin de jouets (*m.*)
traffic circulation (*f.*)
traffic jam embouteillage (*m.*)
train train (*m.*)
train, to s'entraîner
training stage (*m.*)
translate, to traduire
travel agency agence de voyages (*f.*)
travel, to voyager
tray plateau (*m.*)
treatment traitement (*m.*)
treaty traité (*m.*)
tree arbre (*m.*)
trip, business voyage d'affaires (*m.*)
trip, pleasure voyage d'agrément (*m.*)
trunk malle (*f.*)
truth vérité (*f.*)

Tuesdays, on le mardi
turkey dinde (*f.*)
turn on, to allumer

U

umbrella parapluie (*m.*)
unaware, to be ignorer
under the pretext that sous prétexte que
understand, to comprendre
undertake, to entreprendre
unfortunately malheureusement
unknown inconnu
URL address adresse URL (*f.*)
usually d'habitude

V

vacation vacances (*f.pl.*)
value, to apprécier
vase vase (*m.*)
vegetable légume (*m.*)
veil voile (*m.*)
very très
visit, to (place) visiter
visit, to (someone) rendre visite (à quelqu'un)
voice voix (*f.*)
voice mail boîte vocale (*f.*)

W

waist taille (*f.*)
wait, to attendre
walk, to marcher
wall mur (*m.*)
wallet portefeuille (*m.*)
waltz valse (*f.*)
want, to vouloir
war guerre (*f.*)
wardrobe (closet, cupboard) penderie (*f.*), armoire (*f.*)
warn, to prévenir
wash, to laver
waste, to gaspiller
watch, to regarder
watch (wristwatch) montre (*f.*)
watchmaker horloger (*m.*)
water eau (*f.*)
watercolor aquarelle (*f.*)
wave vague (*f.*)
wear, to porter
Web 2.0 Web 2.0 (Web deux point zéro) (*m.*)
Web browser navigateur Web (*m.*)
Web page page Web (*f.*)
Web user internaute (*m./f.*)
webmaster administrateur, administratrice de site (*m./f.*)
website site Web (*m.*)
week semaine (*f.*)
weigh, to peser
welcome, to accueillir
when quand, lorsque

whereas alors que
while alors que, pendant que
white blanc(he)
wholesaler marchand(e) en gros (*m./f.*)
widow veuve (*f.*)
widower veuf (*m.*)
win, to gagner
window fenêtre (*f.*)
wine merchant marchand(e) de vin (*m./f.*)
wipe, to essuyer
wish, to souhaiter
witch sorcier, sorcière (*m./f.*)
witness témoin (*m.*)
Wolof wolof (*m.*)

wood bois (*m.*)
word mot (*m.*)
work (of art) œuvre (*f.*)
work, to travailler
World Wide Web Toile (*f.*)
wrap, to emballer
write, to écrire
wrong, to be avoir tort

Y

yellow jaune
yes oui
young jeune

Answer key

1   The present tense of regular -er verbs

1-1   1. travaille   2. acceptons   3. cherchent   4. apportes   5. bavardez   6. commande   7. habitent   8. déjeune   9. dessinez   10. visitons

1-2   1. Nous refusons l'invitation.   2. Elle annule le voyage.   3. Il parle français.   4. Vous apportez des fleurs.   5. Je coupe le pain.   6. Ils (Elles) déjeunent avec Julie.   7. Il emprunte dix euros.   8. Je commande un dessert.   9. Tu étudies le russe.   10. Ils (Elles) cherchent un bon restaurant.

1-3   1. commençons   2. avancez   3. déplace   4. devançons   5. annonçons   6. effaces   7. remplaçons   8. exercent   9. finançons   10. menace

1-4   1. mélangez   2. range   3. exigeons   4. déménagent   5. héberge   6. corrigez   7. mangeons   8. nages   9. encourageons   10. change

1-5   1. renouvelle   2. emmène   3. achetez   4. ensorcelle   5. espère   6. exagérez   7. s'appelle   8. étincellent   9. répète   10. célébrons

1-6   1. achète   2. travaillent   3. empruntez   4. aimes   5. renonçons   6. J'habite   7. préfère   8. s'appelle   9. bavardons   10. rappelle

1-7   1. i   2. e   3. h   4. a   5. b   6. j   7. c   8. d   9. f   10. g

1-8   1. Nous sommes en train de chanter une chanson.   2. Elle est en train de dessiner un mouton.   3. Je suis en train de travailler dans la cuisine.   4. Tu es en train d'effacer le tableau.   5. Vous êtes en train d'étudier l'histoire européenne.   6. Nous sommes en train de bavarder dans le jardin.   7. Il est en train de corriger les copies.   8. Tu es en train de laver la chemise.   9. Je suis en train de ranger mes affaires.   10. Elle est en train de manger une omelette aux champignons.

1-9   1. Elle chante dans cette chorale depuis trois ans.   2. Je partage cet appartement depuis six mois.   3. Il nage dans cette piscine depuis un mois.   4. J'habite à Montpellier depuis 2004.   5. Il possède cette propriété depuis dix ans.   6. Je regarde cette émission depuis des années.   7. Il travaille dans cette entreprise depuis 2002.   8. Je porte des lunettes depuis dix ans.   9. Il est président depuis 2005.   10. Ce magasin est fermé depuis deux mois.

1-10   1. J'étudie le français.   2. J'épelle mon nom.   3. Ils (Elles) déménagent demain.   4. Elle aime voyager en bateau.   5. Depuis combien de temps étudiez-vous le français?   6. Tu répètes la phrase.   7. Nous finançons le projet.   8. Elle annule la réunion.   9. Depuis combien de temps habitez-vous dans cette maison?   10. Je pèse les légumes.

2   The present tense of -ir and -re verbs

2-1   1. cueillons   2. finissent   3. remplis   4. investissons   5. mentent   6. ouvres   7. réfléchissez   8. sens   9. offrent   10. meurt

2-2   1. h   2. j   3. a   4. e   5. i   6. b   7. d   8. f   9. g   10. c

2-3   1. Nous partons à dix heures.   2. Elle ouvre la porte.   3. Vous cueillez des fleurs dans le jardin de Florence.   4. La voiture ralentit.   5. Nous sortons ce soir.   6. Elle saisit l'occasion.   7. Elle rougit facilement.   8. Ils (Elles) courent vite.   9. Elle résout le mystère.   10. Ils (Elles) dorment dans la chambre de Sonia.

2-4   1. répondons   2. répand   3. rendez   4. vendent   5. descends   6. attends   7. tend   8. perd   9. prétend   10. étendent

2-5   1. h   2. e   3. g   4. i   5. a   6. c   7. b   8. j   9. d   10. f

2-6   1. prenons   2. entreprend   3. apprends   4. comprenez   5. apprennent   6. surprend   7. prenez   8. comprenons   9. prends   10. comprend

2-7   1. Il apprend le chinois.   2. Elle prend le métro tous les jours.   3. Il perd souvent ses clés.   4. J'entends Pierre dans la rue.   5. Il prétend être le frère du roi.   6. Vous répondez rapidement.   7. Elle vend des fleurs.   8. Nous descendons les Champs-Élysées.   9. Je descends.   10. Nous attendons une réponse.

2-8   1. Remplissent-ils les formulaires?   2. Réfléchit-il au problème?   3. Aimez-vous aller au théâtre?   4. Préfère-t-elle voyager en Italie?   5. Écoutes-tu le discours du président?   6. Influencent-ils le public?   7. Annule-t-elle son voyage au Brésil?   8. Travailles-tu le jeudi?   9. Apportez-vous un nouveau livre?   10. Agrandit-elle les photos?

2-9   1. Est-ce qu'ils parlent de la nouvelle transaction?   2. Est-ce qu'elle apprend le portugais?   3. Est-ce que vous commandez une bouteille de vin blanc?   4. Est-ce que tu demandes une augmentation de salaire?   5. Est-ce qu'ils financent un grand projet?   6. Est-ce que vous choisissez une autre direction?   7. Est-ce qu'ils finissent tard?   8. Est-ce qu'il prétend être pauvre?   9. Est-ce qu'ils défendent cette théorie?   10. Est-ce que vous descendez par l'escalier?

2-10   1. Il n'encourage pas ses employés.   2. Ils ne visitent pas le musée.   3. Tu ne gagnes pas à la loterie.   4. Elle n'enlève pas son chapeau.   5. Vous n'exprimez pas vos opinions.   6. Tu ne pèses pas les fruits.   7. Il ne danse pas la valse.   8. Vous ne corrigez pas les copies des étudiants.   9. Nous n'étudions pas l'arabe.   10. Il ne maigrit pas en vacances.

2-11   1. J'apprends le japonais.   2. Il ne parle pas italien.   3. Elle ne mange ni viande ni fromage.   4. Ils (Elles) n'écoutent jamais personne.   5. Vous travaillez tard.   6. Ils (Elles) n'aiment ni le thé ni le café.   7. Comprenez-vous la question?   8. Nous cueillons des fleurs dans le jardin.   9. Il n'enlève jamais son chapeau.   10. Elle ne ment jamais.

3   To be and to have

3-1   1. est   2. sommes   3. sont   4. es   5. sont   6. êtes   7. C'est   8. ne sont pas   9. est   10. suis

3-2   1. Oui, ils sont en retard.   2. Oui, le climat est sec.   3. Oui, je suis libre ce soir.   4. Oui, il est heureux.   5. Oui, elle est sympathique.   6. Oui, ce restaurant français est cher.   7. Oui, je suis fatigué.   8. Oui, vous êtes à la bonne adresse.   9. Oui, ce film est amusant.   10. Oui, le musée est ouvert.

3-3   1. avons   2. n'as pas   3. J'ai   4. avez   5. a   6. ont   7. as   8. n'avons pas   9. n'avez pas   10. J'ai

3-4   1. g   2. j   3. a   4. i   5. b   6. h   7. c   8. e   9. d   10. f

3-5   1. Je suis fatigué(e).   2. Il a très faim.   3. Ils (Elles) ont toujours raison.   4. Sont-ils français? (Sont-elles françaises?)   5. Avez-vous peur de sa réaction?   6. Il a honte.   7. Ils (Elles) ont un chien.   8. Elle a un nouveau chapeau.   9. C'est très cher.   10. Fermez la fenêtre. Nous avons froid.

3-6   1. savez   2. sais   3. ne sait pas   4. savons   5. sais   6. sais   7. ne sait pas   8. Savez   9. sais   10. savez

3-7   1. connaissent   2. connaissons   3. connaît   4. connais   5. connaît   6. connaissez   7. connaissez   8. connais   9. connaît   10. Connaissez

3-8   1. sais   2. sait   3. sais   4. connaissons   5. sais   6. connaissent   7. connaît   8. connaissez   9. sait   10. connaissons

3-9   1. voulons   2. ne peux pas   3. veux   4. pouvons   5. veux   6. pouvez   7. peut   8. veulent   9. voulez   10. peuvent

3-10   1. J'aperçois   2. prévoit   3. pleut   4. voyons   5. déçois   6. promeut   7. vaut   8. faut   9. émeut   10. recevez

3-11   1. Est-ce que tu sais nager?   2. Est-ce qu'il sait faire la cuisine?   3. Je ne sais pas où il est.   4. Est-ce qu'elle peut remplir ce formulaire?   5. Elle connaît Caroline.   6. Est-ce que tu sais cette chanson française par cœur?   7. Il pleut en France.   8. Tu dois arriver à midi.   9. Il prévoit une grande amélioration.   10. Je vois le château.

4 More irregular verbs

4-1   1. allons   2. vont   3. vais   4. va   5. allez   6. va   7. va   8. vais   9. va   10. allez

4-2   1. Nous allons acheter une nouvelle machine à laver.   2. Il va prendre des vacances cet automne.   3. Vous allez investir au Japon.   4. Elle va avoir vingt ans.   5. Cette agence va promouvoir cette marchandise.   6. Il va être président.   7. Nous allons choisir un cadeau.   8. Tu vas dîner au restaurant.   9. Ils vont déménager en janvier.   10. Elle va travailler au centre-ville.

4-3   1. vient   2. viennent   3. viens   4. vient   5. revenez   6. prévient   7. venons   8. devient   9. revenez   10. viens

4-4   1. Je viens de téléphoner à Bernard.   2. Il vient d'annuler son vol.   3. Elle vient de remplacer tous ses meubles.   4. La police vient de révéler le secret.   5. Vous venez de commencer à travailler.   6. Elle vient de manquer le train.   7. Tu viens d'avoir trente ans.   8. Il vient d'achever ses études.   9. Nous venons de parler à la directrice.   10. Ils viennent de voir un bon film.

4-5   1. Vas-tu au cinéma dimanche?   2. Ils (Elles) vont bientôt déménager.   3. Comment vas-tu?   4. Ils (Elles) vont investir au Portugal.   5. Elle vient de commencer un nouveau travail.   6. Ce chapeau te va bien.   7. Ils viennent d'annuler mon vol.   8. Il va à la bibliothèque le samedi.   9. Elle vient d'appeler François.   10. Elle va finir le livre cet après-midi.

4-6   1. c   2. d   3. e   4. a   5. b

4-7   1. fait   2. font   3. fais   4. fait   5. faisons   6. fait   7. fait   8. font   9. faites   10. fait

4-8   1. Je fais lire le dossier.   2. Vous faites laver la voiture.   3. Il fait réparer la télévision.   4. Elle fait investir sa fortune.   5. Je fais envoyer le paquet.   6. Il fait annuler le voyage.   7. Tu fais remplacer l'employé malade.   8. Il fait visiter l'entreprise.   9. Je fais corriger les copies des étudiants.   10. Je fais chanter la chanson.

4-9   1. Ils (Elles) font envoyer la lettre à Paris.   2. Je fais la queue depuis dix minutes.   3. Ils (Elles) tiennent à leurs amis.   4. Il tient à chanter cette chanson.   5. Elle tient un vase.   6. Il tient de son père.   7. Il pleut.   8. Est-ce que vous savez faire la cuisine?   9. Elle fait laver sa voiture.   10. Il fait froid.

5 Devoir and its many facets

5-1   1. doit   2. dois   3. devez   4. doit   5. ne doivent pas   6. dois   7. doit   8. doivent   9. dois   10. dois

5-2   1. Vous devez faire la cuisine ce soir.   2. Elle ne doit pas travailler aujourd'hui.   3. À quelle heure est-ce qu'il doit arriver?   4. Combien est-ce que je vous dois?   5. Pourquoi est-ce qu'il doit vendre sa voiture?   6. Elle doit une excuse à Carole.   7. Est-ce que nous devons connaître ces verbes?   8. Il doit deux mille dollars à la banque.   9. Vous devriez appeler Vincent.   10. Vous ne devriez pas inviter Pierre.

5-3   1. e   2. a   3. d   4. c   5. b

5-4   1. craint   2. feint   3. plaignent   4. ceint   5. feignez   6. craignons   7. peignez   8. craignent   9. teint   10. se plaint

5-5   1. Elle peint la cuisine.   2. Il y a un chien dans la voiture.   3. Ils (Elles) plaignent le pauvre enfant.   4. Dans ce livre, il s'agit du président français.   5. De quoi est-ce qu'il s'agit?   6. Il craint le pire.   7. Il y a des livres sur la table.   8. Est-ce qu'il y a un ordinateur?   9. Est-ce que tu peins les fleurs?   10. Il s'agit de passion.

6 Pronominal verbs

6-1   1. m'habille   2. nous levons   3. se coupe   4. te couches   5. se lavent   6. te peignes   7. vous baladez   8. se reposent   9. nous amusons   10. se détend

6-2   1. se marient   2. vous embrassez   3. nous écrivons   4. se retrouvent   5. se voient   6. nous téléphonons   7. vous quittez   8. nous disputons   9. se détestent   10. nous rencontrons

6-3   1. s'aperçoit   2. se dépêchent   3. t'attends   4. se passe   5. vous servez   6. me rends compte   7. te demandes   8. se dépêche   9. te trompes   10. s'envole

6-4   1. me promener   2. te lever   3. nous rendre compte   4. se souvenir   5. se marier   6. vous demander   7. nous écrire   8. m'habiller   9. vous voir   10. nous plaindre

6-5	1. e 2. a 3. d 4. c 5. b
6-6	1. Lève-toi! 2. Elle s'habille pour la soirée. 3. Elle se coupe les cheveux. 4. Nous nous promenons dans le parc. 5. Ils (Elles) se reposent car leurs jambes sont fatiguées. 6. Il se rase. 7. Ils viennent de se marier. 8. Ils (Elles) s'écrivent. 9. Il est fatigué. Il s'assoit sur un banc. 10. Ils s'aiment.

7   The passé composé

7-1	1. a invité 2. avons refusé 3. as travaillé 4. a compris 5. a apporté 6. J'ai voyagé 7. avez loué 8. a sous-titré 9. avez téléphoné 10. as assisté
7-2	1. ont investi 2. a applaudi 3. ont réfléchi 4. a ralenti 5. ont attendu 6. avons réussi 7. a perdu 8. as grandi 9. a senti 10. a vendu
7-3	1. Ils (Elles) ont vendu la maison en France. 2. J'ai attendu dix minutes. 3. Il a fini le roman. 4. Elle a perdu son dictionnaire. 5. J'ai appelé Marc. 6. Ils (Elles) ont servi un dîner élégant. 7. Il a acheté une voiture. 8. J'ai choisi un très bon fromage. 9. Nous avons regardé le film. 10. Ils (Elles) ont applaudi le comédien.
7-4	1. J'ai pris 2. n'avons pas pu 3. ont suivi 4. a peint 5. a plu 6. avez reçu 7. avons lu 8. J'ai fait 9. a mis 10. a ouvert
7-5	1. e 2. d 3. a 4. b 5. c
7-6	1. est-il monté 2. sommes rentré(e)s 3. est tombée 4. sont descendus 5. sont revenues 6. est-il parti 7. est allée 8. est allé 9. est mort 10. est resté
7-7	1. Elle a lu le journal. 2. Nous sommes allé(e)s à Paris. 3. Ils sont partis (Elles sont parties) hier soir. 4. Il a dû partir à cinq heures. 5. Ils (Elles) ont habité en Italie. 6. Zola est mort en 1902. 7. J'ai écrit une longue lettre. 8. Elle a peint le mur en blanc. 9. Elle est restée à la maison. 10. Il a pris des vacances.
7-8	1. se sont promenés 2. s'est douté 3. se sont maquillées 4. se sont écrit 5. nous sommes arrêté(e)s 6. se sont occupés 7. se sont baladées 8. se sont rencontrés 9. t'es coupé 10. nous sommes demandé
7-9	1. e 2. a 3. d 4. b 5. c
7-10	1. Ils (Elles) ont passé un mois en Chine. 2. Elle s'est évanouie. 3. Ils se sont embrassés. 4. Ils se sont amusés (Elles se sont amusées) à la soirée. 5. Elle a descendu les valises. 6. Il s'est brossé les dents. 7. Il s'est réveillé fatigué. 8. Ils (Elles) se sont écrit régulièrement. 9. Anna s'est arrêtée dix minutes. 10. Il a retourné l'omelette.

8   The imparfait

8-1	1. voyageait 2. faisais 3. étions 4. buvaient 5. J'étais 6. aimions 7. partageaient 8. prenait 9. encourageait 10. alliez
8-2	1. croyait 2. J'étais 3. pensait 4. espéraient 5. avait 6. savais 7. étions 8. paraissiez 9. était 10. faisait
8-3	1. suivions 2. faisais 3. était 4. faisions 5. habitaient 6. buvions 7. assistaient 8. faisait 9. vous voyiez 10. travaillait
8-4	1. faisait 2. dormais 3. bavardions 4. se reposaient 5. parliez 6. étudiait 7. dansaient 8. réfléchissait 9. travaillait 10. J'attendais
8-5	1. Je jouais au tennis tous les jeudis. 2. Tu étudiais quand le téléphone a sonné. 3. Nous dormions quand tout à coup nous avons entendu un bruit fort. 4. Le restaurant était bondé. 5. Il faisait froid à la montagne. 6. Ils (Elles) avaient l'air fatigué. 7. La pièce était fascinante. 8. Elle travaillait aux Galeries Lafayette. 9. Nous attendions l'autobus quand il a commencé à pleuvoir. 10. Elle savait qu'ils (elles) avaient tort.
8-6	1. allait 2. déjeunait 3. apportait 4. attendait 5. commandait 6. faisait 7. ouvrait 8. investissait 9. réfléchissait 10. choisissait
8-7	1. Je suis allé(e) chez le dentiste hier. 2. Quand il était adolescent, il jouait au football. 3. À cette époque-là, ils tenaient une brasserie place d'Italie. 4. Ils ont randonné dans les Alpes le week-end passé. 5. Nous dînions dans ce restaurant tous les samedis. 6. Si on prenait un café? 7. Tu avais l'air fatigué.

8. Chaque jour, il écrivait une lettre à son amie.   9. Je regardais un film quand elle est arrivée.   10. La campagne était si belle.

9   The **futur simple** and the **futur antérieur**

9-1   1. suivrez   2. dînerons   3. entendras   4. cherchera   5. n'oublieront jamais   6. travaillerai   7. rendrons visite   8. finira   9. remplacera   10. partiras

9-2   1. sera   2. fera   3. sauras   4. aurons   5. ira   6. préférera   7. verrons   8. faudra   9. pourra   10. pleuvra

9-3   1. Vous irez à l'opéra quand vos amis seront à Lyon.   2. Nous prendrons une décision dès que la presse annoncera les résultats.   3. L'exposition aura lieu en janvier quand tous les tableaux seront réunis.   4. Le professeur emmènera les élèves au musée dès qu'il pourra.   5. Il devra nous appeler dès qu'il sera en contact avec M. Clément.   6. Tant qu'il y aura des hommes, il y aura des guerres.   7. Elle enseignera le français quand elle habitera au Vietnam.   8. Nous jouerons au bridge quand nous rendrons visite à nos amis.   9. Elle se reposera quand elle aura de longues vacances.   10. Dès qu'il obtiendra l'accord, il partira.

9-4   1. L'avion décollera à onze heures.   2. Tu apprendras à conduire.   3. Je peindrai le salon.   4. Ils sortiront avec des amis.   5. Vous recevrez une invitation.   6. Nous débarquerons à midi.   7. Elle écrira une lettre au président.   8. Tu mettras ton chapeau gris.   9. Ils iront en Bolivie.   10. Il vivra jusqu'à cent ans.

9-5   1. c   2. e   3. a   4. b   5. d

9-6   1. aura appris   2. aura fini   3. aurons visité   4. auront trouvé   5. aura découvert   6. J'aurai répondu   7. se sera reposée   8. auront complété   9. sera mort   10. J'aurai vu

9-7   1. Nous jouerons au tennis.   2. Vous aurez besoin d'acheter une nouvelle voiture.   3. Je suivrai un cours d'histoire.   4. Nous visiterons Venise quand nous serons en Italie.   5. Ils (Elles) iront à Dakar.   6. Nous marcherons le long de la plage.   7. Il étudiera le français quand il sera à Bordeaux.   8. Ils (Elles) verront l'exposition Picasso quand ils (elles) seront à Paris.   9. Elle voyagera en Asie quand elle obtiendra son diplôme.   10. Il deviendra médecin.

9-8   1. n'ira pas   2. fera   3. ne pourra pas   4. gèlera   5. nous promènerons   6. enverrai   7. ferai   8. ira   9. découvriras   10. contacterai

10   The **plus-que-parfait**

10-1   1. J'avais dîné   2. avait expliqué   3. aviez investi   4. étaient arrivées   5. avais décidé   6. avions roulé   7. avait échoué   8. étais allé(e)   9. J'avais obtenu   10. avait bu

10-2   1. avait pris   2. nous étions réveillé(e)s   3. t'étais demandé(e)   4. s'était habillée   5. s'étaient mariés   6. s'étaient couchées   7. s'était souvenu   8. nous étions promené(e)s   9. s'était reposée   10. s'étaient écrites

10-3   1. était tombée   2. avait eu   3. n'avais pas expliqué   4. avait prescrit   5. avait oublié   6. était parti   7. avait invité   8. avait rencontré   9. avait souffert   10. avait reçu

10-4   1. d   2. c   3. e   4. b   5. a

10-5   1. Si seulement vous n'aviez pas été en retard!   2. Si seulement tu avais étudié le français plus jeune!   3. Si seulement nous avions su la vérité!   4. Si seulement elle était restée plus longtemps!   5. Si seulement il avait rendu visite à sa cousine Flore!   6. Si seulement j'avais pris une meilleure décision!   7. Si seulement elle avait expliqué la situation plus clairement!   8. Si seulement vous aviez pu venir à la réception!   9. Si seulement tu avais compris les problèmes!   10. Si seulement il avait conseillé autre chose!

10-6   1. Il a pris le médicament que le médecin avait prescrit.   2. Elle savait qu'ils (elles) avaient fait une erreur.   3. Il était malade car il avait mangé trop de dessert.   4. Je me suis demandé pourquoi elle était restée trois mois à Vienne.   5. Je pensais qu'ils (elles) avaient compris le problème.   6. Si seulement il n'avait pas été en retard!   7. Elle était fatiguée parce qu'elle n'avait dormi que cinq heures.   8. Il avait faim parce qu'il n'avait pas mangé depuis sept heures du matin.   9. Nous pensions qu'il avait vu ce film.   10. Il pensait qu'elle avait lu le livre.

11 The present conditional and the past conditional

11-1   1. irions   2. voyagerait   3. dirions   4. j'aurais   5. mangeraient   6. prendrait   7. serais   8. demanderiez   9. j'écrirais   10. saurais

11-2   1. Iriez-vous   2. Pourrions-nous   3. Pourriez-vous   4. M'achèteriez-vous   5. Signerait-il   6. Pourriez-vous   7. Pourrait-elle   8. Iriez-vous   9. Pourrions-nous   10. Accompagneraient-ils (-elles)

11-3   1. Si j'avais moins de travail, je voyagerais plus.   2. S'ils attendaient, ils obtiendraient un meilleur prix pour leur appartement.   3. Si nous plantions plus de fleurs, nous aurions un plus beau jardin.   4. Si je vendais mon appartement, je pourrais acheter cette maison.   5. S'il pouvait, il déménagerait.   6. Si vous les invitiez, nous serions ravis.   7. Si ma voiture tombait en panne, je piquerais une crise.   8. Si elle avait plus d'argent, elle viendrait avec nous.   9. Si vous vous organisiez autrement, votre vie serait plus facile.   10. Si tu dormais plus, tu aurais de meilleures notes à l'école.

11-4   1. Elle serait contente si tu venais ce soir.   2. Nous ferions une promenade dans le parc s'il faisait beau.   3. Ils prendraient leur retraite s'ils pouvaient.   4. Il accompagnerait Sophie à l'opéra s'il n'était pas occupé.   5. Il y aurait moins de problèmes si vous suiviez mes conseils.   6. Elles iraient au musée s'il était ouvert avant onze heures.   7. Vous finiriez plus tôt si vous travailliez plus efficacement.   8. Nous vous croirions si vous nous disiez la vérité.   9. Elle achèterait cette voiture si elle était moins chère.   10. Tu lui offrirais ce poste si tu avais confiance en lui.

11-5   1. Il irait à Paris s'il avait plus de temps.   2. Elle achèterait ce manteau s'il était moins cher.   3. Nous serions ravi(e)s si tu venais dimanche.   4. J'écrirais une lettre si tu en avais besoin.   5. Le président serait au Brésil aujourd'hui.   6. Ce serait plus joli s'il y avait plus de fleurs.   7. J'inviterais Chloé si j'allais à Paris.   8. Le directeur signerait le contrat.   9. Elle mangerait la soupe si elle avait faim.   10. Il lirait le journal ce matin s'il pouvait.

11-6   1. c   2. d   3. a   4. e   5. b

11-7   1. Nous aurions dîné avec vous si nous avions pu.   2. Elle aurait visité ce musée si elle avait eu plus de temps.   3. Elle aurait vu ce film s'il avait été sous-titré.   4. Ils auraient invité Charles s'il n'avait pas travaillé ce soir-là.   5. Il aurait fait un documentaire sur ce sujet s'il avait trouvé le financement.   6. Ils auraient vendu leur maison si leurs enfants avaient déménagé.   7. Vous seriez arrivé à temps si votre voiture n'était pas tombée en panne.   8. Le directeur aurait démissionné si les ouvriers n'avaient pas fait pression.   9. Cette pièce aurait eu du succès s'il y avait eu plus de temps pour les répétitions.   10. Nous serions venus si nous avions reçu votre invitation plus tôt.

11-8   1. S'il avait fini son projet, il n'aurait pas dû travailler le week-end.   2. Si j'avais mis mon manteau, je n'aurais pas eu si froid.   3. Si vous aviez pu témoigner au tribunal, la situation aurait été différente.   4. Si on n'avait pas guillotiné le roi, l'histoire du pays aurait pris une tournure différente.   5. S'il avait appris sa grammaire, il aurait fait moins de fautes.   6. Si elle s'était présentée aux élections, elle aurait été élue.   7. Si nous avions commandé un couscous, nous n'aurions pas eu faim plus tard.   8. Si elle avait pu, elle aurait été danseuse.   9. Si tu avais été plus pratique, nous aurions voyagé sans bagages.   10. Si j'avais su, je n'aurais pas engagé Daniel.

11-9   1. Le Premier Ministre serait allé en Chine hier.   2. Le témoin aurait donné une version différente à la police.   3. Le cyclone aurait tué deux cents personnes dans cette ville.   4. Le directeur aurait démissionné.   5. La tempête aurait détruit des centaines de maisons.   6. Le chômage baisserait l'année prochaine.   7. Le ministre de la Santé aurait signé la réforme.   8. Les pingouins ne pourraient pas se reproduire en raison du réchauffement climatique.   9. Son nouveau voisin aurait volé sa voiture.   10. Un acteur français aurait acheté une maison en Californie la semaine dernière.

11-10   1. c   2. e   3. a   4. b   5. d

12 *Could, should, would?*

12-1   1. Pourriez-vous aider à nettoyer la maison après la soirée?   2. Nous n'avons pas pu partir en vacances.   3. Je pourrais lui acheter une nouvelle flûte.   4. À cette époque-là, ils (elles) ne pouvaient pas comprendre.   5. Pourrions-nous commencer à manger?   6. Nous pourrions aller voir un film ce soir.   7. Grâce à sa tante riche, elle a pu payer ses études.   8. Je pense qu'elle pourrait mieux faire.   9. Quand vous étiez enfant, vous jouiez avec vos poupées pendant des heures.   10. Pourriez-vous m'apprendre à jouer de la guitare?

12-2 1. Vous devriez apprendre à jouer de la guitare.   2. Ils (Elles) n'auraient pas dû dire cela.   3. Je devrais écrire à Pierre.   4. J'aurais dû leur parler.   5. Pensez-vous que Julien aurait dû vous appeler avant de venir?   6. Je n'aurais pas dû vous appeler si tôt.   7. Nous ne devrions pas prendre la voiture, c'est trop dangereux.   8. Je pense que vous devriez prendre des vacances.   9. Vous devriez louer un piano pour la soirée.   10. Marie pense que son père devrait être présent pour cette occasion.

12-3 1. If he were less lazy, he would have better grades in school.   2. When we were children, our parents would take us on vacation to Morocco every year.   3. Samuel asked for a little more money. His boss would not do it (refused).   4. If Emmanuelle were available, she would come.   5. When she was a student in Paris, she would go to the movies every Sunday.   6. If Sylvie had more money, she would buy herself new shoes.   7. If they had a choice, they would not move.   8. Would you tell me what happened at that meeting?   9. Catherine wanted to turn around, but her husband would not do it (refused).   10. Could you explain to me how this works?

12-4 1. Pourrais-tu lire ce document?   2. Nous devrions acheter des billets pour le concert.   3. Valérie pourrait t'aider!   4. À cette époque-là, elle ne pouvait pas sortir souvent.   5. Pourrais-tu m'envoyer un double de cette lettre?   6. Je lui ai demandé de m'aider; elle n'a pas voulu.   7. Pascal jouerait du violon s'il avait plus de temps.   8. Marie n'a pas pu lui dire la vérité.   9. Quand nous étions enfants, nous jouions sur la plage pendant des heures.   10. Ne penses-tu pas que tu devrais changer de coiffure?

12-5 1. Could you open the door?   2. At that time, he should be home.   3. They could not get tickets.   4. Would you like to participate in this project?   5. I came to pick him up. He would not come with me.   6. If you were not so selfish, you would have more friends.   7. Would you be willing to show me how it works?   8. He could not leave in time.   9. When we were children, we would go to the seashore every summer.   10. He should think before talking.

12-6 1. c   2. a   3. b   4. e   5. d

13   The present subjunctive and the past subjunctive

13-1 1. soit   2. compreniez   3. ne sorte pas   4. finisse   5. gèrent   6. ne soient pas   7. ait   8. soit   9. puisse   10. dise

13-2 1. alliez   2. arriviez   3. acceptions   4. voyagions   5. soit   6. ne disions rien   7. habitent   8. vendiez   9. suive   10. emportions

13-3 1. donniez   2. ne soit pas   3. fasses   4. ne se sentent pas   5. vole   6. puissent   7. ne réponde pas   8. donnent   9. restent   10. puisse

13-4 1. est   2. fasse   3. puissent   4. a   5. fasses   6. aient   7. sont   8. obteniez   9. parliez   10. est

13-5 1. voyagions   2. vous trompez   3. trouvions   4. connaisse   5. achetions   6. ne soit pas   7. ait   8. envoyiez   9. puisse   10. soit

13-6 1. Pourvu qu'il ait raison!   2. Elle est heureuse qu'il puisse étudier le français.   3. Il est possible que vous puissiez acheter ce logiciel ici.   4. Appelez-nous avant que nous allions en France!   5. Il est étrange qu'il soit en retard.   6. Pourvu qu'il puisse venir!   7. Elle veut que vous achetiez cet ordinateur.   8. Bien qu'il soit fatigué, il lit le journal.   9. Bien qu'il fasse quelques fautes, son français est très bon.   10. C'est la plus belle ville que je connaisse.

13-7 1. aies lu   2. ayez pu   3. ait été   4. n'ayez pas vu   5. ait manqué   6. ait réussi   7. ait plagié   8. j'aie pu   9. aient lu   10. ayez dit

13-8 1. Il est content que nous soyons parti(e)s.   2. Nous sommes ravis que tu aies pu venir avec nous.   3. Je ne crois pas qu'il soit allé à l'exposition.   4. Il doute qu'elle ait réussi.   5. Elle a peur qu'il ait eu un accident de moto.   6. Ils sont contents que Laurent se soit marié.   7. Nous sommes désolés que votre sœur ait été malade.   8. Il est douteux qu'ils soient allés en Patagonie.   9. Il est regrettable que leurs enfants aient été si peu reconnaissants.   10. Il est incroyable que vous n'ayez pas su la réponse.

13-9 1. d   2. c   3. a   4. e   5. b

14   The infinitive mood

14-1 1. Écrire ce livre était un défi.   2. Étudier le français est amusant.   3. Travailler quatre jours par semaine est idéal.   4. Trouver un nouveau travail sera difficile.   5. Marcher le long de la Seine est agréable.

6. Se réveiller à cinq heures du matin est trop tôt.   7. Faire la cuisine prend beaucoup de temps.
8. Prendre ce médicament deux fois par jour.   9. Ajouter du poivre.   10. Ne pas mettre d'ail.

14-2   1. à faire la cuisine   2. à danser   3. à parler   4. à éplucher des légumes   5. à travailler pour eux
6. à chercher un autre travail   7. à lire   8. à cueillir des fleurs   9. à rêver   10. à faire les courses

14-3   1. avoir dormi   2. être allé   3. avoir mangé   4. s'être promené   5. avoir regardé   6. être tombé
7. s'être levé   8. avoir préparé   9. être parti   10. avoir allumé

14-4   1. Elle prend des vacances après avoir complété son projet.   2. Il écrit la lettre après avoir consulté son
ami.   3. Je prépare un thé après avoir cueilli des fruits.   4. Ils rendent visite à leurs amis après être allés
au théâtre.   5. Il verse le vin après avoir servi le dîner.   6. Elle se maquille après s'être habillée.
7. Nous dînons après avoir regardé le film à la télévision.   8. Ils se promènent après avoir travaillé.   9. Je
réfléchis après avoir téléphoné.   10. Nous allons chez Julien après avoir choisi un cadeau.

14-5   1. déteste   2. veulent   3. devons   4. peux   5. désirons   6. veux   7. semble   8. penses   9. faut
10. allez

14-6   1. à   2. de   3. à   4. de   5. à   6. de   7. à   8. de   9. de   10. de

14-7   1. Ils (Elles) veulent voyager en France.   2. Il a passé des heures à éplucher des pommes de terre.
3. Faire la cuisine est son passe-temps favori.   4. N'oubliez pas d'ajouter du sel!   5. Il a peur de brûler la
viande.   6. Ils (Elles) ont envie de manger un soufflé au chocolat.   7. Il a cessé de fumer.   8. Ils (Elles)
ont refusé de sortir.   9. Elle apprend à faire la cuisine.   10. Essayez de comprendre la situation!

15   The present participle and the gerund

15-1   1. finissant   2. sachant   3. donnant   4. protégeant   5. faisant   6. ayant   7. avançant   8. étant
9. prononçant   10. vendant

15-2   1. faisant   2. prenant   3. jouant   4. faisant   5. sachant   6. allant   7. se plaignant   8. visitant
9. arrivant   10. pariant

15-3   1. Il a perdu ses clés en marchant dans le parc.   2. N'ayant pas vu le film, je ne peux pas faire de
commentaires.   3. Ils (Elles) ont vu Paul en traversant la rue.   4. Sachant la vérité, elle ne pouvait pas
rester silencieuse.   5. Il a gagné de l'argent en vendant des tableaux.   6. C'était un match fascinant.
7. Ayant fini le livre, il est parti.   8. Ils (Elles) écoutent de la musique en travaillant.   9. Je tricote en
regardant la télévision.   10. Il est tombé en sautant par-dessus le mur.

16   The passé simple

16-1   1. être   2. avoir   3. peindre   4. faire   5. venir   6. lire   7. vouloir   8. savoir   9. plaire
10. éteindre

16-2   1. fut   2. obtinrent   3. explora   4. mourut   5. peignit   6. trembla   7. introduisit   8. eut lieu
9. fit   10. devint

16-3   1. Il vécut dix ans à Amsterdam.   2. Elle introduisit cette nouvelle méthode.   3. Ils (Elles) lurent tous ses
livres.   4. Il mourut en Italie.   5. Il fut surpris.   6. Je voulus le remercier.   7. Elle naquit à Rouen.
8. Ils (Elles) achetèrent un nouveau chevalet.   9. Elle devint portraitiste.   10. Il sourit et partit.

17   The passive voice

17-1   1. Le voleur a été attrapé par le policier.   2. Le traité a été signé par le roi.   3. Un nouveau traitement est
prescrit par le médecin.   4. Le tableau a été volé par le cambrioleur.   5. L'homme au chapeau gris a été
mordu par le chien.   6. L'otage a été pris par l'ennemi.   7. Le canapé a été déchiré par l'enfant.   8. Un
célèbre tableau sera vendu par le marchand d'art.   9. La forteresse est prise par les envahisseurs.   10. Les
étudiants sont félicités par le professeur.

17-2   1. Le chef a fait le gâteau.   2. L'artisan a conçu l'objet.   3. Le roi a érigé le château.   4. L'ambassadeur
signera le document.   5. Le propriétaire a vendu le tableau.   6. Le chat griffe le fauteuil.   7. Le
malfaiteur a payé l'amende.   8. L'antiquaire a volé le vase.   9. Un journaliste écrira le livre.   10. Le
professeur punit les élèves.

17-3 1. Le château est construit par la reine. 2. Le tableau a été volé par un marchand d'art. 3. Un chapeau rose a été retrouvé dans le parc hier. 4. Ce verbe est suivi de l'indicatif. 5. La maison est entourée par la police. 6. Un nouveau remède sera inventé avant 2050. 7. Ce vaccin a été inventé en 1885. 8. La décision a été prise lundi. 9. La lettre a été lue par un témoin. 10. La maison est entourée d'arbres.

18 Indirect speech

18-1 1. Il veut savoir si le programme du parti est bien défini. 2. Il veut savoir si nous allons boycotter les prochaines élections. 3. Il veut savoir si tu vas voter dimanche. 4. Il veut savoir si le ministre de l'éducation a proposé des réformes. 5. Il veut savoir si elle acceptera notre proposition. 6. Il veut savoir si le parti a choisi son candidat. 7. Il veut savoir si les femmes peuvent voter dans ce pays. 8. Il veut savoir si vous viendrez samedi soir. 9. Il veut savoir si elle a fini ses recherches. 10. Il veut savoir si la parité sera jamais réalisée.

18-2 1. Elle annonce qu'elle sera absente mardi. 2. Ils avouent que Paul s'est trompé. 3. La marchande dit que ses produits sont les meilleurs. 4. Tu sais bien qu'elles avaient tort. 5. On se rend compte que le candidat a peu de chance de gagner. 6. Ils ne savent pas si le musée est ouvert. 7. Tu réponds que tu n'avais rien entendu. 8. Elle nous apprend qu'il n'est jamais allé en France. 9. Il nous déclare qu'ils avaient dilapidé leur fortune. 10. Il ignore où le peintre habite.

18-3 1. J'ai entendu dire que tu avais accepté leur offre la semaine dernière. 2. J'ai entendu dire qu'elle avait vendu sa voiture hier. 3. J'ai entendu dire que tu travaillerais à Chicago l'an prochain. 4. J'ai entendu dire qu'elle irait en Asie demain. 5. J'ai entendu dire qu'ils s'étaient mariés le mois dernier. 6. J'ai entendu dire qu'il faisait froid à Moscou aujourd'hui. 7. J'ai entendu dire qu'ils s'installeraient au Canada l'an prochain. 8. J'ai entendu dire qu'il avait quitté son poste vendredi dernier. 9. J'ai entendu dire qu'elle était la candidate favorite en ce moment. 10. J'ai entendu dire que tu avais pris beaucoup de photos hier soir.

18-4 1. Ils (Elles) savent que vous habitez à Paris. 2. J'ai entendu dire que vous habitiez à Paris. 3. J'ai entendu dire que vous aviez habité à Paris en 1995. 4. J'ai entendu dire que vous iriez à Paris l'année prochaine. 5. Il dit que son chat est adorable. 6. J'ai entendu dire que vous aviez un chat. 7. J'ai entendu dire que vous aviez un chat quand vous habitiez boulevard Victor Hugo. 8. J'ai entendu dire que votre sœur vous donnerait son chat. 9. On m'a dit que vous aviez voté pour moi. 10. Nous nous rendons compte qu'elle a une chance de gagner.

19 The imperative mood

19-1 1. Prends le train de neuf heures! 2. Regardez le film à la télé ce soir! 3. Dînons sur la terrasse! 4. Achète le journal! 5. Buvons à sa santé! 6. Expliquez les conditions! 7. Ne cours pas si vite! 8. Épelle ton nom! 9. Prêtez votre dictionnaire à Marie! 10. N'invite pas Denis!

19-2 1. Lave-toi les mains! 2. Baladez-vous dans la forêt. 3. Écrivons-nous plus souvent! 4. Ne te couche pas trop tard! 5. Réveillez-vous à cinq heures! 6. Habille-toi vite! 7. Ne vous trompez pas de route! 8. Retrouvons-nous devant la Brasserie Lipp! 9. Dépêche-toi! 10. Rencontrons-nous un jour à Paris!

19-3 1. N'oublie pas ton passeport! 2. Reposons-nous sur le banc! 3. Apportez votre carte d'identité! 4. Dis-nous son prénom! 5. Prends ce médicament! 6. Ne soyez pas en retard! 7. Allons en Italie! 8. Ferme la porte! 9. Attendez-moi! 10. Écrivez votre adresse sur l'enveloppe!

20 Articles and nouns

20-1 1. des 2. du 3. des 4. de la 5. de l' 6. des 7. du 8. des 9. des 10. de la

20-2 1. le 2. le 3. la 4. la 5. le 6. la 7. le 8. le 9. la 10. le

20-3 1. le roi 2. le frère 3. le grand-père 4. le vendeur 5. le décorateur 6. le neveu 7. le fils 8. le rédacteur 9. le Brésilien 10. le prince

20-4 1. la directrice 2. ma coiffeuse 3. la pharmacienne 4. la tante de Paul 5. ma sœur 6. son institutrice 7. la reine 8. ma cousine 9. une femme 10. la bouchère

20-5 1. la 2. la 3. le 4. l' (f.) 5. le 6. la 7. l' (f.) 8. l'(f.) 9. le 10. la

20-6 1. en 2. en 3. en 4. au 5. au 6. en 7. en 8. en 9. au 10. en

20-7 1. Marie habite à Lyon, en France. 2. Christina habite à Istanbul, en Turquie. 3. Fatima habite à Tunis, en Tunisie. 4. Laurent habite à Varsovie, en Pologne. 5. Vincent habite à Caracas, au Venezuela. 6. Nancy habite à Toronto, au Canada. 7. Xavier habite à Mexico, au Mexique. 8. Patrick habite à Boston, aux États-Unis. 9. Henri habite à Sydney, en Australie. 10. Martha habite à Berlin, en Allemagne.

20-8 1. d' 2. d' 3. de 4. d' 5. du 6. du 7. des 8. d' 9. de 10. du

20-9 1. Elle habite dans un village en Irlande. 2. Son frère habite en Russie. 3. Il a étudié en France. 4. Elle est allée en Normandie l'été dernier. 5. Ils (Elles) ont voyagé en Grèce en mai. 6. Ils (Elles) importent des produits d'Argentine. 7. Leur fils travaille en Californie. 8. Elle a pris cette photo au Japon. 9. Ils (Elles) construisent un pont dans un village au Sénégal. 10. Allons en Chine!

21 All the pronouns

21-1 1. Elle les achète. 2. Il le consulte. 3. Nous le soutenons. 4. Ils la construisent. 5. Je l'ouvre. 6. Elle la conduit. 7. Il les accepte. 8. Nous la comprenons. 9. Tu le visites. 10. Elle l'étudie.

21-2 1. Il me remercie. 2. L'écrivain les envoie. 3. Ils (Elles) nous invitent. 4. Nous l'acceptons. 5. Elle les a appelé(e)s. 6. Apportez-les! 7. Je vais l'acheter. 8. Ne le (la) vendez pas! 9. Nous devons le (la) voir. 10. La connaissez-vous?

21-3 1. La grand-mère leur a raconté une histoire. 2. Nous lui avons fait un cadeau. 3. Je lui ferai parvenir le dossier dès que possible. 4. Nous lui enverrons des fleurs. 5. Ce théâtre lui appartient. 6. Est-ce que tu lui as écrit? 7. Téléphonez-lui aussitôt que possible! 8. Ne lui mentionnez rien! 9. Il leur annoncera sa décision demain. 10. Il leur donnera le scénario en fin de journée.

21-4 1. Apporte-moi un livre! 2. Ne les appelle pas après huit heures du soir! 3. Envoie-nous ta nouvelle pièce! 4. Je lui écrirai une lettre. 5. Elle me donnera une réponse lundi. 6. Il ne m'a pas rendu les livres. 7. Ce stylo lui appartient. 8. Il ne nous parle pas. 9. Ils (Elles) nous ont raconté une bonne histoire. 10. Ils (Elles) te prêteront leur maison pour le week-end.

21-5 1. Elle s'y habitue. 2. Tu devrais y prêter attention. 3. Nous nous y intéressons. 4. Je m'y abonne. 5. Elle y tient. 6. Nous n'y croyons pas. 7. Il n'y pense jamais. 8. Ils n'y obéissent pas. 9. Elle y réfléchira. 10. Pourquoi n'y avez-vous jamais répondu?

21-6 1. J'en ai parlé. 2. Ils en ont envie. 3. Nous en avons besoin. 4. Il s'en est approché très lentement. 5. Je m'en chargerai. 6. Tu t'en sers? 7. Il en a peur. 8. Je ne m'en souviens pas. 9. Elle s'en est occupée. 10. Il ne pourra jamais s'en débarrasser.

21-7 1. e 2. d 3. a 4. c 5. b

21-8 1. Ne lui en parlez pas! 2. Elle lui en a emprunté. 3. Je le lui ferai parvenir. 4. Patrick les lui a racontées. 5. Le musicien la lui a envoyée. 6. L'ouvrier la lui a donnée. 7. Je la lui ai demandée. 8. Il la lui vendra. 9. Le médecin le lui a prescrit. 10. Je le leur recommande.

21-9 1. J'y pense. 2. Il ne s'y intéresse pas. 3. Elle s'en est occupée. 4. Je te l'ai envoyée. 5. Nous le leur avons donné. 6. Je m'en sers tous les jours. 7. Il en a parlé. 8. J'en ai besoin. 9. Elle m'en a emprunté. 10. Ils (Elles) nous en ont donné.

21-10 1. C'est lui qui a gagné... 2. C'est moi qui prendrai... 3. C'est vous qui écrirez... 4. C'est nous qui préparons... 5. C'est toi qui as fait... 6. C'est elle qui lui fait... 7. C'est moi qui vous ai invité. 8. C'est eux qui sont... 9. C'est elles qui s'occuperont... 10. C'est lui qui fait...

21-11 1. Il ira en France avec moi. 2. Moi, je déteste le café! 3. Elle travaille pour nous. 4. À qui est ce livre? 5. Fais-le toi-même! 6. Je ne peux pas prendre cette décision sans toi. 7. Il est plus grand que toi. 8. Je pense à elle. 9. Ils (Elles) ont peur de lui. 10. Elle l'a dit elle-même.

21-12 1. Moi non plus. 2. Eux aussi. 3. Elle aussi. 4. Elles aussi. 5. Nous aussi.

22 Adjectives and comparisons

22-1 1. Ta grand-mère est française? —Non, elle est italienne. 2. Ces fenêtres sont propres? —Non, ces fenêtres sont sales. 3. Sa femme est blonde? —Non, elle est rousse. 4. Il porte ses chaussures noires? —Non, il porte des chaussures bleu marine. 5. C'est une situation sérieuse? —Oui, c'est une situation très sérieuse. 6. C'est une histoire tragique? —Non, c'est une histoire amusante. 7. C'est un long voyage? —Non, c'est assez court. 8. Votre projet est ambitieux. —Non, c'est la directrice qui est ambitieuse. 9. Ses idées sont bonnes? —Oui, ses idées sont meilleures que les nôtres.   10. Ton travail est ennuyeux? —Non, mon travail est très intéressant.

22-2   1. vieilles   2. adorable   3. fascinant   4. intéressant   5. folle

22-3   1. française   2. charmante   3. amoureuse   4. belle   5. agressive   6. active   7. folle
8. généreuse   9. rousse   10. douée

22-4   1. Je suis plus optimiste que lui.   2. Cécile est aussi efficace que Carole.   3. Ce vin-ci est meilleur que ce vin-là.   4. Sa sœur est aussi intelligente qu'elle.   5. Votre chambre est moins chère que la mienne.
6. Arnaud a autant d'argent que vous?   7. Ce prix est le meilleur!   8. Marie a moins de paires de chaussures que toi.   9. Elle est plus organisée que lui.   10. Cet appartement est le plus beau de l'immeuble.

22-5   1. Charlotte est plus grande que Lucie.   2. Charles est aussi drôle que Xavier.   3. Véronique est moins optimiste que Sébastien.   4. Lucien est plus intelligent que sa sœur.   5. Élodie est aussi bronzée que Thérèse.

22-6   1. C'est une bonne idée.   2. Ils (Elles) ont acheté une vieille maison en Normandie.   3. Ce jeune homme est ambitieux.   4. Cette chemise blanche est à moi.   5. Sa tante aime les vieilles chansons françaises.
6. Je n'ai pas votre nouvelle adresse.   7. L'Angleterre est plus petite que la France.   8. Elle n'aime pas cette veste jaune.   9. Elle est aussi ambitieuse que lui.   10. Cette histoire est ennuyeuse.

22-7   1. e   2. d   3. a   4. b   5. c

23   Demonstrative adjectives and pronouns

23-1   1. cette   2. ce   3. cette   4. ce   5. ces   6. Cette   7. ce   8. ces   9. Cette/ce   10. Ce

23-2   1. cette pâtisserie-ci / cette pâtisserie-là   2. ce jouet-ci / ce jouet-là   3. Ce cousin-ci / ce cousin-là
4. Cette maison-ci / cette maison-là   5. Ce neveu-ci / ce neveu-là   6. cette belle-sœur-ci / cette belle-sœur-là   7. ce roman-ci / ce roman-là   8. ce jeu-ci / ce jeu-là   9. Cette poupée-ci / cette poupée-là
10. cette carte-ci / cette carte-là

23-3   1. sa   2. son   3. son   4. Sa   5. notre   6. votre   7. Votre   8. ma   9. leur   10. Leurs

23-4   1. b, d   2. e   3. b, d   4. a, c   5. a, c

23-5   1. Les siens   2. Les miens   3. le mien   4. le vôtre   5. le tien   6. les leurs   7. les nôtres   8. le sien
9. le mien   10. le sien

23-6   1. Ma famille est plus grande que la vôtre.   2. Notre situation est plus difficile que la sienne.   3. Ses frères sont plus jeunes qu'elle.   4. Leur ville est plus propre que la nôtre.   5. Mon exercice est plus avancé que le leur.   6. Votre chien est plus beau que le sien.   7. Nos voisins sont plus sympathiques que les vôtres.   8. Vos hivers sont plus froids que les nôtres.   9. Leurs produits sont plus chers que les vôtres.
10. Vos enfants sont plus actifs que les miens.

23-7   1. —Quelle robe vas-tu porter? —Celle que j'ai achetée à Paris.   2. —Que pensez-vous de son nouveau roman? —C'est affreux!   3. —En quoi sont ces bagues? —Celle-ci est en or et celle-là est en argent.
4. —Que penses-tu de ma nouvelle maison? —C'est belle!   5. —Quels plats pouvons-nous préparer?
—Nous pouvons préparer ceux que tu préfères.   6. —Ces films sont disponibles? —Celui-ci est disponible mais pas celui-là.   7. —Sont-ils sous-titrés? —Celui-ci est sous-titré en français et celui-là en allemand.
8. Leurs enfants aiment les jeux mais pas ceux qui sont difficiles.   9. Regarde ces deux livres. Penses-tu que ma mère aimerait celui-ci ou celui-là?   10. Voici deux bracelets. Celui-ci est indien. Celui-là est égyptien.

23-8   1. Celle-ci est rose. Celle-là est blanche.   2. Ceux-ci sont inconnus. Ceux-là sont célèbres.   3. Celui-ci est jeune. Celui-là est plus âgé.   4. Celui-ci est trop tôt. Celui-là est trop tard.   5. Celui-ci est un best-seller. Celui-là est épuisé.   6. Celui-ci est vieux. Celui-là est le dernier modèle.   7. Celle-ci est trop claire. Celle-là est trop foncée.   8. Ceux-ci sont bien écrits. Ceux-là sont mal écrits.   9. Celle-ci est légère. Celle-là est lourde.   10. Ceux-ci sont bons. Ceux-là sont nuls.

23-9   1. Après dix années difficiles, elle est retournée chez les siens.   2. Mon ami René n'est pas à l'aise parmi les siens.   3. Son jeune chien a encore fait des siennes!   4. Leur petite-fille a encore fait des siennes à l'école!
5. À la tienne! C'est ton anniversaire.   6. Tu vas tout perdre si tu n'y mets pas du tien!   7. S'il n'y met pas du sien, la présentation sera un désastre!

24 Relative pronouns

24-1 1. suis 2. suit 3. avons 4. peuvent 5. sait 6. ai 7. devez 8. fait 9. écris 10. veulent

24-2 1. qui 2. qu' 3. qui 4. qui 5. que 6. qui 7. que 8. qui 9. que 10. qu'

24-3 1. c 2. e 3. a 4. b 5. d

24-4 1. pour qui / pour laquelle 2. par laquelle 3. avec lequel 4. à laquelle 5. avec lesquels 6. dans lequel 7. auquel 8. chez qui / chez lesquels 9. à quoi 10. sans qui / sans laquelle

24-5 1. dont 2. que 3. dont 4. qui 5. dont 6. qui 7. dont 8. que 9. qu' 10. dont

24-6 1. Je peux me souvenir de l'année où il a ouvert son magasin (sa boutique). 2. Le lustre qu'il a acheté est pour le salon. 3. L'outil avec lequel elle travaille est très vieux. 4. C'est vous qui êtes le (la) propriétaire? 5. Le fauteuil dans lequel vous êtes assis(e) appartenait à mon grand-père. 6. La ville où ils (elles) habitent est très belle. 7. Je connais la personne dont il parle. 8. C'est le seul détail dont je me souviens. 9. Les documents dont vous avez besoin sont chez Valérie. 10. Je ne sais pas à quoi il pense.

24-7 1. Ce à quoi 2. Ce dont 3. Ce qu' 4. Ce dont 5. Ce dont 6. Ce qui 7. Ce que 8. Ce qui 9. Ce dont 10. Ce que

24-8 1. Ce qu'il veut, c'est plus de temps libre. 2. Ce dont le souffleur de verre se sert est dans l'autre atelier. 3. Ce dont je ne peux pas me souvenir, c'est de cet incident en Camargue. 4. Ce à quoi je m'attendais était différent. 5. Ce dont il a besoin, c'est de ce livre. 6. Ce dont ils (elles) parlent est intéressant. 7. Ce qu'il fait est difficile. 8. Ce à quoi elle s'intéresse, c'est à cette collection d'art. 9. Ce qu'ils (elles) aiment, c'est le chocolat. 10. Ce qui s'est passé hier soir est très triste.

24-9 1. qui 2. dont 3. laquelle 4. Ce dont 5. qui 6. ce que 7. qui 8. auxquels 9. que 10. Ce qui

25 Adverbs and expressions of time, frequency, and location

25-1 1. demain / demain soir 2. la semaine prochaine / la semaine prochaine 3. aujourd'hui / aujourd'hui 4. tous les jours / tous les deux jours 5. tard 6. souvent / rarement 7. parfois / jamais 8. en ce moment / en ce moment 9. la semaine prochaine / après-demain 10. hier / avant-hier

25-2 1. Aujourd'hui, c'est le premier jour de l'hiver. 2. Elle voyage souvent. 3. Je ne suis jamais à l'heure. Je suis toujours en retard. 4. Il arrive après-demain. 5. Son rendez-vous est dans deux semaines. 6. Nous travaillons demain, mais nous ne travaillons pas après-demain. 7. Ils (Elles) ont vendu leur maison la semaine dernière. 8. Est-ce que tu vas à l'opéra ce soir? 9. Tu es tôt. Je ne suis pas prêt(e). 10. La boulangerie sera fermée la semaine prochaine.

25-3 1. Depuis quand 2. Depuis combien de temps 3. Depuis quand 4. Depuis combien de temps 5. Depuis quand 6. Depuis combien de temps / depuis 7. Depuis quand 8. Depuis quand 9. Depuis combien de temps 10. depuis

25-4 1. Je travaille pour cette agence de voyages depuis cinq ans. 2. Je cherche un nouvel appartement depuis le mois de janvier. 3. Je vais chez cet opticien depuis des années. 4. Nous sommes mariés depuis quatorze ans. 5. Nous nous connaissons depuis neuf ans. 6. Je t'attends depuis quarante-cinq minutes. 7. Je prends cette ligne de métro depuis cinq ans. 8. Le coiffeur est situé par ici depuis six mois. 9. Je ne fume plus depuis la semaine dernière. 10. Il est en vacances depuis trois semaines.

25-5 1. Il y a une demi-heure que j'attends. 2. Il y a quatre mois que Valérie a sa voiture. 3. Il y a dix jours que nous essayons de joindre le banquier. 4. Il y a deux jours qu'il est en voyage d'affaires. 5. Il y a un an que Sophie étudie le chinois. 6. Il y a cinq ans qu'elle veut adopter un enfant. 7. Il y a des semaines que nous cherchons un appartement. 8. Il y a trois mois que j'attends votre réponse. 9. Il y a longtemps que ses idées sont dénuées d'intérêt. 10. Il y a une semaine que le chien de nos voisins est perdu.

25-6 1. Ils ont souvent voyagé en Asie. 2. On a bien mangé chez eux. 3. Elle a beaucoup dépensé. 4. Il a rarement lu des romans policiers. 5. Nous n'avons pas assez travaillé. 6. J'ai trop parlé. 7. Elle a très peu écrit. 8. Tu es souvent allé(e) au théâtre. 9. Il s'est toujours très mal exprimé. 10. Nous avons bien aimé la maison.

25-7 1. Combien de 2. Comment 3. Qui 4. Que 5. Combien 6. Où 7. Quand 8. Pourquoi 9. Quand 10. Qui

25-8 1. Il a planté des fleurs partout.   2. Voulez-vous vivre ici?   3. Ma voiture est garée juste derrière la vôtre.   4. Nous irons ailleurs.   5. Il est dehors.   6. J'habite près de la rivière.   7. Vous habitez trop loin.   8. Je vois des choses bizarres çà et là.   9. Il est devant vous.   10. Venez vous asseoir près de moi.

26   Numbers

26-1 1. six   2. quatorze   3. vingt-trois   4. vingt-huit   5. trente-cinq   6. trente-neuf   7. quarante et un   8. quarante-six   9. quarante-neuf   10. cinquante-deux

26-2 1. He lost for the third time.   2. I live on the thirty-first floor.   3. She sold her second car.   4. It's his fifty-eighth birthday.   5. We skied for the first time.   6. It's the fourth time we have run into each other on the street.   7. He got forty-eighth place.   8. I love Beethoven's Ninth Symphony.   9. He lives at the corner of Twenty-third Street and Seventh Avenue.   10. Is it his second year?

26-3 1. 53   2. 59   3. 62   4. 70   5. 71   6. 78   7. 83   8. 87   9. 90   10. 93

26-4 1. cent un   2. cent quatorze   3. cent vingt-six   4. cent trente-neuf   5. cent quarante-cinq   6. cent cinquante-six   7. cent soixante   8. cent soixante dix-huit   9. cent quatre-vingt-un   10. cent quatre-vingt-dix-neuf

26-5 1. deux cent douze   2. trois cent quinze   3. quatre cent vingt   4. cinq cent trente et un   5. six cent vingt-trois   6. sept cent quatre-vingt-dix   7. huit cent quarante-huit   8. neuf cent quatre   9. six cent quarante-cinq   10. cent un

26-6 1. deux cent cinq   2. trois cent quatre-vingt-neuf   3. quatre cent cinquante-six   4. cinq cent quatre   5. six cent soixante-dix-huit   6. sept cent quarante-cinq   7. huit cents   8. huit cent quinze   9. neuf cent un   10. neuf cent quarante

26-7 1. mille cinq   2. deux mille quatre cent cinquante-six   3. trois mille vingt et un   4. quatre mille sept cent quatre-vingt-neuf   5. dix mille quatre cent cinquante   6. vingt-quatre mille huit   7. cent soixante-dix mille huit cent quatre-vingt-dix   8. un million deux cent trente mille   9. trente million trente mille   10. un milliard six cent millions

26-8 1. deux mille quinze   2. cent cinquante mille   3. mille neuf cent soixante-dix-huit   4. deux mille sept   5. un milliard   6. mille cinq cents   7. deux mille six / un million   8. mille huit cent quatre-vingt-cinq   9. cinq mille   10. six milliards

27   Pot pourri

27-1 1. de   2. de   3. sur   4. à   5. de   6. à   7. de   8. en   9. à   10. de

27-2 1. I miss Paul.   2. My brother did not keep his word.   3. This writer lacks talent.   4. I missed the beginning of the course.   5. The boss failed to do his duty.

27-3 1. Quoi que tu dises...   2. Quelle que soit sa décision...   3. Qui que tu sois...   4. Où que tu ailles...   5. Qui qu'elle soit...   6. Quoi que tu penses...   7. Où qu'ils (elles) habitent...   8. Quelle que soit leur suggestion...   9. Qui que tu sois...   10. Quoi que ta mère puisse penser (Quoi que pense ta mère)...

27-4 1. Quitte à ne pas dormir, je vais avec toi à cette soirée.   2. Il démissionnera quitte à avoir des problèmes financiers.   3. Il a beau être intelligent, il est très seul.   4. Ils (Elles) ont beau être ami(e)s, ils (elles) ne peuvent pas parler politique ensemble.   5. Je prendrai deux ans de congé quitte à perdre mon poste.   6. Ils (Elles) ont eu beau essayer, ils (elles) ont échoué.   7. Cette théière a beau être magnifique, ça ne vaut pas 200 euros.   8. Tu as beau jurer de dire la vérité, j'ai toujours des doutes.   9. Quitte à t'ennuyer, j'ai besoin de te poser quelques questions.   10. Il ne quittera pas la pièce quitte à déranger tout le monde.